Mirror on the Stage

MIRROR ON THE STAGE

The Pulitzer Plays as an Approach to American Drama

by Thomas P. Adler

Purdue University Press
West Lafayette, Indiana

Book and jacket designed by Marlene Kennedy

Copyright © 1987 by Purdue Research Foundation, West Lafayette, Indiana 47907. All rights reserved. Unless permission is granted, this material shall not be copied, reproduced, or coded for reproduction by any electrical, mechanical, or chemical process, or combination thereof, now known or later developed.

Published 1987

Library of Congress Cataloging-in-Publication Data

Adler, Thomas P.
  Mirror on the stage.

  Bibliography: p.
  Includes index.
  1. American drama—20th century—History and criticism.   2. Pulitzer prizes.   I. Title.
PS350.A35   1986   812'.5'09   86-21170
ISBN 0-911198-84-9

Printed in the United States of America

Second Printing, January 1989

*In memory of
my Mother and my Father*

Contents

	Preface	ix
	Acknowledgments	xv
1.	Nora's American Cousins	1
2.	Supportive Illusions/Romantic Delusions	23
3.	The Ethic of Happiness	38
4.	"Over There"—and Over Here	53
5.	The Fifth Horseman of the Apocalypse—Race	68
6.	The Political Animal	85
7.	Whatever Happened to the American Dream?	96
8.	The Varieties of Religious Experience	113
9.	The Idea of Progress	127
10.	From Modernism to Metatheatre—Art and Artists in Modern American Drama	142
	Appendix	155
	Notes	157
	Index	165

Preface

The comparatively low estate in which American drama is currently held by some critics of literature, and the benign neglect that it suffers from at the hands of others, have not gone unnoticed even in the popular press. In a somber reflection entitled "The Play's Not the Thing" (*The New York Times Book Review*, December 26, 1982), D. J. R. Bruckner reminds readers that whereas "serious critics of European literature would never think of ignoring the plays of Camus and Genet and Frisch and Handke, in the curriculum of literary criticism American plays are not given much credit"; consequently, "intelligent criticism of plays as literature" is no longer helping sustain and nurture American theatre as it once did. Even more recently, Frank Rich ("To Make Serious Theater 'Serious' Issues Aren't Enough," *The New York Times*, February 19, 1984) singles out as the most "disturbing" of the "ills" besetting American theatre "the widespread perception that... American theater no longer plays a central part in our cultural ferment." By pointing, however, to such contemporary writers as Lanford Wilson, Marsha Norman, David Mamet, and Sam Shepard (all of whom have, incidentally, received the Pulitzer Prize for drama within the last several years), Rich argues that there still are "playwrights who write about issues that matter—or who connect with the rest of our literature, past and present—or who swim with the modernist and postmodernist currents of international art."

The treatment of American drama as the ugly stepchild of American literature might be traced to any number of sources, but none is more decisive than the truism that American drama—like any drama—must begin its life first as plays in and for the theatre rather than as texts for the study or the library. This is as true of Shepard as it was of Sophocles and Shakespeare and Shaw: if plays are not first popular with audiences in the theatre, the likelihood that they will ever find their way into the literature anthologies, into the canon of a nation's literature, is greatly reduced. That this in no way need diminish them *as* literature is a hurdle that some academic critics find difficult to clear—and one, ironically, made nearly insurmountable once a play wins a major award. Granted, as critics have lost no time in pointing out, the award of a Pulitzer Prize, for instance, is no necessary index to the literary quality of a play. John Simon, for one, believes "that if a play, for example, received a Pulitzer, the tendency among the cultivated was to regard it, not always justly, with suspicion, and to reckon its author as a confirmed middlebrow" (*Singularities: Essays on the Theater/1964–1974*, Random House, 1975). And yet, the Pulitzer plays provide a far more reliable accounting of the nature and development of serious American drama than the equivalent novels do of classic American fiction. Many major novelists (Fitzgerald, for one) never won, and several others (Hemingway and Faulkner, for instance) only won for lesser works. Of the playwrights, however, with any continuing claim on critical, as distinct from purely popular, attention, only four (Clifford Odets, Lillian Hellman, Arthur Kopit, and David Rabe) have not received the award. True, some playwrights who should not have won have: and several dramas that should have won (*The Iceman Cometh, The Glass Menagerie, Who's Afraid of Virginia Woolf?*—and perhaps *Indians* and *Sticks and Bones*) have not. But, with few exceptions, the dramas usually thought of as 'classic' American plays—*Our Town, Long Day's Journey Into Night, Death of a Salesman, A Streetcar Named Desire*—have all been honored with the prize.

Furthermore, the award-winning dramas exhibit greater technical and thematic variety and more diversity in their attitudes and points of view than would appear to be true of the prize novels—perhaps because the juries recommending the plays generally have been more conscious of the impact—for good or ill—of the Pulitzer Prize upon the state of theatre in America. As W. J. Stuckey argues in *The Pulitzer Prize Novels: A Critical Backward Look* (University of Oklahoma Press, 1981), a paramount concern among the fiction winners has been edification and uplift, the enshrining of hard work, honesty, and endurance as avenues to the material success that confirms inner virtue. While such emphases do appear sporadically in the prize dramas, they are seldom treated uncritically; the playwrights seem to be less conservative and more aware of the political and social and moral deficiencies of the American system.

Three earlier books include extensive material on the Pulitzer dramas. John Toohey's *A History of the Pulitzer Prize Plays* (The Citadel Press, 1957) is, as its title suggests, mainly a visual scrapbook of memorabilia about the winners, though it does quote representative excerpts from the daily and periodical reviews, with some additional evaluative judgments by Toohey as to the merits of individual works. In *The Pulitzer Prizes: A History of the Awards in Books, Drama, Music, and Journalism, Based on the Private Files Over Six Decades* (Columbia University Press, 1974), John Hohenberg presents mainly a factual record of the prize. He traces the alterations in the terminology of the drama citation: from its inception in 1917 when the award was to go to "the original American play, performed in New York, which shall best represent the educational value and power of the stage in raising the standard of good morals, good taste, and good manners"; through a period beginning in 1929 when the clause about "raising the standard . . ." was omitted; to the present form adopted in 1964: "For a distinguished play by an American author, preferably original in its source and dealing with American life."

Over the years, the drama juries responsible for recommending choices to the Advisory Board of the Graduate School of Journalism at Columbia for their ratification have been composed primarily of notable theatre reviewers, augmented occasionally by academic critics, though usually not by practicing playwrights, with the obvious exception of W. Somerset Maugham. The roster of those who have served includes William Lyon Phelps, Stark Young, Oscar Campbell, Joseph Wood Krutch, John Mason Brown, John Gassner, Maurice Valency, Elliott Norton, Henry Hewes, Brendan Gill, and Walter Kerr, many of whom have written widely and well on drama and theatre. Because of the preponderance of daily and weekly reviewers among jury members, the texts likely to be privileged over others tend to be, though not exclusively, the same ones that have gone on to become commercial and popular successes as a result of initially favorable reviews. The power, perhaps excessive, of reviewers to shape the canon of American dramatic literature by largely determining what will remain open and thus what will be seen and eventually read is not in question; and an evaluation of the precise nature and extent of their influence, for better or for worse, on American dramatists is matter for another study. The valorization of a work that results from the award of a Pulitzer, however, will probably have a shaping impact upon what other playwrights (except perhaps those of the very first rank) come to think of as available and acceptable subjects and styles for the commercial theatre. Although the chapters that follow suggest evidence of such cross-fertilization, the tracing of influences is not a primary concern here.

In his record of the awards, Hohenberg includes salient comments from the jury reports about the winning works, airing as well the major disputes among jury members and revealing the workings of the advisory board, composed of newspaper publishers and editors and a lesser number of university (not always Columbia) officials, as it either ratified or rejected the nominations, or in some instances recommended a different choice of its own. This work makes no attempt to retrace that material, despite its fascination, and so it is brought in only peripherally in the few cases where it has a particular bearing on the literary judgment of a work. *Mirror on the Stage*, then, is not a criticism of the award itself—despite several oversights and wrongheaded decisions—but is rather a critical reading and interpretation of the plays that have won the award and an indication, as the subtitle to this study suggests, of what these works reveal more generally about the nature of American drama.

Now ten years old, Jane Bonin's study, *Major Themes in Prize-Winning American Drama* (The Scarecrow Press, 1975), is, at one and the same time, both broader and narrower than this present book: broader because she surveys winners not only of the Pulitzer but of the Drama Critics Circle, Tony, and Obie Awards as well; narrower because she does not provide thorough, self-contained analyses of the plays, instead fragmenting her discussion of each of them in order to approach them topically, so that one aspect of a particular work will be discussed in one place and another aspect in another. Furthermore, she intends, in her words, to "explore America's most popular body of culturally acceptable plays for attitudes they contain." *Mirror on the Stage*, instead of reading the American experience through its plays, remains first and last a reading *of* American drama. Rather than use these plays as the primary texts for writing an American intellectual history, this study makes a contribution to such a social and cultural history only insofar as it paints a few of the tiles that compose the vast mosaic of American life as seen through its artifacts.

Instead of establishing arbitrary topics and then pigeonholing the prize-winning plays into them, the ten categories for discussion were arrived at inductively, by first analyzing and interpreting each of the fifty-seven works that received the Pulitzer between 1918 and 1985 to understand its dominant focus. The resulting ten subjects were than arranged to move from the more individual and specific to the more universal and general. The first three chapters—"Nora's American Cousins," "Supportive Illusions/Romantic Delusions," and "The Ethic of Happiness"—treat largely personal issues; the next four—"'Over There'—And Over Here," "The Fifth Horseman of the Apocalypse—Race," "The Political Animal," and "Whatever Happened to the American Dream?"—explore more social topics; the next two—"The Varieties of Religious Experience" and "The Idea of Progress"—consider more cosmic concerns; and the last one, "From Modernism to Metatheatre—Art and Artists in Modern American Drama," serves also as a conclusion since it subsumes plays handled in all the other chapters. The remarks about individual works can be read as discrete explications—not that each brief section pretends by any means to say everything there is to be said about each of the plays, although even in the case of the better-known works most frequently discussed elsewhere, an attempt has been made to say something new and fresh.

Decisions were necessarily made about the overriding emphasis of certain plays and, therefore, about the context in which they would be considered (*South Pacific* and *Talley's Folly*, to choose just one instance, might have been placed in the chapter on war rather than in the one about race). Yet a thematic approach such as the one adopted here, unlike a strictly chronological one, allows shifting attention away from these works as representative of prevailing attitudes at a specific period in America's social and cultural history—which, again, is Bonin's focus. What is more important, this encourages an intertextual approach: it permits drawing relationships that might otherwise not become apparent among plays widely separated in time; it allows for alluding freely to other works that did not win the award, including a number that probably should have; and it opens up the possibility of following recurrent motifs—such as the game-of-life metaphor or the reverse-evolutionary metaphor that denotes moral decline, the link between the failure of fathers in cultivating matters of the heart and the failure of the American Dream, and the connection between the passage of time and reduced possibilities for human choice and change, among others.

To the extent that drama—and in this the Pulitzer plays are no different—by its very nature is mimetic ("an imitation of an action in the form of an action"), the theatrical artifact mirrors life. Moreover, every theatre audience ideally confronts an image of itself through experiencing a play, so the space inhabited by the audience and even the consciousness of each member of that audience become "stages" for the action. Since drama mirrors as well the playwright and his or her particular point of view, along with expressing society and its values, the award of a Pulitzer ordinarily reflects what is being thought by the American popular imagination. That is, however, only a subsidiary concern of this current study, in which each of the prize-winning plays is analyzed and evaluated first as an end in itself rather than as a means of examining American culture or sociology, though some hints in that direction do appear in the introductions and conclusions to each chapter. What is of greatest interest is the way that many of these dramas render their audience conscious of being in the theatre by throwing back an image of themselves as an audience. Relatively few of these plays actually have an on-stage mirror that reflects the actors and/or audience; when such mirrors literally are present, they function as a metaphor for the nature of the dramatic occasion itself which, to a greater or lesser degree, images reality. In those instances when an audience does see itself reflected in a mirror, their consciousness of themselves as an audience and of the stage space as extending across the footlights and into the auditorium is made explicit and emphatic, forcing them to entertain epistemological questions about seeing and knowing the self and reality outside of the self. The concluding chapter draws attention to the way in which many of these works force the audience, in C. W. E. Bigsby's words, to "theatricalize itself," as well as to the widespread and rather surprising phenomenon of these playwrights' concern—even in works of essentially popular entertainment—with aesthetic questions about the nature of art and the vocation of the artist. To an unexpected degree, American dramatists write plays about plays and the theatrical experience.

Acknowledgments

For initially suggesting that I undertake this study, I owe a debt to my longtime friend and colleague Bill Stuckey. I am also grateful to the National Endowment for the Humanities for the award of a summer stipend that facilitated my beginning the research on this project and to Purdue University for a sabbatical leave that permitted me to do much of the initial writing.

My thanks go as well to Anita Ashendel for her expertise in copyediting, to Marlene Kennedy for her talent in design, and to Verna Emery and Janice Becker of the Purdue Press for their care in seeing my work through publication. As always, my greatest debt is to my family, to sons, Jeremy and Chris, and to my wife, Winnie—without whom, nothing.

Several brief sections of *Mirror on the Stage* have appeared previously in print. I appreciate being given permission to use here, in revised form, material from the following essays:

"Through a Glass Darkly: O'Neill's Aesthetic Theory as Seen Through His Writer Characters," from *Arizona Quarterly*, vol. 32, no. 2, Summer 1976, copyright by the *Arizona Quarterly*.

"'The Mystery of Things': The Varieties of Religious Experience in Modern American Drama," from *Themes in Drama 5: Drama and Religion*, edited by James Redmond, 1983. Copyrighted by and reprinted with permission by Cambridge University Press.

"The Mirror as Stage Prop in Modern Drama," from *Comparative Drama*, vol. 14, no. 4, Winter 1980–81, copyright by *Comparative Drama*.

"Albee's *Seascape:* Humanity at the Second Threshold," from *Renascence*, vol. 31, no. 2, Winter 1979, copyright by *Renascence*.

"Theatre Looking at Theatre: A Self-Image of the Post–World War II American Drama," from *Claudel Studies*, vol. 9, no. 1, 1982, copyright by *Claudel Studies*.

...for the poet is representative. He stands among partial men for the complete man, and apprises us not of his wealth, but of the common wealth. The young man reveres men of genius, because, to speak truly, they are more himself than he is. They receive of the soul as he also receives, but they more. . . . He is isolated among his contemporaries by truth and by his art, but with this consolation in his pursuits, that they will draw all men sooner or later. For all men live by truth and stand in need of expression. In love, in art, in avarice, in politics, in labor, in games, we study to utter our painful secret. The man is only half himself, the other half is his expression.

        Ralph Waldo Emerson, "The Poet"

. . .it is just the literature that we read for "amusement," or "purely for pleasure" that may have the greatest or least suspected influence upon us. . . . Hence it is that the influence of popular novelists, and of popular plays of contemporary life, requires to be scrutinized most closely. . . .Though we may read literature merely for pleasure, of "entertainment" or of "aesthetic enjoyment," this reading never affects simply a sort of special sense: it affects us as entire human beings; it affects our moral and religious existence.

        T. S. Eliot, "Religion and Literature"

1

Nora's American Cousins

Near the end of Henrik Ibsen's *A Doll's House*, Helmer pleads with Nora, "Before all else, you're a wife and mother." As she prepares to slam the door and walk out to mold her own destiny, Nora responds: "I don't believe in that anymore. I believe that, before all else, I'm a human being, no less than you—or anyway, I ought to try to become one."[1] Since he was promoting the need for each person—man and woman alike—to arrive at a sense of selfhood, Ibsen would not want to be regarded, in any narrow sense of the term, as a feminist playwright. And yet, according to Janet Brown in *Feminist Drama: Definitions and Critical Analysis*, his *Doll's House* does display a "feminist" aesthetic, not simply because it is a play about a woman or one presenting characters sympathetic to women, but rather because its protagonist "struggle[s] for autonomy," for the "death and rebirth of the woman herself as subject instead of object" in an "'unjust socio-sexual hierarchy' where women are powerless."[2] The world outside the house that Nora ventures into was, of course, formed and shaped by the identical value system that curtailed her life within. It was a system which, in Virginia Woolf's description, required that a woman mold herself into being "the Angel in the House," a woman "intensely sympathetic," "immensely charming," "utterly unselfish," and "above all...pure, who has absolutely no mind of [her] own," especially as concerns "human relations, morality, sex."[3] Because the system has allowed Nora only very minimal economic independence—and that through scrimping and subterfuge—she cannot really be considered free within its confines. Woolf might be seen as echoing Ibsen—even to the point of employing the same image of the woman shutting the door—when she writes in *A Room of One's Own* "that it is much more important to be oneself than anything else";[4] she argues that economic self-sufficiency "seemed infinitely...more important" than political emancipation that secured the right to vote, because "money dignifies what is frivolous if unpaid for" (pp. 37, 68). The patriarchal system, built on the premise that for one group to be superior there must exist another that is inferior, creates by keeping women economically powerless a dependency of the mind as well, since "intellectual freedom depends upon material things" (p. 112). Only when a woman can finally close the door behind her and enter "a room of [her] own" will she secure "the power to think for herself" (p. 110).

Jesse Lynch Williams's *Why Marry?*, the first play ever to win a Pulitzer (no award was made in 1917)—along with *Miss Lulu Bett* of three years later and *Craig's Wife* of five years after that—analyzes in much the same way Woolf does how the social structure of the time limits the options open to women for finding security, both economic and emotional. The only answer is to marry, and to marry well, yet this ordinarily entails submitting to "financial force" or ownership in the way that women in earlier times were prey to "physical force." Williams combines the comedy-of-manners form with the social-problem play, perhaps with George Bernard Shaw in mind as his model; what results, however, is a rather tedious and only occasionally crisp play—yet in some ways a work far ahead of its time, addressing such issues as unequal pay for equal work and the practice of living together without benefit of matrimony. Through five marriage (and/or engagement) relationships, Williams dramatizes, or more accurately discourses upon, some diametrically opposed views of the institution of marriage.

John, the wealthy philanthropist who subscribes to a kind of economic Darwinism (those with the most money are the fittest), regards Lucy, his wife, as a possession, and though in private she might rail against it, Lucy seems to accept that a married woman's only vocation and sphere are "in the home."[5] John's sister Jean, referred to as the true woman, plays the seduction game with Rex Baker, a rich playboy whom she does not really love, recognizing fully that she is entering into a relationship of legalized prostitution in which she will sell her body in obedient submission. Their uncle, Judge Everett, has been married for years, but he and his wife have decided that they are happier apart than together, so she is off in Reno getting a divorce; in this instance, divorce appears to be made in heaven, and they pride themselves on being no longer hypocritical before the world—though they do stay married in the end. Dour cousin Theodore, a clergyman who believes sex a "necessary evil," has had to place his wife, Mary, in a sanatorium after raising a large brood of children, their poverty and misfortune accepted as part of life's necessary suffering. Williams has so far treated his audience, then, to a practical, a cynical, an antisentimental, and a traditional if somewhat pathetic view of marriage.

The fifth couple, John's other sister, Helen, and the brilliant scientist whom she works with, Ernest Hamilton, provide what was for its day a radical point of view. Helen is a New Woman of "independent views" who can more than hold her own economically as well as intellectually in the man's world of science, though she is far from the "sexless freak" others take her to be. And Ernest is perfectly willing to respect her intelligence as the equal of his; he refuses to make her into his slave and credits her contribution by listing her as co-author of the article detailing their latest scientific advance. As much, however, as they are in love, neither believes in marriage. They recognize that you do not contract by law what is better secured by love, that oftentimes a "legal union" simply signifies a "spiritual separation," that "modern marriage" is often tantamount to "divorce"—John and Lucy provide adequate proof of that. Both Helen and Ernest act unselfishly in their temporary decision to remain unmarried but share the same bed. Along with understanding that he cannot boast of a mind like a woman's that responds to affection, Ernest realizes that to marry Helen would only threaten her career and his own as well. For her part, Helen believes that she is doing right in the eyes of God, which she does not equate with any church. Organized religion, in fact, comes off none too well in the play. When the scientist and the minister sit down to discuss things, Ernest argues that love is equal to religion, that the sexual instinct prompts creativity in other areas of life, and that the sexual urge to procreate makes man most like God. With a kind of Shavian fervor, he claims it is "the one eternal thing we mortals share" (p. 26) with the divine. Williams portrays the traditional religious responses as inadequate: Theodore will not sanction Helen and Ernest's arrangement, though based on love; however, for economic considerations, he will perform the ceremony uniting Rex and Jean, as if ritual could bless what is essentially profane. The scientist reveals himself as more truly religious than the clergyman.

Society in Williams's play has reduced marriage to a sacrament of property, making it more respectable to sell self, as Jean will do, than to give self to one another, as Helen and Ernest do. That same society would exact a price of ostracization if they should go forward with their intention of living together. Yet Williams seems unable to follow his thesis through to a logically satisfying conclusion, evidently feeling that he must subscribe to, rather than attempt to change, the predispositions of his audience. So Helen and Ernest do marry, almost accidentally, by swearing their love before God; but since Everett is a judge he can legalize the union, though it can hardly be made more sacred than it has been all along. They have been tricked into the form for appearance's sake. The play ends with a Brechtian challenge. A problem has been aired, but no solution is proffered: "Unless society wakes up and reforms its rules and regulations of marriage," propounds the judge, "marriage is doomed.... Respectability has triumphed this time, but let Society take warning and beware!" (pp. 44, 51).

In *A Room of One's Own,* Woolf quotes the poetic lament of Lady Winchilsea (born 1661) that "'the dull manage of a servile house / Is held by some our utmost art and use'" (p. 62). Up until very recently, one of the best examples in all of American drama of the transformation of such an "angel of the house" into a rebellious Nora-like figure appeared in one of the earliest Pulitzer plays, the winner for 1921. Zona Gale adapted *Miss Lulu Bett* from her novel of the same name, making it the first of several exceptions to the rule that the drama Pulitzer be given to an "original" work (*The Old Maid, South Pacific, Look Homeward, Angel, The Diary of Anne Frank,* and *All the Way Home* are later ones). The adaptation is legendary for the speed of its composition—eight days—and for the location of its first performance under the aegis of impresario David Belasco—Sing-Sing penitentiary. That the play had a link to the woman's rights movement of the first two decades of this century and that its author was a woman did not go unnoticed by the drama jury that voted the prize; indeed, the second fact appears to have been decisive in the deliberations. *Lulu Bett* forms part of the literature of the small midwestern town, popularized by such writers as Sinclair Lewis and Sherwood Anderson. As a comedy of manners, but of bourgeois rather than upper-class mores (as is generally true of American stage comedy, with some obvious exceptions such as the plays of Philip Barry and S. N. Behrman), it satirizes the stifling and stultifying atmosphere of the narrow-minded, provincial town. *Lulu Bett* is notable as well for its observation of naturalistic details, for its originality and daring in putting on stage the banalities of everyday conversation—and even for beginning two of its acts with precisely the same situation and virtually identical dialogue, thus antedating techniques later applauded as original in Eugene Ionesco and Harold Pinter.

Gale's central figure, a thirty-four-year-old spinster lacking financial resources of her own, finds herself a virtual slave in the household of her brother-in-law and sister, Dwight and Ina Deacon. Her life is so circumscribed that her "keepers" object to her extravagance of bringing a potted tulip into the house; rebelling silently, and perhaps foreshadowing the ending, "she takes [the] flowerpot from the table and throws it out the window"[6] as a signal that she possesses a will of her own. She literally keeps the household going, aware of her deprivations but wanting nothing more than to "care" for someone, to be "needed" by someone.

Even though her mother has kept her single—to protect her from the pain that she herself experienced in losing four of six children—Lulu insists that she is "Miss...from choice" (p. 34), "choice" being a favorite word with her. Possessing a dry, laconic humor, often directed at herself, she does not believe that anyone would really want to marry her, but, of course, Dwight's brother, Ninian, arriving for a visit, almost immediately does; he recognizes what a gem Lulu is, and for reasons other than just her expert cooking. Ninian, while telling the Deacons' younger daughter, Monona, about fantasies of planting diamond mines, conceives the idea of taking the family and Lulu to the theatre. As they prepare to leave, Ninian and Lulu playfully and unselfconsciously recite the traditional form of the marriage vows, only to have Dwight remind them (à la Everett in *Why Marry?*) that he is a magistrate and that they are now legally married in this "Cinderella" tale. Playacting becomes reality, with Ninian the artist responsible for the transformation of Lulu from her fixed role. The plucky Mrs. Bett can only remark: "This is what comes of going to the theatre" (p. 72).

As it turns out, however, Ninian, whom Mrs. Bett calls a "whited centipede" (p. 152), was married long ago to a woman whom he has not seen in fifteen years. Yet he is honest with Lulu and sends her back home. Dwight, a pompous, tendentious, and ultimately cruel little man-about-town, fears scandal and turns Lulu's situation against her, so that it reflects badly on her character and judgment rather than on his or his family's. He makes Lulu agree that Ninian deserted her because of some deficiency on her part and that she was the fool for marrying someone already married. Dwight preaches a doctrine of everything for the family, but the way he pontificates and mocks his children and in-laws reveals him, like Ina, as a hypocritical social-climber, worried about the outward image that he projects. Gale thus begins in *Lulu Bett* a deromanticizing of the family that will continue in much of American drama; what should be a nourishing fount for its members is often awash in selfishness and recrimination.

The desentimentalizing continues also in the subplot involving the Deacons' older daughter, Diana, a flirtatious teenager with an excessively romantic notion of men gained largely from her reading. Like Lulu herself, Di is mocked and made fun of by Dwight; she intends to escape from this through marriage to Bobby, though her rejection of him after an abortive elopement points towards the unhappy ending of the original version of Gale's play. For the third act exists in two different versions, one written after the adverse criticism following the premiere. Gale's novel ended with Lulu marrying Cornish, a somewhat effeminate man of good character but little promise; in her first ending for the stage version—and clearly the superior one of the two—Cornish offers to marry Lulu after she receives a letter from Ninian confirming that his first wife is still living. Lulu rejects him, however, at least for now, to go off and work to search for an authentic self, "gone," as Mrs. Bett says, "to call her soul her own" (p. 154) and "to see out of [her] own eyes" (p. 182). The "angel of the house" has made the choice to try her way in the world. This is a true emancipation, a freedom from constraint, but also an avenue *to* something, to possession of herself, undertaken with the blessing of her mother, who claims that Lulu should have done it years ago. Lulu has, to paraphrase Saint Paul, "put on the new woman." In the sentimental revision demanded by some critics and the public, Ninian returns with word that his wife has long been dead, and he and Lulu live happily ever after in married respectability. Gale somewhat lamely justified her capitulation to popular taste on the grounds of truth to life, arguing that "if a play is to present life—it must not always end an episode unhappily, because life does not always do so."[7]

The protagonist's determination to go her solitary way, yet this time not only without the support of Thelma, her mother, but in actual defiance of it, also informs Marsha Norman's two-character *'night, Mother,* the 1983 Pulitzer winner which ran first at Harvard's American Repertory Theatre before moving to Broadway. With its absolute adherence to the unities of time (an hour and a half), place (the living room and kitchen of the Cates's lower-middle-class home seen in a wide-angle set), and action (a daughter's calm leave-taking of her mother as she prepares to commit suicide), Norman's family drama provides an impeccable example of what has come to be called "new American realism" on stage. Audiences are kept particularly aware that stage-time and real-time perfectly coincide; a number of strategically placed clocks show that their sojourn in the theatre between 8:15 and 9:45 occurs simultaneously with the action in the Cates home. This fosters the illusion that the action is happening now, in the present tense, an inexorable movement that the audience might want to prevent or at least delay but that they finally come to understand is inevitable. Yet one element in the stage setting, the entrance to the bedroom where Jessie will shoot herself at play's end, is handled symbolically and somewhat expressionistically: "an ordinary door that opens onto absolute nothingness... is the point of all the action...and the lighting should make it disappear completely at times and draw the entire set into it at others."[8] Moreover, the wide black border framing the set creates the impression of a shadow box, adding to the audience's sense of themselves as helpless watchers.

Jessie's matter-of-fact announcement that she will take her own life later in the evening contrasts with her mother's instinctive recoiling against a decision that she finds irrational and yet, try as she will, cannot alter. Thelma demands that Jessie continue to live for *her,* whereas Jessie determines that now she must die for *herself.* Thelma dredges up every imaginable panacea for Jessie's unhappiness and emptiness—from getting rid of the newspaper and TV or rearranging the furniture to getting a driver's license or a job or a dog or a place of her own—in the process whining and cajoling and resorting to childish temper tantrums such as throwing pots and pans around the kitchen. Thelma's insistence that Jessie continue to live derives not from any moral abhorrence over the act of suicide, but rather from her own unfulfilled emotional life and her own fear of mortality: her husband, Jessie's father, was almost always silent with her, while she looked on in jealousy at the easy camaraderie between father and daughter; when she herself must confront the terrible "quiet" that is death, she vows that they will have to "drag [her] screaming and...screeching into [her] grave" (p. 78). The neatly arranged clutter in Thelma's living room—the bric-a-brac and momentos that substitute for a lived life—reflects a rage for order as a feeble shelter against the terrors unleashed by Jessie's announcement. Perhaps as a protection against further rejection and hurt, Thelma exists on the surface of things; she lives a spiritually empty, unexamined life: "I don't know what I'm here for, but then I don't think about it" (p. 49). If Thelma's world can so easily tumble apart, perhaps the imposed order and control were never more than tenuous and illusory all along.

For Jessie, dying will mean a being born into a self that she has chosen, an essential identity that has thus far eluded her. As she plaintively says, "I'm what was worth waiting for and I didn't make it. . . . I'm not going to show up, so there's no reason to stay" (p. 76). Jessie regards herself up to this point as wholly defined by the decisions of others who keep intruding on her life and using her, instead of allowing her to "belong" to herself, beginning with Thelma's misconceived decision not to tell Jessie that her epileptic seizures (from which, significantly, her father also suffered) began long ago and not recently as the result of an accident. Importantly, Jessie's physical and psychological maladies are now under control, for her choice must spring from strength, not weakness, from full knowledge, not depressive whim. Jessie's methodical way of getting through this last night of her life might at first seem too emotionally distanced, almost somnambulistic, yet her outer control is no mask but a reflection of her inner assurance. Although the audience hear of Jessie's failed marriage to a man she still loves and of her wayward teenage son who, like Jessie herself, "look[s] out at the world and. . .see[s] the same thing: not Fair" (p. 60), Norman downplays Jessie's self-pity. Her suicide is not a cop-out; she insists that she is "*'not'* giving up" (p. 75). Neither is the play itself a tract about an individual's right to choose suicide over an intolerable life—or, what is ethically more problematic, one that is tolerable. Rather, Jessie's suicide becomes an ultimate act of existential definition of self; it is something she does not "*have to*" do, but which she chooses to do just the same. Here, poet Robert Lowell's lines, "the lovely, / peculiar power to choose life and die,"[9] are applicable, for Jessie finally belongs only to herself and creates whatever meaning she might have by committing suicide, a more authentic act than any other in her life.

That she dies using her Daddy's gun indicates his continuing grip over her and the way that no other man in Jessie's life could measure up to him, as well as how he failed her by dying. In the same way, Jessie will desert her mother by dying and thereby perhaps retaliate against Thelma for never having loved her husband. Jessie's activities on this last night of her life cannot quell Thelma's essential fear, even though Jessie reassures her mother that this night will be like any other: she will kiss her and say "'night, Mother" and then go into the bedroom. Significantly, however, because Thelma will not allow Jessie to "go gently into that good night,"[10] the kiss never comes. Even if Norman did not have Dylan Thomas's famous poem in mind when she titled her play, the comparison proves instructive. Thelma, like Thomas's persona, would have Jessie "rage" at death instead of going "easy." Jessie, however, sees the night that is death as "good" not only in the sense of its being final, but as an ethical good as well: by dying, she will have defined herself as an adult *woman*, whereas Thelma, as she admits too late in her epiphanic curtain line, has always needed to control and keep Jessie a child: "Forgive me. I thought you were mine" (p. 89).

If her daughter's suicide plunges Thelma into a nighttime of guilt and self-recrimination over her inadequacy to prevent it—as she believes Jessie's father would have been able to do had he still been alive—as well as guilt over her failure to recognize that Jessie was "so alone," perhaps paradoxically she wins the audience's sympathy because her reaction is akin to their own. Jessie's chilling serenity as she embraces "absolute nothingness" and closes and locks the door behind her might render her too unique and exceptional for audience identification. The bedroom into which she retreats might be seen as a variation on the inner stage, an appropriate location for that most solipsistic of all actions. Nevertheless, as with Nora, the courageous act of closing the door on the past and the present and going beyond into the unknown future is what remains important, for it is a means of defining the self. The aftermath—what will be found on the other side of the door—must remain ambiguous, unseen. That *'night, Mother* moves its audience without the least trace of the maudlin is a tribute to Norman's spare, understated style, sparked by unexpected humor and the unblinking way she follows these two women to their separate, yet linked, destinies.

If Gale's Lulu and Williams's Helen are favorably presented—one gaining her independence outside of marriage and the other maintaining it within, and neither at anyone else's expense—four other female protagonists of Pulitzer plays seem able to achieve what passes for selfhood only by victimizing someone of the opposite sex. Woolf remarks that the woman suffrage movement "roused in men an extraordinary desire for self-assertion," and that "when one is challenged...one retaliates" (p. 103). And this may indeed help account for the virulent portraits of women as emasculators in *Craig's Wife,* in the wake of women's winning the right to vote, and in *The Gin Game,* an extreme response, perhaps, to the militant feminism of the early 1970s. Woolf also finds a causal link between the experience of war and a radical realignment of male/female roles, seeing the shattering of the illlusions under which men and women guided their relationships with one another as occurring coincident with "the guns fired in August 1914" by which the stereotypical pattern of "romance was killed" (p. 15). The Second World War, during which women literally replaced men in the work force at home only to be displaced again once men returned from the battlefields abroad, may have been equally traumatic in questioning traditional perceptions of sex roles; the consequent insecurity and threat to the male self-image may, in fact, have motivated such plays as the rather violently antifeminist *The Shrike.*

In James Thurber's famous drawing captioned simply "Home," a diminutive man arriving back at what should be his "castle," evidently from work or from a night out with the boys, timorously approaches the front porch of a large three-story house, the back wall of which is formed by the head, shoulders, and arms of a wife looking as though she waits to devour him; the house, in fact, appears to be an extension or appendage of the woman. Thurber's cartoon—a nightmare of castration anxiety—might serve as a visual epigraph for George Kelly's 1926 prize play, *Craig's Wife,* a portrait of a woman so obsessed with possessing a territory of her own that she turns into a monster, a perverted Juno who has converted her house into an idol or a shrine, variously called "God Almighty," "Temple of the Lord," "Holy of Holies," or "sanctum sanctorum." It is not a house for the living, but for the dead, where, as one of the characters remarks, the "rooms have died—and are laid out."[11] This is home as tomb, not as warm, sheltering womb.

Yet if Harriet Craig is a monster, she is so not simply because of a flaw in her own character (though there are many), but because of a fault in a society built on the "powerlessness of the woman alone"[12] which decrees that a woman's only guarantee of her own protection and economic security is a house. Not that Mrs. Craig is simply a victim of society or of her stepmother who came in and laid claim to her own mother's house. For Kelly gives Mrs. Craig faults aplenty. In this meticulously detailed and naturalistic well-made play, Kelly dissects Mrs. Craig so minutely that she becomes a grotesque harridan, so imbalanced on the side of the rapacious are all her qualities. Although Kelly attempts to provide some psychological motivation, the effect more nearly resembles caricature. Why would Walter so recently have taken for a wife so frigid a woman as Mrs. Craig, especially against the advice of his now-deceased mother and maiden aunt—except, perhaps, from a need to replace the mother? If so, he has found a totally cold substitute who distrusts feelings and things of the heart because she sees—and to some degree accurately—that an unchecked Victorian romanticism and sentimentality have partly been responsible for opening the way to "the almost primitive feminine dependence and subjection" (p. 326). Furthermore, affairs of the heart are messy and not tractable to the fanatical orderliness that she can impose on inanimate objects.

For Mrs. Craig, money reigns superior to human affection and practicality to love. Although Walter warns that pragmatism and utilitarianism eventually fracture even the closest relationships, Mrs. Craig counsels her unmarried niece Ethel to consider financial advantage above all else in selecting a husband; if she chooses a poor man, as Fredericks, a college professor, is, he will only feel guilty and indebted. Marry to gain security for self, particularly if you are a woman, is Mrs. Craig's watchword. And once married, no matter how good the man, dominate him, for the things that he brings to the marriage, such as the house, are more important than the man himself. Equally important are social status and respectability, so practice whatever subterfuge and hypocrisy are necessary to avoid scandal. Mary McCarthy correctly associates Kelly's play with Jonsonian comedy, for Kelly's central character is possessed of a dominant trait, exaggerated almost to the point of unbelievability, that consumes her in the way an Elizabethan humor or dominant passion would: "a human trait has been carried to the point of inhumanity."[13]

At one juncture, Walter, who sees the attempt to unman him for what it is, suggests that his wife desires only to "control the very destiny of a man" (p. 363)—words that echo the motive of Ibsen's heroine in *Hedda Gabler*. Harriet does, indeed, manipulate everyone. Like Hedda, Harriet's neuroses reveal themselves in certain recurrent gestures, such as hands fluttering up to arrange the hair. Yet Hedda's attempts to control other destinies have a largeness about them that Harriet's lack, and so Hedda contains possibilities for tragedy absent from Harriet. Kelly's conclusion, furthermore, is moralistic in a way that Ibsen's is not. When Harriet latches the door of the empty house, closing herself in rather than venturing out as Nora does, she is alone in a circumscribed world from which everyone else has either escaped or been banished by her cruelty. The final image is funereal; if not a willed expiation and entombment like that of Lavinia in Eugene O'Neill's *Mourning Becomes Electra*, it possesses, as Winifred Dusenbury notes, a nicely ironic ring to it,[14] since Harriet now has what she always wanted, or thought she wanted: a house all to herself. As she walks through the house trailing petals from the white roses a neighbor has left for the aunt, the wilting flowers suggest Harriet's own death-in-life. Kelly's epigraph from Jane Austen tells all: "People who live to themselves, Harriet, are generally left to themselves." Mrs. Craig now presides over a house that death has entered, though society and its conventions have been at least partially responsible for creating this living embodiment of Thurber's monster.

Joseph Kramm takes the theatre metaphor—that Gale applies only sketchily in *Lulu Bett*—and works it out more deliberately in *The Shrike*, his 1952 Pulitzer play about another domineering monster like Harriet. The stage provides a logical metaphor for Kramm's work, since one of the two main characters, Jim Downs, faced now with the choice between commitment to a state mental institution or complete submission to his shrewish wife, was a theatrical director before the war interrupted his career. For the past several years, he has been attempting a comeback in a society that worships its youths and reserves for them its best opportunities. So Jim experiences what today might be termed a "midlife crisis." Added to his general malaise and sense of *angst*, to his perception that few, if any, chances for achievement remain open to him, are the collapse of his marriage to Ann and his near penury. After his failed suicide attempt (he knows he took exactly 156 pills because he counted them), he is confined to a ward at City Hospital and treated as a criminal since failing in an attempt to kill oneself is against the law. Jim confounds the doctors and nurses by refusing, like Jessie in *'night, Mother*, to think in conventional moral terms: to him, to take one's life when there is no reason to continue to exist violates no moral sanction. But to the others, Jim's blatant disregard for life threatens social stability. Although *The Shrike* may not be as direct a reaction against McCarthyism as Arthur Miller's *The Crucible* of the next theatrical season, it might still be a veiled attack on the increasing suspicion of and contempt for diversity of thought and belief in the early 1950s. And if the sanatorium in Mary Chase's *Harvey* of several seasons earlier was presented in an almost farcical manner, the one Kramm depicts partakes of a Kafkaesque nightmare.

Kramm equates the ward for the insane, with its rules and regimentation, first, with the army, second, with a prison, and third—and most subtly—with a theatre, suggesting that the asylum is a microcosm of the world and an analogue to it. His method for establishing the microcosmic level of this very circumscribed portion of reality becomes, however, too pat and predictable: the other patient-inmates are both black and white and a perfect mix of nationalities—Jewish, Greek, Spanish, though the last bears an Irish name. (Not only is the Greek conventionally "swarthy," but the two blacks, in an excess of sentimentality that becomes patronizing, are, respectively "wonderfully graceful" and "the gentlest man in the world.")[15]

The asylum most resembles a theatre since both are places of pretense. Observed constantly by an ever-present audience of doctors, nurses, attendants, and other patients, those committed for treatment must continually play a role, for only if they act according to society's rules will society deem them sane. Consequently, society forces them, at best, to be untrue to themselves so that they will appear normal and, at worst, to become mad if they are not already so, and thus to be permanently separated from the so-called sane people. But the so-called sane are normal only because they live in the outside world and are in the majority. The audience in the theatre at first comfortably associate themselves with the doctors onstage, until to do so forces them to question their own sanity when it becomes clear, through the destruction of Jim Downs, that society's masquerade of sanity is a ruse.

The true source of Jim's destruction, however, is his wife, Ann, who is motivated not simply by jealousy of Jim's mistress, Charlotte—though her desperate "fear of loneliness" (p. 67) partially explains her need to possess and control Jim completely—but more deeply by her desire to avenge the sacrifice of her life and her career for her husband's at the expense of having cultivated "a room of [her] own." At one time an actress, she gave up any future in the theatre, since a two-career marriage did not seem feasible (just why never is revealed, and they have no children). The years have turned her into a Strindbergian vampire. Faced with the choice of continued incarceration or release into Ann's custody, Jim capitulates and chooses the latter. "Freedom" from the hospital into the control of Ann will, ironically, be a more insidious dependency and imprisonment than any other.

Discussion perhaps makes *The Shrike* appear richer and more multileveled than it is. The plot is creaky and contrived; Jim's attempted suicide, for instance, converges with his first real opportunity in years for employment as a director. The language is bland to the point of being nondescript—and not, apparently, out of any attempt to catch the banalities of everyday speech as was true in *Lulu Bett*. Character revelation is minimal, not because these people are enigmatic, but because there simply is nothing more to know about them; Ann's motivation for her excessively hateful actions is especially strained. And her emasculation of Jim cannot be explored on a symbolic level, as can that, for example, of the archetypal Mommy in Edward Albee's *American Dream*. The play probably appealed initially because of its surface naturalism, yet the doctors incredibly do not penetrate Ann's conniving and effectively allow her to dictate their decisions—though the hellish treatment of the mentally ill patient, feared by society more than "one who's been to jail" (p. 166), might have appealed to some as propaganda for a more humane attitude. In any case, Kramm, like a number of other Pulitzer winners, has not been heard from significantly again.

Kitti Frings, the skillful adapter of Thomas Wolfe's massive *Look Homeward, Angel* to the stage in 1957, earlier crafted the screenplay for *The Shrike*, and so it is perhaps not unexpected that echoes of Ann can be found in the domineering wife and mother, Eliza Gant, who tries to deny man his art, whether it be sculpture or writing, and thus his life. *Angel* breaks the predictable pattern of most "portrait of the artist as a young man" works: here it is not the artist's mother who is the supportive and sensitive influence, but rather the father who serves as artist exemplar. Eliza, on the contrary, possesses the business acumen and the masculine gestures that accompany it. Like Harriet Craig, she has turned her hearth, a rooming house in Altamont, into hell, making it a workhouse for the family, whose only responsibility is catering to the boarders' whims. The paying customers provide a surrogate family for Eliza, closer than her own family precisely because they do pay, but also because Eliza is afraid to love. Since to love necessitates opening oneself to being hurt and disappointed by the loved one, Eliza determines to turn her family into strangers who demand no commitment or risk. Her relationship with her husband, the Falstaffian Gant sadly come to "the rag end of [his] life,"[16] replays the Strindbergian battle of the sexes; she is the "stronger," seen by her husband as "a snake" and bloodsucker.

Eliza's sons must search for substitute mothers at the same time they seek escape from the prison that she runs, where they perform such demeaning jobs as huckstering for customers. So Ben, whose consumption symbolizes the way he has been "drowned" in the home of his mother, must go in search of an Earth Mother figure, whom he finds in the unsentimental Mrs. "Fatty" Pert. Ben tries to be a guide to his younger brother, Eugene (the authorial figure), much as Jamie Tyrone is to his sibling Edmund in *Long Day's Journey Into Night*, though Ben does so with tenderness and without the vindictiveness that Jamie exhibits. Eugene, like his father, is a romantic, enamored of women, especially of the new boarder, Laura Jones. His affair with her (she fails to tell him this is a last fling before her marriage) essentially secures a means of escaping the human condition of being "strangers," as well as of breaking away from Eliza's hold and going *to* something not yet clearly defined. He longs for the freedom symbolized by the sound of the train whistle—which plunges him into a Whitmanesque verbal rapture—and by the locale of his father's artist studio. Laura does let him go, just as Eliza also eventually must, but necessary freedom means movement from loneliness among people to an aloneness that might be productive and educative for the young artist. Before his older brother and mentor dies in a movingly handled scene,

Eugene learns from Ben that the only escape possible must be to owning oneself—a less sentimental kind of response than the running away from the past which Tom Wingfield undertakes in *Glass Menagerie*, a memory play that provides a touchstone for this type of drama in American literature. As Ben tells Eugene, "The world is nowhere, no one, Gene! *You* are your world (p. 298).

In Gant's studio stands a serene-looking stone angel, symbol of both idealism and permanence, that Gant the unfulfilled artist has been trying to copy unsuccessfully for years. As the artifact of beauty that counters Eliza's businesslike obsession with money, the angel represents, on one level, Gant's first wife, Cynthia, or at least the memory of her, though now distorted by time. The play, in fact, focuses mainly on time and loss. The passage of time inevitably entails loss, but there can be gain in that loss, as Eugene discovers. A "photograph" of life as it was and is lived is only potentially a work of art. It must be subjected to a transmutative process, as Eugene will attempt to do as he makes his own life the subject matter of his art, seeking after the transcendent—if elusive—form of the angel sculpture.

The Strindbergian male/female conflict already apparent in *Craig's Wife*, *The Shrike*, and *Look Homeward, Angel* continues in D. L. Coburn's *The Gin Game*, awarded the 1978 Pulitzer for drama. It is one of several recent plays—part of a loose movement begun by Albee in *The Sandbox* and *The American Dream*, continuing through Robert Anderson's *I Never Sang for My Father*, and perhaps culminating in Arthur Kopit's *Wings*—to consider at least peripherally the plight of the aged and infirm in American society. As residents of a county-run nursing home, the two characters experience—and comment on—the loneliness (solitaire is a favorite pastime), the neglectful children who do not visit, the awful food, the nurses who treat the elderly like children, the well-meaning do-gooders who take the aged into their homes in search of extended families, the complainers who thrive on misery. Weller Martin categorizes such an existence as a demeaning sentence to death-before-death, calling the home "a warehouse for the intellectually and emotionally dead" and bemoaning "the same damn empty look, face after face. . . . like rows of wrinkled pumpkin heads."[17] Coburn's major concern, however, is larger and more archetypal than the provocative castigation of society's failure. Mostly, as his title indicates, the work examines the inadequacy of the life-as-a-game metaphor, for to quantify people always into winners and losers necessarily diminishes the quality of life—both in and outside the nursing home. The card game that constitutes the play's ongoing action becomes ultimately a vicious Strindbergian battle of the sexes, a fight for life in the face of old age and death in which there are only losers. For to win, the woman as titular champion must adopt the worst aspects of the male, descending to the level of the enemy. Coburn perhaps thus warns his audiences against a too militant feminism. But nothing is ever only a game; as Fonsia Dorsey implies, something more than cards is at stake. More broadly, if less emphatically, the play also reveals man's tendency to flee to the cloak of providence, chance, or luck rather than accept personal responsibility.

Weller and Fonsia begin as perfect foils for one another: he, a rather crude, feisty old codger, but with a strain of sardonic humor; she, a creature of refinement both in manners (inherited from her father) and in morals. Weller walks with a cane, a prop literally supporting a weak leg though used aggressively and vindictively in a feeble attempt to demonstrate his strength and finally symbolically broken to indicate his defeat. Weller responds ever more violently to threats to his conception of himself; not only is he unmanned by the economic system—victimized by a business partner and now diminished by having to accept welfare—but emasculated by Fonsia as well. Winning gin game after gin game, she reduces his dignity, since the game was his assertion to himself of his value as a human being. If he is a sore loser who overreacts like a petulant child, it is a symptom of his terror at being treated as if he were dead and useless before he really is. His defiance at the end, however, is puny rather than Promethean, since he has resorted to something external to himself—winning—as his chosen means for establishing self-respect.

Fonsia, also victimized by the system, is, nevertheless, even more a victim of herself. As she manipulates Weller and strips away his dignity, unintentionally at first, since she does not understand the fragility of his self-esteem, but increasingly with growing satisfaction and maliciousness, she diminishes herself, falling into excesses of rage and vulgarity that before she prided herself on rising above. Coburn errs in presenting little more than a stereotype of the castrating wife and mother who fights with her ex-husband for control of their son, makes her son feel like the "lowest piece of crap" (p. 62), and vengefully prevents him from getting any of her inheritance by giving it to a church. In a slip of the tongue, the woman who always demanded that people take responsibility for their actions tries to shirk hers, rationalizing that she was simply "unlucky" in her men. As she sinks further and further to Weller's level (indicated by her language that regresses from "hell" and "goddamn it" through "bastard" to "fuck"), she at first feels frightened by these sudden outbursts, but then gleefully uses them as chants of victory and triumph. Yet at the poignant close she reaches (much like Thelma in 'night, Mother) a painful cry of recognition, "Oh, no," and the audience pities someone who is so petty up until the very end of her life, who has come to so little after so long. If the experience of releasing all the anger and frustration seems to have been cathartic for her, it remains true that Coburn achieves his comic effects cheaply, through expletives from the mouths of the aged. And although skillful performances can make it a brilliant *tour de force* for an acting duo, the play itself has benefited, like so many others in Broadway's recent lean years, from an inflation in criticism that takes the small, successful work and raises it preemptively to the level of importance.

The last two plays in this group—widely separated from each other in time—uncharacteristically present female protagonists whose fulfillment comes from sacrificing themselves so that a man they love can attain selfhood. Owen Davis designated *Icebound,* his regional New England drama and winner of the 1923 prize (over Elmer Rice's expressionistic *Adding Machine*), a "folk play," although it could more precisely be linked with the local-color tradition, solidified in fiction by Sarah Orne Jewett and Hamlin Garland and reflected in popular film entertainment of the day by D. W. Griffith's *Way Down East.* Set in Veazie, New Hampshire, *Icebound* is naturalistic in its dialogue and other techniques, as well as in its philosophy, for the physical setting serves not only as an emotional barometer of the people, but actually determines their character. During much of the play, whose action spans late October through late March, the landscape remains frozen and snowbound, symbolic of the lives of the Jordan family. They could not be any other way: "That's what nature's done for us Jordans,—brought us into the world half froze before we was born . . . . . . so's we could live the hard, mean life we have to live."[18]

As the play opens, the family gathers in the parlor, a room as "cheerless" as their God and opened only for funerals, to await the death of the matriarch. Money, the question of who will inherit, consumes these "crow buzzards"; though not so evil as the despicable Hubbards in Lillian Hellman's *The Little Foxes,* the Jordans, too, are despoilers eating the earth, "living out of this soil for more than a hundred years, and never putting anything back" (p. 220). Davis peoples his stage with Northern grotesques, content to leave most of them caricatures, truthful but flat. In this conventionally plotted play, the return of the black sheep, the younger brother, Ben, who fled from the law after a drunken spree that ended in a barn burning, provokes a fear that he will inherit the land since, despite his failings, he most resembles the mother. Mrs. Jordan, who dies alone before Ben can reach her bedside, remains unseen but is spoken of as an emotionally repressed, frigid woman unable to express love and equally afraid to receive it. To be strong, she thinks, means to be unemotional—at least toward other human beings, for she does share with Ben a natural affinity for animals; Ben's attempt to reduce these creatures' pain and ease their lot becomes for him a saving grace. Hardly less alienated and disillusioned is Ben's elder spinster sister, Ella; thwarted in fulfilling herself and displaced from her limited role of caring for their mother, taken over by cousin Jane Crosby, she now pursues a demeaning career as a hatmaker, thinking possessions will bring salvation: "I've been stuck here till I'm almost forty, worse than if I was dead.... Now I'm going to buy things—everything I want" (p. 198).

In a neat twist of the plot, Ben does not get the inheritance, at least not at first, but Jane is willed it in trust since Ben would only squander it. Mrs. Jordan recognized Jane as the forceful outsider capable of saving her son, but only by sacrificing herself, by being "a woman who will hold out her heart to him and let him trample on it, as he has done on mine" (p. 217). Jane, possessing the fiber of the Jordans without their emotional constraint, becomes consumed with her role of restoring to Ben a measure of self-respect by instilling him with a strong work ethic and turning the estate over to him once he takes hold of his life.

Structurally, in a technique Gale employed earlier, the beginning of the third act exactly repeats the first, the characters grouped on stage in identical positions waiting to hear Jane's disposition of the money. Ben, at first tempted to become hard as the Jordans have always been, questions whether he will be able to escape the family curse. Poised against the stifling atmosphere of the bleak and wintry New England house is the joy of life, the sun and laughter and music Ben experienced in France during the war, when he became infatuated with a girl in a "sort of blue" dress. Allowing herself one small luxury, Jane buys herself a similar dress for her birthday, only to walk in and discover, in a compellingly ironic moment, Ben kissing his flirtatious step-niece, Nettie, who has donned the dress. Tempted to throw his life away in hedonistic self-satisfaction, Ben taunts Jane. But his resolve is only temporarily deflected, and in an unsentimentally handled—if unlikely—ending, Jane stays on as his wife. Davis, unfortunately, relies too heavily on the cyclic symbolism of spring's return to carry the weight of convincing his audience about the rightness of the match.

Despite the passage of thirty years and a shift in geographical setting from North to South, there exist obvious similarities between *Icebound* and the 1955 winner, Tennessee Williams's *Cat on a Hot Tin Roof,* in plot (both center on death and questions of inheritance), in character configurations (both look at relationships between a parent and a favored child and between a woman and an alienated man whom she tries to reform), and in thematic motifs (both examine lack of communication and emotional estrangement and the kind of love that bridges such a gulf). Yet Williams has written a drama considerably richer and more complex than Davis's in meaning and character psychology, as well as in its multifold use of visual stage symbols. Though Williams, like Davis, fills out his cast with a number of humorously or satirically conceived caricatures, in this instance Southern grotesques, he recognizes and exploits the possibility of multiple protagonists through three compelling characters and the interactions among them. As Williams expresses it in one of his stage directions: "I'm trying to catch the true quality of experience in a group of people, that cloudy, flickering, evanescent—fiercely charged!—interplay of live human beings in the thundercloud of a common crisis."[19]

Significantly, the play begins on Big Daddy's sixty-fifth birthday, but since nearly everyone else knows that he is dying of cancer, the household has the oppressive aura of death about it—though much of this aura will be dispelled, especially in the Broadway version of act 3, by the symbolic use of the birthday. Like Ephraim Cabot in O'Neill's *Desire Under the Elms*, Big Daddy as patriarch of the family possesses a great, bounding lust for life, tenaciously clinging to it because, as he says, it "is important. There's nothing else to hold onto" (p. 63). And, again like Ephraim, he desires to pass on that life as a way of gaining immortality, of surviving after death by leaving something of himself behind. Big Daddy comments that man alone among all the animals is conscious of his death, of his finiteness, and so time becomes an enemy to be conquered, in a purely biologic and secular way through progeny, through passing on the Mississippi delta plantation that he loves to a son who is like him and who will see that the inheritance is nurtured in the way Big Daddy wants. Vying for the land are Daddy's sons, Gooper and Brick (and their respective wives, Mae and Maggie). His cancer symbolizes, at least in part, the greed eating up the family; Gooper and his baby factory, Mae, with their brood of little "no-necked monsters" bearing "dogs' names" (maybe next time Mae will "drop a litter") resemble in their avariciousness the despoilers Davis sketched.

Brick, although like Ben the favorite son, has also become a black sheep. A former football star and sometime sports announcer, he hobbles around on a crutch after an accident jumping the hurdles, trying to recapture the faded days of former glory. If the crutch supports him in his physical disability, drink until he hears the click of forgetfulness softens his state of spiritual disrepair. "A monumental monstrosity peculiar to our times, a *huge* console combination of radio-phonograph. . .TV set *and* liquor cabinet. . . . a very complete and compact little shrine to virtually all the comforts and illusions behind which we hide" (pp. xiii-xiv) makes visual man's reliance on artificial supports or defense mechanisms instead of human help and compassion. In the act 2 confrontation, Brick, his crutch knocked out from under him, will finally be forced to accept his father's hand.

Brick attempts to flee from his moral culpability in the death of his friend Skipper, who harbored homosexual longings for Brick—although there is every reason to believe Brick when he says that on his part it was nothing but a "pure" friendship. Several critics, particularly John Simon and Foster Hirsch,[20] have accused Williams of dishonesty in not pursuing openly the question of Brick's latent homosexuality. Williams would answer in part by saying that "some mystery should be left in the revelation of a character in a play, just as a great deal of mystery is always left in the revelation of character in life, even in one's own character to himself" (p. 85). Furthermore, homosexuality seems finally as little at issue here as in Robert Anderson's *Tea and Sympathy* of a few seasons earlier. What Williams concentrates upon is Brick's failure to respond with compassion to Skipper when he called just before his suicide—evidently to confess his feelings. But Brick, apparently fearful of hearing his friendship tarnished by being named something else and, what is worse, of having his own insecurities bolstered, hung up on Skipper; he now suffers from guilt over his part in his friend's death, as well as from disgust over the general condition of "mendacity" that contributes to the malaise of the times. Having given up on himself, he wallows in self-pity and blames his wife, Maggie, who once out of jealousy even went to bed with Skipper, both as a means of getting closer to Brick and to prove to Brick that Skipper was indeed a homosexual. Now Brick has turned from Maggie, though she is determined he will father their child.

Williams, drawing a static heroine who functions mainly as a catalyst, characterizes Maggie as a tenacious, tough-skinned woman unafraid to tell the truth; according to her own assessment, she is "not good," yet she does claim to be totally "honest." Although not completely free from greed (she endured a childhood of deprivation that left her wanting security), her actions in the play are more altruistic than selfish; eaten up with longing, she determines not to let her marriage fail—for the sake of Brick and Big Daddy as well as herself. Maggie shares with Big Daddy his sensuality and sympathizes with his dream of continuity through physical regeneration. She will risk all to restore Brick's self-respect and faith in his manhood: "Oh, you weak people, you weak, beautiful people!—who give up,—What you want is someone to—take hold of you—Gently, gently, with love! And—I *do* love you, Brick, I do! (p. 123). Maggie, blending strength and compassion, would seem to exemplify Woolf's ideal of the "woman who [has] intercourse with the man in her" (p. 102).

Just as Gale wrote a new third act after *Miss Lulu Bett* opened, Williams wrote a new third act during rehearsals of *Cat* at the insistence of director Elia Kazan. Essentially, the new version, along with bringing Big Daddy back onto stage to assert his renewed strength in the face of death (and tell his ribald elephant tale), leaves Broadway audiences more certain of Maggie's success in accomplishing Brick's regeneration. When she asserts in the new concluding act that there is "life" in her, she is not yet pregnant, and so she appears to be lying. Yet this lie is a potential truth, for her love and determination to redeem Brick, to hand his life back to him "like something gold [he] let go of" (p. 158), is the life that she exudes; and Big Daddy—who hates all lies and liars—confirms its presence when he proclaims, "Uh-huh, this girl has life in her body, that's no lie" (p. 153). The potential for giving life physically will become actual when, having thrown out Brick's liquor bottles, she leads him off to bed. Brick himself "admires" her and recognizes her creativity. This last birthday of a dying man becomes, then, his son's birth day into manhood, looking towards a grandchild's birth.

Along with Williams's persistent emphasis on the destructive effect of a predatory family on the sensitive individual, on the need to endure even in the face of shattered ideals, on the lack of communication and the human condition of "solitary confinement," on the painful nature of facing the truth, and on the destructive effects of a guilt that is allowed to fester, *Cat* defines several different levels of love. Williams pictures in Maggie's love for Brick a mature love characterized by not being afraid to criticize the other creatively, yet accepting the other humanely and nonjudgmentally. Their renewed love is grounded in and glories in the physical (the "big double bed" is a central prop in the stage setting), but it also offers the possibility for transcending, while never forgetting, the purely physical. Maggie refuses to give up on Brick because she realizes that her fulfillment as a woman is tied to his fate. Her definition and completion as a woman can come only from her success in making him whole. If this seems perhaps a far cry from what is ordinarily considered emancipation, Maggie *regards herself* as totally independent, pursuing her freely chosen role. Williams clearly admires his heroine for this, so *Cat* helps demonstrate that the selfhood Nora sought can take more than one form—and can exist within, as well as outside, the marriage relationship. Although among the Pulitzer plays the earliest ones, such as *Why Marry?* and especially *Miss Lulu Bett*, may most accurately express the "feminist" viewpoint, *Cat* remains (along with *'night, Mother*) superior drama and among the worthiest recipients of the prize.

Considered chronologically, these nine plays—whose award dates of 1918 through 1983 span virtually the whole history of the Pulitzer—do not evidence (as some might wish) any neat progression from the unemancipated to the emancipated woman. Yet most of the permutations, except that of the totally submissive female, occur somewhere along the way. Jane from *Icebound* and Maggie from *Cat* dramatize the woman who only discovers the source of self-fulfillment in the knowledge that she has helped her husband reaffirm his own sense of dignity and manhood. Four other female characters exhibit symptoms of the emasculating wife and/or mother: Ann, by her total victory in *The Shrike*, might obtain precisely what she wants; the triumph of Harriet in *Craig's Wife* and Fonsia in *Gin Game* is, however, essentially hollow, while Eliza's defeat in *Angel*—her inability to be at one and the same time loving wife and mother as well as calculating, successful businesswoman—is treated with the greatest poignancy. Helen from *Why Marry?*, on the other hand, exemplifies the "new woman" who is intellectually and socially and economically the equal of man, able to integrate seamlessly marriage and a career, if not motherhood, while the protagonist of *Miss Lulu Bett* decides, at least for the time being, that working on her own and living free from marriage is the best means for her of achieving a sense of self, of becoming, in Nora's words, "a human being."

Although Jessie from *'night, Mother* appears totally unconcerned or even oblivious about the link between having money of one's own and the freedom to be oneself, most of these women understand—in concert with Woolf—that money confers power. When a society, like that of Ibsen's Nora, makes control of financial affairs a male prerogative, then this becomes one means of subjugating women. Can a woman call her soul her own when she depends upon another (father or husband or brother or son) to feed her body? Even works whose domain is the family are not without their sociopolitical ramifications; as Miller remarks of *Cat on a Hot Tin Roof*: "The struggle in that play is around who is capable of carrying on this society. And without the power and politics, that play can't exist."[21] Maggie, however, like Jane in *Icebound*, by her own choice holds the money/power in trust only until the man she is determined to help redeem can take hold of himself sufficiently to exercise financial authority. For two of these women, Harriet Craig and Ann, financial dependence only seems to contribute to their shrewishness; for two others, Eliza and Fonsia, having money, on the other hand, just exacerbates their emasculating tendencies. In other words, women in these plays do not necessarily wield their financial power any more equitably or compassionately than men do. Only in the case of Helen and Lulu does working for money of their own become an essential ingredient of attaining selfhood.

Along with this primary focus on the ways in which women define themselves, these plays touch upon several secondary thematic patterns: an ironic criticism of social and moral hypocrisy, whether in the form of upper-class airs or small-town provincialism, as in *Why Marry?*, *Craig's Wife*, and *Lulu Bett*; the regenerative and transformative power of a love that is willing, if need be, to criticize compassionately, as in *Icebound* and *Cat*; the disillusionment that comes, often in middle age, from seeing that the days of glory, if not opportunity, are past, as in *The Shrike* and *Cat*; lack of communication between the generations, as in *'night, Mother*, *Gin Game*, and *Cat*. Also woven in the plays are a few of the primary motifs—the ideal of art as a protection against the destructive power of time and as an intuition of the supernatural, as in *Look Homeward, Angel;* the world-as-theatre metaphor, as in *Lulu Bett* and *The Shrike*—that become recurrent staples of the Pulitzer Prize dramas.

Though none of these works violates the convention of the assumed presence of an imaginary fourth wall separating stage from auditorium, several of them do play, to a greater or lesser degree, on the audience's awareness of being within a theatre. *Why Marry?* may end with a Brechtian challenge to the audience to reform the social system, particularly in the area of sexual mores, yet the closing line is directed not to them but to the characters onstage, and so no crossing of the footlights occurs. Nor do the characters in *Cat on a Hot Tin Roof,* despite the partially nonrealistic set with walls open to the sky that helps to universalize the action, ever acknowledge the audience's presence. This boundary between characters and audience is maintained as well in *Miss Lulu Bett* and *The Shrike,* even while they employ the life-as-a-stage metaphor: in the first, Mrs. Bett hints that the act of theatergoing is contagious and that playacting might be carried over into real life with surprisingly satisfying results; in the second, role playing is diagnosed in more negative terms as a necessary concession to protect oneself from the shortcomings and prejudices of society.

At the beginning and end of *Look Homeward, Angel,* the link between onstage characters and audience is handled more fluidly: both when young Eugene narrates one of his stories to open the play and when he converses with the spirit of his dead brother, Ben, to close it, he could be talking to himself; but he (and Ben) could just as easily be addressing the audience, telling them that the passage of time entails change and loss yet also mercifully brings forgetfulness and that life is a struggle to find the only permanence that exists—the self. While naturalistic in its precise rendering of detail, *'night, Mother* insists at the same time on keeping its audience aware of themselves as in a theatre, through the way that it frames the proscenium stage with the wide shadow-box border, as well as through the way lighting symbolically emphasizes the door through which Jessie will exit at the end. From one point of view, the door leads to an inner stage where, as in the Elizabethan theatre, the emotional climax of the play will be acted out. Yet Jessie's closing of the door is an even more definitive assertion of freedom than Nora's, for she goes into a world whose absolute value she alone can determine, rather than out into one whose patriarchal value system will continue to fight her every step of the way.

2

Supportive Illusions/ Romantic Delusions

Lionel Trilling once remarked that "'all literature tends to be concerned with the question of reality. . . .what really is and what merely seems.'"[1] To say, however, that a play, or any work of literature, is about the illusion/reality dichotomy is to say everything and yet nothing, for simply by its very existence every product of the imagination somehow comments about the nature of art versus life. Yet certain dramas, most notably several by William Shakespeare and many by Luigi Pirandello, are more openly philosophical in their approach. One of the major American plays in that tradition—and one of the handful of works that run counter to the ideological tameness of most modern American drama when seen beside its Continental, and even British, cousins—is O'Neill's *The Iceman Cometh,* eligible for a Pulitzer in 1947, a year when no award was given. (Also eligible that year was Miller's *All My Sons.*) It can be argued that O'Neill's massive work is not primarily about illusion/reality, that it concerns instead the way a totally uncritical and forgiving love (Evelyn's for Hickey) can be destructive rather than creative, as well as man's need (in this case, Hickey's and Parritt's) to be judged so that expiation for guilt can follow. On the question, though, of illusion/reality, O'Neill apparently follows Ibsen's notion of "life-lies" in *The Wild Duck* when he intimates that a life of illusion can sometimes be preferable to a life spent facing the truth, that, in fact, only a relatively few truly heroic individuals are equipped to confront the truth with any kind of regularity and consistency. As T. S. Eliot says, "Humankind cannot bear very much reality." Sometimes, therefore, it may be desirable *not* to pull the saving grace of illusions out from under other persons, particularly if they are aware that they live in illusion, if they can distinguish that illusion from the truth, and if they do not harm anyone else by clinging to the illusion. As *Iceman* dramatizes, the truth-bringer (Hickey) can be a death-bringer for most.

In *Who's Afraid of Virginia Woolf?*, which should have, and indeed would have, won the Pulitzer for 1963 had not the advisory board rejected the drama jury's recommendation—resulting in the courageous resignation of both John Gassner and John Mason Brown, two of the most eminent and respected drama jurors ever—Albee explores the same issue of whether the destruction of illusion might ever mean salvation rather than death. In *Iceman*, Harry Hope's birthday celebration quickly becomes a wake as Hickey strips away saving illusions. In *Virginia Woolf*, there emerges the same play on birthday/deathday when George determines to destroy his and Martha's illusory child, on the day that it would have come into its maturity, so that their relationship can henceforth be built on a more creative foundation of mutual love and support and so that their young guests, Nick and Honey, will recognize the emptiness of their marriage without the unitive agency of a real child. The theatre, a house of make-believe, might by its very nature seem to exist as a statement in support of some universal need for illusion; and the playwright, as fabricator and artificer, might be seen as its chief accomplice in this. Yet *Virginia Woolf* uses the theatre and the artist (both Albee and George) to challenge the audience's dependence on illusion. George's recitation of the requiem mass for the dead "child" becomes a ritual burial of art/illusion as escape and a ritual rebirth of the union between husbands and wives: it is not simply that truth has replaced illusion, but that love, rather than lies, will now be trusted and tried as the basis for human relationships. In *Virginia Woolf* only love remains to fill the void left by the loss of illusion and to assuage the fear of the unknown. The condition of Albee's four characters is finally not unlike that of O'Neill's Larry Slade. When Larry asserts at the close of *Iceman* that he is Hickey's "only real convert to death,"[2] he affirms his conviction that he is one of those rare people who can live condemned to know the truth about others and about himself, free now from the illusion of detachment and from the fear of death as the final end and meaning of life. This is not necessarily as nihilistic a position as some commentators would hold: living with that awareness proffers man a "hopeless hope"—perhaps the most he can expect in O'Neill, but enough to make him potentially heroic.

The award of the 1945 drama prize to Mary Chase's *Harvey* can probably best be explained by the escapist mood of the war years that favored entertainment and forgetfulness above all else—though, perhaps surprisingly, *Harvey* makes a serious point not unlike that of *Iceman*: for some people, illusions are not only harmless but helpful. It goes even further by suggesting that the illusion-less are the really deprived. Though *Harvey* finally ran for 1,775 performances, its winning the Pulitzer must rank as very nearly the least defensible in the history of the prize, since that year the jury passed over Williams's now-classic *Glass Menagerie.* Many critics like McCarthy not only judge *Harvey* as utterly "lacking in artistic merit,"[3] but also generally question its theatrical merit as farce. Despite its flimsiness as drama, Chase's play remains a paean to the imagination and to man's power to create metaphor. Since the title character, a pooka in the form of a six-foot white rabbit, never appears on stage (only sounds and props, such as a hat with holes in it for the ears, indicate his presence), watching the play demands not simply a willing suspension of disbelief but an imaginative participation by the audience, who must accept what they cannot see. The point is made, then, that surface reality tells only a part of the story, and those who accept only experiential, empirical knowledge, who attempt to remove all mystery and magic from life, become fools rather than wise.

The theatre has always been a house of illusions capable, if the playwright so desires, of whisking an audience away from their everyday reality; in this way, going to the theatre becomes analogous to the journey that the characters in romantic comedy oftentimes take when they leave their usual habitat for a distant green world. Here, the audience and the characters enter not a green world, but a sanatorium. Dr. Chumley, who owns the rest home where the second two acts occur, emphasizes that the so-called worldly wise often suffer from an inability to distinguish the reasonable from the irrational. Ironically, the "fools" living in illusion most nearly approach sanity, and the psychiatrists themselves, bent on freeing people from their psychoses and neuroses and denying them any life-giving and creative fantasies, are the object of Chase's criticism—though admittedly not as extreme a criticism as in *The Shrike,* which broached the same topic. To say "it stands to reason" is deceptive. Veta, the staid, matronly sister of Elwood Dowd, whose faithful companion Harvey is, stresses that reality is somehow *less* than the totality of life. Referring to the portrait of their mother in the stage set, she distinguishes between a photograph that simply records the surface and a painting that "captures not only the reality but the dream behind" that reality; it is such "dreams that keep us going. That separate us from the beasts."[4] Later, Elwood significantly replaces his mother's painting with one of Harvey, the fruit of his imagination made concrete. Elwood claims that the rabbit revealed itself to him, as it would to any individual alive enough to recognize it. Whereas Hickey in O'Neill's drama acts as a false saviour, trying to strip others of their saving illusions, Harvey possesses the ability to inspire people to undertake "wonderful" projects that would otherwise not be attempted.

Although Veta, too, has seen Harvey all the while, she commits Elwood to Chumley's rest because her eccentric brother wreaks havoc on all the proprieties and pretensions of her social set. Eventually Veta, who has been in Elwood's camp all along, is joined in her support of Elwood by Chumley himself, after he has been converted by the "miracle" occurring around the sanatorium; on the other hand, Myrtle, her convention-ridden daughter, Dr. Sanderson, and the Judge all oppose Elwood. Sanderson, as his vocation demands, urges a return to reality, to an almost Puritan acceptance of one's "duties and responsibilities." Even some critics—excessively outraged by the libertarian emphasis and not recognizing the farcical exaggerations of an essentially harmless play— fall into line behind Sanderson, arguing that to accept Elwood's escapist approach to life threatens the American system of values. Lillian Horstein, for instance, solemnly protests, "To glamorize neuroses, psychoses, and even murders and to make them subject of light laughter by means of dramatic art and clever stage business indicate a moral shallowness and intellectual futility...the first signs of decadence,"[5] while George Jean Nathan less sententiously calls *Harvey* "the greatest intemperance document that the American stage has ever offered."[6] (Harvey will certainly never appear to either of them.)

It takes the Cabbie to state explicitly that Sanderson's cure would be worse than the disease, that the injections to return the patient to sanity destroy a person's "faith" and ability to have "fun." Veta echoes this, claiming that normal human beings are "bastards," the kind who, if they ruled the world, would cause dissension and war. Elwood simply suffers a more aggravated case of a disease that everyone might benefit from—a liberal dose of life-saving and humanizing illusion. The only differential that Chase would seem to admit between the people in her world is the quality of their imagination, which exists in proportion to and is a measure of their humanity. Despite everything that can be said for her viewpoint, this type of play by its very nature oversimplifies and ignores entirely the opposite possibility: that illusions can be harmful and that maybe the only heroism finally does come from an uncompromising refusal to be sheltered by the dream. In short, her unambiguously upbeat philosophy allows no room for admitting that the iceman does come. Moreover, this narrow vision, while it might be temporarily satisfying, is conveyed in a work that never challenges the audience to regard it as more than an amusing trifle.

Many of the Pulitzer plays, including some of the earliest winners, are, however, decidedly more substantial than Chase's. With the possible exception of Susan Glaspell's one-act plays *Trifles* and *Suppressed Desires,* and his own one-act plays of the sea, Eugene O'Neill's *Beyond the Horizon,* recipient in 1920 of the second drama Pulitzer (none was awarded in either 1917 or 1919), is the first work by an American playwright to provide evidence that American drama can attain a literary as well as a theatrical position. Stated abstractly, *Horizon* considers what happens when an all-consuming dream is denied, when the almost visionary impulse of the poet is not acted upon. O'Neill concretizes this in the conflict between two brothers who each make an inauthentic choice: Robert Mayo, possessed by "a touch of the poet," who yearns to wander freely on a voyage of discovery in search of the secret "beyond the horizon"; and Andrew, who finds fulfillment in farming, rooted and wedded to the good, clean earth. Theirs is the archetypal conflict between the romantic and the realist—between the sensitive, nonmaterialistic impulse and the practical, businesslike one that O'Neill often dramatizes. Linked to this is the more universal search for some place to belong, for a sense of oneness with self and mystic union with something outside of and greater than self that also constitutes one of O'Neill's recurrent motifs.

Robert's means of escape will be a three-year voyage at sea, undertaken not for financial gain, the only motivation that his cunning father could imagine, and not even to come into touch with some cosmic mystery. Rather, he intends unselfishly to remove himself from Ruth, whom he loves, since he knows that Andy loves her, too, and believes that she loves Andy. Yet when he tells Ruth about leaving, he misreads her banal and cliched romantic response as a declaration of her love for himself and so chooses to remain. The romantic dream is, however, a false poetry, a lesser good, and by choosing it Robert fates himself to never belonging anywhere, except in death. Instead of fighting for Ruth, Andy flinches from the pain of seeing her with Robert and himself embarks on the voyage. Despite old man Mayo's portrayal as an authoritarian and ruthless father (whom Andy resembles, just as Robert, in a pattern typical in O'Neill, emulates the soft and compassionate mother), he serves as a choral figure, warning Andy that he is "running against his nature"[7] and will come to regret being untrue to himself. As is frequently the case in O'Neill, the ethical perceptions of the father are valid, rebel as youth might against the rough surface qualities of the man. Both sons, of course, have betrayed their nature: Andrew returns from having hated the sea and, now that life on the farm seems trifling to him, determines to go off to Argentina and seek his fortune; Robert's marriage has become another Strindbergian battle zone, Ruth hating him for having distracted her from love of Andy, and Robert accusing her of never having provided the support he needed. The farm has gone to seed and become a wasteland, imprisoning Robert both physically and spiritually. When their daughter, Mary, dies five years after the initial wrong choice, Robert curses God and questions the meaning of suffering and its relationship to Providence; if unmitigated suffering exists for life's misbegotten creatures, then the suffering itself becomes meaningless and irrelevant, since no interlude of joy exists against which to measure it. Only in contrast to something better can pain be meaningful, and if it is not meaningful, then existence itself becomes unthinkable. As is invariably true in O'Neill, character becomes destiny: the initial choices that Robert and Andrew make to go against their natures determine their fate.

When Andy returns penniless to the farm where his brother is dying of consumption, he tells Ruth that she must lie creatively to spare Robert, confessing she loves him and has always loved only him. For himself, Robert can only travel "beyond the horizon" in death, full of unreconciled impotent rage at Fate, but certain of winning release and being free at last. Andy, having excoriated Ruth, takes pity on her, saying they must help one another and then perhaps someday... (the implication being that the tale might still have a happy ending). Already here, love equals service, a definition that O'Neill never moves very far beyond in his work; in fact, there appears to be a deep distrust of any married love not founded on service of wife to husband, a condition that might be seen as a regression, the wife acting as mother to satisfy the needs of her husband/son. O'Neill, nevertheless, clearly views this as preferable to the romanticized concept of love that first attracted Ruth to Robert. As Jane Bonin notes, "The culprit is romantic love, which causes the characters to make wrong choices. . . . romantic love becomes an infantile disease."[8]

Horizon opens at sunset and closes at sunrise with Robert exclaiming, like Oswald at the end of Ibsen's *Ghosts,* "The sun!" Yet, as if to counteract any too facile dependence on the pathetic fallacy, O'Neill makes the old gnarled apple tree that was budding into leaf and straining heavenward at the play's opening lifeless and seemingly dead in the October dawn. The contradictory images (sunset/budding; sunrise/dying) underscore the pattern of gain as well as loss, life as well as death, fate as well as free choice—an ambiguous doubleness to life. O'Neill consistently employs his settings and stage time symbolically; here, he carefully (some might argue too schematically) alternates between indoor and outdoor scenes to indicate the fragmentation and lack of harmony between the inner and outer man in his characters. Robert never finds peace inside the home, suggesting his lack of truth to his inner self, his delusion in the choice of object to which he commits himself. Thus O'Neill conveys the central meaning of his play visually, in a work that helped catapult American drama to maturity.

While *Horizon* focuses on two men who love the same woman, Zoë Akins's faithful and deft dramatization of Edith Wharton's *The Old Maid* concerns two women who love the same man. Both examine the pull between material values and a higher ideal and the life of regret that follows when marriage fails to fulfill the dream. The choice of *The Old Maid* for the 1935 prize, even more so than that of *Harvey* a decade later, was controversial and much maligned, not because the play, old-fashioned and sentimental as it now seems, lacks merit in structure and characterization, but because of the strength of the contenders: *The Children's Hour* by Hellman and *Awake and Sing!* by Clifford Odets (neither of whom ever won a Pulitzer), along with Robert Sherwood's *The Petrified Forest* and Maxwell Anderson's *Valley Forge*. The decision, which has been deemed "the silliest and most disgraceful... because of the unmentioned censorship that eliminated consideration of a genuine American classic"[9] (that is, *Children's Hour* for its ostensible lesbianism), met not only with an enraged critical outcry but also was instrumental in prompting the establishment of the Drama Critics Circle—which gave their first award to Anderson's *Winterset* in 1936, the year Sherwood won his first Pulitzer for *Idiot's Delight*.

Akins places less emphasis than Wharton on the social manners and mores of upper-class New Yorkers in the 1850s to 1880s; furthermore, she alters the narrative strategy by beginning chronologically with Delia's marriage to James Ralston, rather than presenting it retrospectively as in the novella; this permits her to open and close with a wedding sequence, thus effectively emphasizing the area of human experience that Charlotte, the title character, is denied. In marrying James, Delia chooses security and practicality over the love she felt for the artist Clem Spender, to whose bohemian lifestyle she refused to accommodate herself. The Ralstons, in fact, perfectly exemplify the Protestant ethic of success and how this becomes synonymous with the American Dream; James's aunt, Mrs. Mingott, claims the family came to America "with every intention of living for a bank account instead of dying for a creed."[10] As in O'Neill, there exists an unbridgeable gap between art and business, poetry and practicality; Clem, in fact, finally loses the spark of the poet by marrying a rich girl.

For a wedding present, Clem sends to Delia, via Charlotte, a blue cameo picturing Psyche and Eros. The cameo is Akins's invention, and the myth of the mortal woman of surpassing beauty who lacks the faith and trust necessary to keep the god of love by her side relates to Delia's inability to offer Clem sufficient time to prove himself as an artist, and thus losing him. Just as Psyche spends the rest of her life looking for Cupid, Delia seeks something of Clem's that she can call her own, finding it in the illegitimate child of Clem and Charlotte. In contrast to Delia, Charlotte vows that she would have waited all her life for Clem, whom she secretly loved, though she also admits she would choose to "be an old maid because the man [she] love[d]" (p. 11) did not love her in return, as Clem did not. Delia will sacrifice the ideal for practicality, Charlotte will not; she refuses to reduce it by allowing it to be anything less than perfect. To be an old maid in a society where marriage confers upon a woman her identity is to condemn oneself to a life of desperate loneliness, although marriage, as Charlotte discovers, usually entails the financial dependency of the wife upon the husband.

Like the humanitarian women in George Eliot's novels, Charlotte compensates for her loss by altruistically devoting herself to running a nursery for children—including her own Tina, whose identity no one knows. She even decides to forego marriage to Jim's brother, Joe, when it becomes clear that he would no longer allow her to run the nursery (something society would not tolerate in the wife of a Ralston) and that he indeed resents her emotional attachment to the children, not because of jealousy but out of distrust over any open display of emotion. (Jim gives expression to a more odious side of the capitalist class when he proposes that the masses of people going hungry because the banks have stopped payments be shot down like "mad dogs.") Delia, seeing Tina as her one remaining connection with Clem, invites Charlotte and Tina into her home to live. Attempting to recapture the dream she denied by rejecting Clem, she now tries to possess Tina. Charlotte, to keep secret the truth of Tina's parentage, deliberately makes herself into a churlish old maid, only to have her daughter taunt her as someone who has "never known anything about love" (p. 77). On the eve of Tina's marriage to a man very much like Clem (the next generation replays the preceding one almost too neatly), she resists the temptation to reveal her identity and have Tina address her as "Mother" just once. For this, she is rewarded by Delia's one unselfish action: Delia begs Tina to keep her "very last kiss" goodbye for Charlotte, so that Charlotte will not regret the choice she made in sacrificing everything for her daughter.

As is true in *Beyond the Horizon*, both central characters receive ample recompense for the choice they make. Charlotte, who clung to the dream and would not allow it to be compromised, is up to the last moment treated shabbily at the hands of Tina; Delia is excoriated by the other characters for succumbing, like Ibsen's Hedda, to the "sacrilegious thing of wanting to lay so much as a finger on another person's destiny" (p. 56) as her means of avenging herself on the world for her decision to renounce the romantic dream and relinquish Clem.

Works focusing on mothers and daughters, such as *The Old Maid*, are much less common in American drama than those about father/son or mother/son conflicts. Of the other plays awarded the drama Pulitzer, only William Inge's 1953 prize-winning *Picnic*—and to a lesser degree Norman's *'night, Mother*, Beth Henley's *Crimes of the Heart*, and Paul Zindel's *Effect of Gamma Rays on Man-in-the-Moon Marigolds*—detail the influence of mothers upon their daughters. *Picnic*, like Inge's other works distinctive for its midwestern setting and characters, might have been called, to reverse Ernest Hemingway, "women without men"—not because it contains no important male characters, but because the men are, for much of the play, circumscribed, even created, by the image that the women have of them. Inge himself remarks, "'The women seemed to have created a world of their own, a world in which they seemed to be pretending men did not exist."'[11] What delimits these women is their almost total subjugation to the curse of the romantic imagination—a malady that afflicts such other characters as Amanda in *Glass Menagerie* and Mary in *Long Day's Journey Into Night*.

In *Picnic*, Flo Owens, the mother of two teenage daughters, attempts to control the parameters of their existence by instilling in them a romantic ideal to pursue as their grail: to "live in a palace with a doting husband who'll spend his life making [them] happy."[12] As an ideal, this finds its source in serialized women's fiction as canonized by Hollywood. At heart it is an image very much tied to domesticity, countered in this play by the pull towards freedom and independence—symbolized by the train whistle heard in the distance, with its equally unreal promise of happiness somewhere over the rainbow. These two options, romantic escape versus domesticity, are represented by Flo's daughters, Madge and Millie, who exhibit the classic but now cliched split between beauty and brains. If Flo, partly as a way of finding a chance to live her youth over again and experience the love she never felt, only dreams of "pretty things" for her girls, Madge actually hopes to be "discovered" by Hollywood. But she and her awkward and unpretty younger sister both acknowledge their incompleteness, each envying what the other has. Madge never considers, however, that her incompleteness might reside in a certain spiritual vacuity; such a perception would probably be totally beyond this restless young woman, who gazes narcissistically at her image in a mirror to validate her existence.

The young men are presented in an equally schematic fashion, underlining Inge's fondness for foil characters. Alan, Madge's boyfriend, is a well-to-do intellectual, while Hal, whose arrival as the cock in the henhouse sets the women in a tizzy, is the muscle-bound, swaggering jock, barechested or tee-shirted in the tradition of Stanley Kowalski, a goodhearted, Hollywood-bound derelict who has never quite found himself. The triangular conflict his arrival initiates ends when, much to Flo's dismay, Madge deserts the security Alan promises to follow Hal and the whistle that beckons.[13] Women, Flo seems to be saying, may escape to the realm of their romantic illusions in their daydreams, yet they must not in reality, where domestic slavery is still the order of the day. What makes a woman like Madge so ill-prepared for marriage, however, is precisely the romantic dream that Flo has fostered; married life with Hal will clearly not be what Madge expects. Millie, moreover, becomes so depressed and confused over the sexual mating games going on around her that she vows never to open herself up to potential hurt by marrying, committing herself instead to the lonely life of the artist. (The audience recognizes this as simply a temporary adolescent overreaction, perhaps revealing Inge's own intuition about the solitary fate of the writer.) Flo's neighbor, Helen Potts, whose mother had her marriage annulled so that Helen's only role would be as daughter/martyr and never as wife/mother, stands as a reminder to Flo of what can result from the undue and basically selfish influence of mother upon daughter.

Essentially, Inge intends in *Picnic* to show that women finally cannot do without men, much as they might like to fool themselves into thinking that they can. In the subplot, which Inge handles with the complexity of a double plot, the spinster schoolteacher, Rosemary, desperate over the awareness of time running out, sacrifices her freedom and independence to marriage. Although oftentimes blatant, Inge's symbolism is not lacking in theatrical effectiveness. The time is early autumn, when the fruit is beginning to ripen, yet the prime is brief; as Flo remarks, one minute a woman is "twenty-one" (like Madge), "then forty" (like Rosemary). With the younger and middle-aged generations both onstage, *Picnic* becomes a ritual of youth supplanting age, and the somewhat pathetic older women must accept, however grudgingly, the passing of time. Helen, for instance, finds herself drawn in by the cult of youth; she thinks the idea of a Labor Day picnic with the young couples is romantic, and yet she feels uneasy over her sexual attraction to Hal. Rosemary, who puts up a front of propriety by chiseling the sexual organs off the school's statue of a gladiator and by objecting strenuously to degenerate books by the likes of D. H. Lawrence, masks her own sexual deprivation in an emasculating attitude that prevents her beau, Howard, from getting fresh with her, which is how she keeps at bay her fear of sex. Yet Hal's appearance somehow liberates her.

Inge brilliantly dramatizes the dynamics of these relationships—in a work sometimes too busy and full of incident and detail—through the dance at its center. If the play is partly seasonal ritual, it is mating ritual as well; and the dance, in which sexual roles are temporarily thrown askew, is a contest of the sexes, eventuating in a reconfirmation of the image of woman as traditionally subservient to the man, even pleading to be allowed that unchallenging identity. (The uneasy feeling remains that this might be Inge's male wish fulfillment, caused by a fear of the castrating female.) At the beginning of the dance, Rosemary is with Millie, since she has no man to dance with, but she leads, as she thinks she must; nor will she tolerate a parody of her and Millie when Hal and Howard imitate them in drag. In a pathetic attempt to prove her youth, a jealous Rosemary later pulls Hal away from Millie and dances with him, finally turning on him and literally ripping off his shirt when she realizes the impossibility of setting back the clock and possessing him. Meanwhile, Alan, by appearing in an apron, visually displaces the macho image that would confirm him as an appropriate husband for Madge. In her desperation, Rosemary eventually pleads with the weak mama's boy, Howard—a far cry from Hal—to assert his feelings, take her as his wife, and thus save her from a life of profligacy and one-night stands. Yet once they are married, she will undoubtedly dominate, and Howard will probably return to the bottle. If Inge's men finally think they have broken free, it is only to fulfill a stereotypical role that the women are responsible for creating and perpetuating. The myth of maleness, though differently understood by both sexes, is finally destructive for both.

As satisfying as *Picnic* is in its characterization, Tennessee Williams's *A Streetcar Named Desire,* the Pulitzer play of five seasons earlier (1948), may legitimately be called the finest work ever to win the award, possessing, along with technical brilliance, what much modern American drama lacks: the psychological and thematic complexity usually associated only with the novel. Setting his play in New Orleans, Williams dramatizes what results when a Southern woman's dream of refinement meets and is challenged by the brutality of the real world—a brutality in which she, at one point at least, unintentionally participates. Williams structures his drama around dichotomies of character, imagery, and ideas as a means of expressing how fragmentation of experience and dissociation of sensibility inevitably lead to an imbalance. To deny any part of existence, to refuse to admit life's organicism and see experience instead in terms of unresolvable antinomies ("either/or" rather than "both/and"), constitutes modern man's major illness.

Blanche DuBois, the illusionist, confronts Stanley Kowalski, the literalist. She insists on the place of "magic" in life: "I don't want realism. I want magic! Yes, yes, magic! I try to give that to people. I misrepresent things to them. I don't tell the truth, I tell what *ought* to be truth."[14] As Harold Clurman notes, she is "the potential artist in all of us. . . . Her lies are part of her will to beauty; her wretched romanticism is a futile reaching toward a fullness of life."[15] At one point, in an attempt to recapture life as it was—or as she remembers its having been—at the family plantation, Belle Reve (that is, "beautiful dream"), Blanche attires herself in the long white satin evening gown, the silver slippers, the rhinestone tiara; but in a symbolic action, she breaks the hand mirror, for art cannot camouflage life or stop time, and reality will always betray the dream. Belle Reve was lost through "the epic fornications" of her ancestors, and all the old generation have fallen victim to "the Grim Reaper." Blanche has also endured the death of her young husband, Allan, who shot himself after she discovered him in the arms of his homosexual lover; impulsively, she had yelled, "You disgust me" (p. 96). Gradually, she has come to understand her failure to respond nonjudgmentally to another in time of need. She lacked the infinite compassion later exemplified by Hannah in *Night of the Iguana,* whose unselfish answer to the request by the underwear fetishist, "Nothing human disgusts me unless it's unkind, cruel,"[16] exists as a touchstone for measuring the morality of an action in Williams's world. Although Blanche can truthfully say that she has never fallen prey to "deliberate cruelty," she feels guilty and is haunted by the strains of the "varsouviana" polka, playing when Allan pulled the trigger. If Brick in *Cat on a Hot Tin Roof* drinks until he hears the "click" blocking out his failure to answer Skipper's similar call for help, Blanche assuages her sense of failure by running from "death" to "desire," from thanatos to eros, through a series of liaisons with young soldiers that eventually get her fired from her teaching position. Yet Blanche deludes herself by attempting to deny that this sensual side, which runs counter to her dream of purity and gentility, is really a part of her nature. The repressed sensual side demands expression in excess, finally even in violence.

If Blanche is fragile, nervous, and mothlike, in need of soft lights to shade over the ravages of time (to tear the paper lantern that reduces the harsh glare of the naked bulb, as twice happens, is to violate Blanche herself), her brother-in-law, Stanley, is virile, steely, apelike, wearer of "gaudy shirts" that are the "richly feathered plummage" of the male bird; the first image of him is as "the gaudy seedbearer " bringing the fresh meat home from the hunt. Such striking opposites can only come together in the violence of rape; as Stanley says, they have "had this date with each other from the beginning" (p. 130), ever since Blanche intruded on the territory of her sister, Stella, and brother-in-law. Yet the Stanley-in-Blanche, the side she tries to deny in her abhorrence of his vulgarity and lack of refinement, finds expression in the red satin robe that she wears, for she is also temptress, seductress, coquette. And if Blanche has her red robe, Stanley displays a softer side in his neo-Lawrentian love for Stella, a kind of pagan naturalism that invigorates her and guarantees new life for their family line in the accommodation and adaptation that old must make to new, both on a personal and a societal level. (From one perspective, *Streetcar*, like *Glass Menagerie*, is not just about its protagonists, but also about the genteel civilization of the South under siege by the brutal North. It is Chekhovian in the sense of charting the passing of a way of life; by comparing the white woods of Belle Reve to "an orchard in spring," Williams even alludes verbally to *The Cherry Orchard*.)

Blanche's last chance to make real the "magic" in her life comes in her relationship with Mitch, who seems ready to marry her and restore the self-respect she lost through failing Allan. Appropriately, she sings in the well-known lyric from "Paper Moon," "It wouldn't be make-believe / If you believed in me!" (p. 99). Blanche says of their relationship, in which physical sexuality would be a saving grace and affirmation of existence, "Sometimes—there's God—so quickly" (p. 96). When Mitch discovers Blanche's past indiscretions, however, he fails her as she failed Allan; ironically, he treats her like the refined lady she claims to be by acting the perfect gentleman who could never marry the fallen woman. Williams dramatizes expressionistically her extreme vulnerability and the mental disintegration she undergoes by the screeching of cats, the locomotive headlights, the jungle cries, the grotesque reflections, the piano out of tune. Yet, because there remain grace and beauty within her and, as Blanche herself affirms, because she is not totally "destitute," she is proffered in return a promise of gentility and humanity by the doctor who leads her off to the sanatorium. Blanche's curtain line, "I have always depended on the kindness of strangers" (p. 142), is set off against the final, harsh line of the play, "This game is seven-card stud" (p. 142), as the men resume their poker hand. For Williams, the Blanches of this world will always be preferable to the Stanleys who increasingly threaten their existence. In a passage central to the play thematically, Blanche utters Williams's reformulation of Shakespeare's "What a piece of work is man" soliloquy from *Hamlet*. Although her remarks echo faintly the Christian humanistic religious idiom, her phraseology employs the evolutionary metaphor that recurs frequently in American drama: "Maybe we are a long way from being made in God's image, but... there has been *some* progress.... Such things as art—as poetry and music—such kinds of new light have come into the world.... In some kinds of people some tenderer feelings have had some little beginning! That we have got to make grow!...In this dark march toward whatever it is we're approaching. ...Don't—don't hang back with the brutes!" (p. 72). This jeremiad to modern civilization on the brink of aesthetic and moral backsliding comes not from the mouth of the literalist, but from the heart of the artist/idealist.

O'Neill's ambiguous attitude in *Iceman Cometh* towards living in illusion can serve as a warning against applying any preconceived moral categories and judgments to the characters in these five plays. The audience's perspective must fluctuate given the contexts and differing emphases of the particular drama: to fail to pursue the ideal proper for oneself, as Robert and Andy do in *Horizon*, may result in personal destruction; and yet, on the other hand, to pursue a faulty ideal wholeheartedly, as Flo does for her daughters in *Picnic*, can be just as destructive. The difference rests in the quality of the dream or illusion. Robert's ideal—to reach a cosmic harmony that it is given only to the poetic spirit to achieve—is a far cry from Flo's mundane romantic delusion that canonizes the soap opera mentality. Delia in *The Old Maid*, by choosing the practicality that money confers over the less tangible illumination of the artist, experiences a sense of regret so strong that she must meddle destructively in the lives of others to assuage her loss; if Charlotte fares much less well in material terms by committing herself unwaveringly to the dream of marriage with the artist or no one, she is at least free from moral culpability. The characters in these three plays who fail do so not because they follow the dream unremittingly but because they misunderstand the way in which their romantic dreams distort reality and do not see that subscribing to an overly romantic notion, particularly of love, actually ill-prepares them to live in reality. Ultimately the dream may be debilitating because it prevents their pursuing not only more realistic but also more humane goals.

The two other works discussed here propose, as do *Horizon* and *Old Maid*, a relationship between the product of the artist's creative imagination and what is commonly called illusion. In the whimsical *Harvey*, illusion is firmly linked with the artistic vision that can have a practical effect on people's lives by making their actions gentler and more humane. In *Streetcar Named Desire*, the artist/illusionist, Blanche, possesses greater moral awareness than the nonillusionist, Stanley. After the violence of the rape—the most brutal, prosaic act in the play—she is plunged permanently into a dreamworld that will be for her a restful haven; her permanent state of delusion becomes a blessing that the real world of excessive rationality can never provide. Her exit from the world, though an act of grace for her, leaves material civilization, however, even further deprived of the life-giving insight that only the artist can provide. Both these plays applaud the metaphor-making ability that is man's special gift, setting him above all other creatures and permitting him to see beyond experiential phenomena into the realm of the spiritual.

Because Harry Hope's saloon in *The Iceman Cometh* is a palace of illusions, James Watson has likened it to a theatre, "a mid-kingdom of dream . . . set apart in time and space from the world outside," complete with "an outer [front barroom] and inner [back room] stage . . . separated . . . by a curtain."[17] The habituees are both actors who play parts and an audience who suspend their disbelief to support and sustain one another in their role playing. In Watson's view, it is the world as theatre, created by the common consent of the residents, that Hickey very nearly manages to destroy in *Iceman*, which is self-consciously "a play about plays" (p. 231). George and Martha's living room in *Who's Afraid of Virginia Woolf?* is, likewise, obviously a playing space, complete, as Hirsch notices, with actors (the host and hostess) who "perform"' for Nick and Honey; the young guests, in turn, provide "an audience for George and Martha."[18] The curtain rising to reveal a "set in darkness" before the "lights are switched on"[19] may, indeed, replicate the darkening of the theatre before the rising of the curtain, thus emphasizing for the audience that they are one step removed from reality and distanced from an action they are somehow conscious of themselves as watching.

What Watson claims about *Iceman*'s "faith in the ordered illusion of art [such that] objective truth is insanity, sanity is art, and art is the sole hope for man in a world gone mad" (p. 237) could certainly apply equally as well to *Harvey* and even—albeit less unambiguously—to *Streetcar Named Desire*. *Harvey* deliberately plays on the audience's awareness of entering the world of the imagination when they escape to the theatre; the place that illusion built becomes a redemptive realm, so the loss of theatre would entail deprivation. In *Streetcar*, the world of magic that Blanche insists upon weaving around herself might be analogous to the web in which the theatre audience temporarily is caught, but only up to a point: at the play's close, illusion is mercifully the only reality left for Blanche, whereas for the audience there can be no final escape, even in art, from the world of Stanley's "seven-card stud."

In neither *Harvey* nor *Streetcar*, however, is the audience's awareness of itself really a central concern in the way that the illusion-making process is. And the closeness of these illusions to sustaining myths would seem to suggest that America is a peculiarly myth-ridden society, using some of these myths—like Blanche's of the genteel South—as a substitute for a long cultural tradition and heritage that would allow Americans to feel less temporary about themselves. These plays might be seen in part as examinations of the extent to which certain defining myths have or have not retained their potency. From this perspective, *Iceman* would test the continued validity of the myth of a saviour outside of oneself, while *Virginia Woolf* would explore the abstract myth of liberal humanism divorced from social action. All of these works repeatedly question those organizing myths by which, for better or for worse, the characters and the audience alike sustain themselves: in *Harvey*, the myth of rationality, of facticity as superior to fantasy; in *Beyond the Horizon*, the myth of spatial dislocation as guarantee of freedom—which it shares with *Picnic*; in *The Old Maid*, the myth of materialism, of getting and keeping, as holding promise of security; in *Picnic*, the myths of domesticity and maleness as defined by Hollywood; and in *Streetcar*, the myth of the absolute disjunction between culture and vulgarity. The recurrent tension is between the material and the immaterial, and almost always, to the detriment of the individuals involved, the society sanctions power and money at the expense of beauty and art.

The Ethic
of Happiness

The works discussed in each of the other chapters in this study—those on women, illusions/delusions, war, race, politics, the American Dream, religion, the idea of progress, art and artists—span virtually the entire history of modern American drama. With the exception of Henley's *Crimes of the Heart*, those in this chapter on "the ethic of happiness" tend to cluster not just between the two world wars but in the decade from the mid-1920s to the mid-1930s. In *The Modern Temper*, published at the end of the 1920s, Joseph Wood Krutch diagnoses the fracture of the intellect from the spirit that came about with the advance of the scientific method. Instead of providing a new certainty in the realm of ethics and human values, the emphasis upon reason and the quantifying of data left man even more isolated from the wellsprings of human action and less sure of himself. When Krutch, who served as a member of the Pulitzer drama jury from 1945 to 1950, reissued his book twenty-five years after its first appearance, he delineated its "thesis" in this way: "The universe revealed by science, especially the sciences of biology and psychology, is one in which the human spirit cannot find a comfortable home. That spirit breathes freely only in a universe where what philosophers call Value Judgments are of supreme importance. It needs to believe, for instance, that right and wrong are real, that Love is more than a biological function, that the human mind is capable of reason rather than merely of rationalization, and that it has the power to will and to choose instead of being compelled merely to react in the fashion predetermined by its conditioning."[1] In Krutch's assessment, science's attempt to provide rational answers leaves man's emotional and moral hungers unsatisfied.

Not only was the time of these plays a period of philosophical questioning but of moral relativism as well, when man increasingly turned from orthodox religious systems towards the dictates of the individual human conscience as the sole norm for conduct, embracing a situational ethic. What came to be a dependence on "happiness" as the gauge of the moral rightness or wrongness of an action—with all its possibilities for distortion and dilution by egoistic and narcissistic concerns—resulted not just from a breakdown of absolutes but from the increased interest as well in psychology, particularly that of Sigmund Freud and Carl Jung. As Walter Meserve notes, a "free expression of self was, of course, part of the new psychology."[2] The half-dozen works examined in this chapter all focus on the question of what constitutes happiness, that elusive state which Freud saw as idyllically available only to "the child in its mother's womb" when, in Krutch's words, "into his consciousness no conflict has yet entered, for he knows no limitations to his desires, and the universe is exactly as he wishes it to be" (p. 3). These plays, however, exhibit sharply divergent emphases on the wisdom and morality of adopting such an ideal of happiness as a valid ethical norm by which to live.

Of these works, Moss Hart and George S. Kaufman's *You Can't Take It With You*, winner of the 1937 Pulitzer, expresses the least concern with the deeper ramifications of individual choice. Kaufman and Hart specify that the New York abode of the middle-class Sycamore family is a "house where you do as you like,"[3] which is precisely what this zany, appealing family does. Penny Sycamore took up playwriting eleven years ago and has since completed eight scripts with such unpromising titles as *Sex in a Monastery*, composing at a desk adorned by a skull paperweight and pet cats named Groucho and Harpo. Her husband, Paul, builds with an erector set and makes fireworks in the basement with Mr. DePinna, the iceman who arrived eight years before and stayed, first as a model for Penny's still unfinished *Discus Thrower* painting. Penny and Paul's daughter Essie studies ballet under a Russian emigré and makes the candy peddled by her husband, Ed, a Trotskyite xylophone player and amateur printer. Presiding over the unconventional household is Grandpa Vanderhof, who keeps pet snakes, plays darts, and attends Columbia University commencements. Assorted visitors include a drunken nymphomaniac actress and an exiled Russian grand duchess. Every excellent farce, which *You Can't Take It With You* assuredly is, possesses an internal logic of its own that prevents its becoming so fantastic that it cannot make its point. This family, as Grandpa states it, has fabricated its existence on a belief that "life is simple and beautiful if you just let it come to you" (p. 156).

Anyone who abides by traditional values within such a family becomes, paradoxically, the oddball, a role here filled by the nonconformist daughter Alice; while recognizing that her family is "gay, fun, and has a kind of nobility about them" (p. 149), she somehow "has escaped the tinge of mild insanity" (p. 141) and even works for a living. Her engagement to the idealistic Yale- and Cambridge-educated Tony Kirby provides the love interest, though Alice senses that their families are just "too different" to permit a marriage. Tony, admiring Alice's family more than she does, deliberately brings his staid parents to the Sycamore house the night before they are expected—though dinner in any event would probably feature corn flakes. But Tony hopes the visit will serve as a catalyst for his father, whose hobby of raising orchids is the only evidence that remains of his desire at fourteen to be a trapeze artist and at eighteen to play the saxophone. The play mourns the accommodation virtually all people make with their youthful dreams and the unfortunate demise of rebelliousness that usually accompanies maturity. Grandpa tutors Mr. Kirby to reject a lifestyle comprised of "doing things you don't want to do" (p. 172) rather than seeking the fun in life.

Not that Grandpa totally dismisses the work ethic for all citizens, but only for himself, advising, "let people who really like to work do it." In biblical terms, he would number himself among, and value more highly, the Marys of this world rather than the Marthas. He has escaped the "jungle" out there because he was not having any "fun," and so money has come to signify for him the root of all evil in this post-depression-era play. He expresses his anarchic impulses against a paternalistic society by refusing to pay taxes because he does not see any benefits accruing to him from armaments and the like. Perhaps he can even get a refund from the IRS once it is discovered that he gave his own name to the anonymous milkman who arrived at the house years ago and stayed until he died.

In his prayer before meals that concludes both acts 1 and 3, Grandpa inoffensively addresses God as a kind of benevolent Chairman of the Board: "Sir, all we ask is just to go along and be happy in our own sort of way" (pp. 146, 175). Although Alice raises the question of whether "to be happy [is] enough" (p. 167), no serious probing towards an answer occurs; on the surface, Kaufman and Hart resoundingly say "yes." To plumb any deeper would risk destroying the farce.

The moral consequences of adopting an ethic of happiness are, however, much in evidence in the earliest of these works. Sidney Howard won the award in 1925 for *They Knew What They Wanted* over two plays destined to be of more lasting interest: Maxwell Anderson and Laurence Stallings's realistic war drama, *What Price Glory?*, which Howard himself judged "the great American play,"[4] and O'Neill's *Desire Under the Elms*, with which Howard's work shares strong similarities in plot. Both look at a May/December marriage in which an old man is cuckolded by a stepson or substitute son, with the bride bearing the child of the young man.

Howard's straightforward treatment of narrowly conceived characters painted in broad, emotional strokes later fed easily into Frank Loesser's 1956 operetta, *The Most Happy Fella*—which, at this juncture, seems a more enduring work than Howard's play. The love triangle is a simple and predictable one: Mexican Catholic Tony, the sixty-year-old owner of a vineyard in the Napa Valley, attracts Amy to his estate through letters, one of which includes a photograph of Joe, his ranch hand who is sympathetic to the cause of the Wobblies. Amy naturally thinks she is to marry the younger man. Tony suffers an accident on the way to meet her, breaking both legs; despite this, the wedding occurs as planned, but Joe and Amy spend the night together. Amy nurses Tony back to health, finally revealing she is pregnant with Joe's child. Tony begs Amy to remain with him, which she does, while Joe goes off to Frisco and greater involvement in the workers' cause.

Tony, with his immense *joie de vivre*, desires a child in his late age so that, like Big Daddy in *Cat*, he will have someone to leave his land to; for him, a "good wife," "gett' rich'—even if as a by-product of Prohibition—'an' raisin' playnta kids'"[5] equal happiness. For Amy, happiness means "a good safe home" (p. 297) where she can escape the desperation of eking out a living in the city; in the country, she hopes to find somewhere she can "belong'—exactly what O'Neill's Abby wants in *Desire*, though Amy is less motivated by greed. Joe, who finds the involvement he needs in some cause outside himself through activism in the workers' movement, proclaims all of them satisfied at the end: "there ain't none of us got any kick comin'" (p. 316).

Howard introduces but leaves largely unexplored a number of thematic motifs. Nothing, for instance, comes of the conflict between religion and science in the persons of the Doctor and Father McKee; nor is much made of the seasonal cycle (Tony raised up in the spring from the dead, the grape harvest in autumn) or of the tension between the Mediterranean and American cultures. Father McKee's agreeing with Tony that no matter who rules, "gover'ment's always gover'ment," and that, in Hobbesian fashion, there will always be a state of war, hints at the social background and unrest. Tony and Amy both espouse a vengeful notion of the deity, he justifying his accident as a punishment for having deceived Amy, she claiming to deserve the humiliation of bearing Joe's child for having betrayed Tony. That they forgive one another demonstrates their developing love.

For the theatre of his time, Howard proposes a rather advanced notion of moral freedom. Tony's live-and-let-live attitude reflects his belief that people should not impose their standards upon others; from this he develops an affective norm for human action, saying that a "mistake in da head is no matter" (p. 316) because the motive of the heart is all that counts. The play is, then, antirational, celebrating the truth of one's emotions and instincts by setting up feelings as the normative measure for right and wrong. These characters discover that happiness not only is possible, it is attainable—they get what they wanted—and the attainment need not necessarily require living by society's conventional manners and mores. It may, in fact, even require violating them in favor of a higher morality determined by the promptings of the heart.

Human affection serves as the measure of morality in Elmer Rice's 1929 prize play *Street Scene* as well. Rice, who earlier embraced expressionism in *The Adding Machine,* successfully experiments this time with extreme realism or naturalism in an attempt to present onstage an entire milieu (here that of the urban tenement). What results is the first of America's important ghetto dramas, in the tradition of Maxim Gorky's *The Lower Depths* and O'Casey's *Dublin Trilogy* and forerunner of Odet's *Awake and Sing!* and any number of black plays from the 1960s and 1970s. Rice conceived of the work as a "landscape with figures," making the apartment house (only the outside is visible) "an integral part of the play."[6] Audiences found Jo Mielziner's set so realistic—he based his drawings on an actual West Sixty-fifth Street locale—that they swore it was their own brownstone up on stage. Yet creating and sustaining this extreme naturalism in setting and atmosphere (with almost constant city noises in the background) proved not as great a problem for Rice as scoring the dialogue for over forty speaking voices, linked only by the accident of inhabiting the same building, and then integrating them with fifty walk-on parts.

The people in the windows and on the front stoops one hot June evening and the following morning form a microcosm of lower- and middle-class urban life, complete with its caring and its apathy, its acts of kindness but also its gossip and petty prejudices: a nervous husband and his unseen wife, giving birth to their first child; a deserted mother and her two children, waiting to be evicted and thrown on charity; a childless Italian woman and her generous, happy-go-lucky musician husband; a spinster schoolteacher with a touch of a martyr complex and her Jewish father, writer of radical tracts for Marxist publications; an unmarried daughter who sacrifices to care for an infirm mother; and a vicious busybody whose two grown children are worse than the worst excesses she criticizes in others. Although types, they are individuals.

The melodramatic central plot involves a love triangle and double murder. Mrs. Murrant, who enjoys music and dancing, argues the need for humaneness, for establishing and nurturing a sense of community, and for "trying to get something out of life";[7] her husband—authoritarian, brooding, life-denying—fails to satisfy her gentler impulses. His watchword is "law an' order," and so he looks with suspicion upon anyone who exercises personal freedom or overtly expresses emotion. He returns unexpectedly to their apartment, discovers his emotionally starved wife and Sankey together, and shoots them both. Although Mrs. Murrant's relationship is adulterous, Rice has so dramatized her aloneness and so orchestrated their relationship against the purely sexual one between two minor characters, that audiences will not judge her harshly. Mrs. Murrant's action is further mitigated through contrast with the solely self-serving overtures Mr. Easter makes to her daughter, Rose. Sharing her mother's belief in the need for kindness and generosity, Rose is pursued as well by the love-struck and misanthropic young student, Sam Kaplan, who decries the world as a vale of tears created by man's misdoing. Since life is only pain, without possibility of any happiness, he concludes that it lacks any purpose. Because all faith is only an illusion, he espouses rationalism; any belief that "somebody. . .sort of loves us and looks after us" he judges "nothing but superstition—the lies that people tell themselves, because reality is too terrible for them to face" (p. 587). In short, he condemns the illusions, both religious and political, that others use to placate their awareness of the void.

Rice explores the relationship between environment, human action, and the quality of life as the central issue of his play. The urban setting seems to deaden; no possibility exists for aloneness or solitude, but there is, as Dusenbury suggests,[8] loneliness even though—or, more accurately, because—these people are forced to exist in close proximity to one another. Old man Kaplan blames these conditions on capitalism and "bourgeois morelity" [sic] that would throw helpless people out on the street rather than encourage them to act with Christian charity; such savagery leads him to conclude that humanity really is not civilized. Yet sufficient doubt remains over whether equal distribution of wealth is the answer; like O'Casey, Rice evidently believes that it is not a different social system which will guarantee happiness, but only an essential alteration in man himself. And it seems dubious whether Rose's decision to escape from the city to the suburbs for a romantic communion with nature can supply the answer—any more than the similar escape routes taken by other idealistic youths in social plays of the 1930s can. Rose finally realizes that the major change must be to take possession of herself, no matter where she is. Although this does not preclude a relationship with another, loving someone else and even being loved cannot substitute for owning herself: "loving and belonging aren't the same thing" (p. 596). A change in place cannot by itself, however, effect a spiritual alteration.

Rice masterfully orchestrates his action, especially at the close of his acts. At the end of act 2, after the murder has occurred and the dying and dead are carried out, the marshall carts the evicted Hildebrand's furniture out onto the street; both actions result from an un-Christian cruelty and inhumanity. At the close of act 1, Rose establishes a symbolic analogue for the entire play. She tells Sam of walking through the park and seeing a lilac bush with a few blooms still on it, reminding her of Walt Whitman's poem that Sam once recited. With his characteristic melancholy, he immediately recalls the line, "I mourned and yet shall mourn, with ever returning Spring," but she insists he recite the part about the farmhouse that ends: "A sprig with its flowers I break." She continues: "That's just what I felt like doing—breaking off a little bunch of flowers. But then I thought that maybe a policeman or somebody would see me...so I didn't" (p. 568). An unnecessarily repressive legalism on the part of society prevents the full joy of life. A moment later they hear the screams of Mrs. Buchanan giving birth. Society prevents joy, but Nature, too, brings pain. Only human generosity and love can endure and prevail over both, and only in these does happiness reside.

Unhappiness that springs from loneliness also pervades Beth Henley's 1981 award-winning *Crimes of the Heart*, which premiered two years earlier at the Actors Theatre in Louisville. Henley's three MaGrath sisters, who bear little relation to Anton Chekhov's, have lived for years in Hazelhurst, Mississippi, under the onus of their mother's suicide that made the national news. Those outside the family, and even some within like first cousin Chick Boyle, foster the notion that the event somehow molded or imposed a pattern upon the MaGrath girls; and the sisters themselves do little to discount that interpretation. What might be just a touch of eccentricity or hint of darkly comic Southern grotesquerie in their behavior thus comes to be regarded as instability or even worse. When the action opens, the youngest sibling, Babe Botrelle, has just added to the family's notoriety by shooting her husband, Zackery, a member of the state legislature, because she "just didn't like his stinking looks!"[9] Yet this "crime" is by no means the worst of those uncovered during the play—the things people do to one another, and to themselves, in a desperate search for love. As Ihab Hassan remarks in another context, "Who has not smashed another, asking for love?" Hovering over these three sisters, along with the spirit of their mother, is their Old Granddaddy, with whom they have made their home and who has, perhaps unwittingly, controlled and limited their lives more decisively than the shadow of their mother's suicide.

Granddaddy always wanted Babe to marry into society, but life with the brutalizing Zackery left her feeling "just...so lonely" that she fell into an affair with a fifteen-year-old black. After Zackery bars him from their home, the child-woman Babe—who had "wanted a team of white horses to ride Mama's coffin to her grave" (p. 59)—contemplates following her mother's example, but decides to kill Zackery instead (he survives). Barnette Lloyd, her defense attorney and, significantly, the only person to call her by her given name, Becky, possesses evidence of Zackery's shady dealings; for love of Becky, he chooses, however, to sacrifice the joy of a personal vendetta against the man who ruined his father's life and who now threatens to make public photos of Babe and her lover.

Granddaddy always wanted Meg, the middle sister, to be a singing star, yet, despite Barnette's claim that she possessed "some special sort of vision" (p. 34), she never had much of a career—her lies to Granddaddy notwithstanding—and so she returns home after her release from a psychiatric hospital. Meg had found their mother hanging in the basement, and her defense against the trauma was to hide behind a defiant humor and harden herself to the misery of others, since to vent her feelings would have signalled weakness rather than strength. To prove her imperviousness, she spent her dimes on ice cream cones rather than donate them to crippled children. Deliberately thwarting her instinct to care, she even walked out on "Doc" Porter after the collapse of a building during the hurricane brought his career to an end. Now, although "Doc" is happily married to a "damn Yankee," they share one night of love in the back of his pickup truck, and Meg vows to finally tell Granddaddy the somber truth about herself rather than falsify things just "to see him smiling and happy" (p. 58), though in his comatose state he will never hear.

Granddaddy always wanted the shy, eldest sister, Lenny—celebrating her thirtieth birthday on the day the play opens—to devote her life to caring for him. By making her self-conscious of the diseased ovaries that prevent her from ever conceiving a child, he has, in effect, caused her to break off a barely begun relationship with Charlie, whom she met through a lonely hearts club. Lenny, in her need to be needed, convinces herself that Granddaddy does this to protect her from hurt, yet she still feels "I'll never be happy!" (p. 67). She is as alone, and as afraid of being lonely, as Babe is. Life for Henley's three sisters has become a search after strategems to get through the miserable days of emotional starvation. Finally, the answer for Lenny, as for Babe and Meg, is reconciliation with herself and others. If Lenny has always envied and resented the talented Meg, she comes to her defense when the judgmental Chick, worried about public opinion, berates her scandalous behavior with "Doc." And Lenny discovers, like Sally in *Talley's Folly*, that Charlie never wanted any "little snot-nosed pig" anyway.

The contrivance of so many decisive events in the lives of the MaGrath girls converging on one day and of the basically upbeat resolutions of each of their multiple problems threatens to topple *Crimes* into farcical soap opera. Just barely forestalling this descent into caricature are the rich texture, the complex motivations, and the rightness of the small details: Lenny's sadness over the inopportune death of her horse; Meg's biting into all the candies in Lenny's giftbox, clearly marked cremes, in search of a caramel; Babe and Lenny's nervous giddiness under pressure when Granddaddy suffers his paralyzing stroke. Along with her skill in individualizing characters, Henley adeptly uses symbolic actions and props.

She begins and ends *Crimes* with a ritual: at the opening, the solitary Lenny unsuccessfully tries to put one candle into a birthday cookie; at the close, the three sisters together celebrate Lenny's "being born" with a dance and a huge, candle-laden cake. Now reluctant to hurt or judge one another, they are interdependent and supportive of one another. The communion-like sharing of the birthday cake concretizes the emotional sustenance they give each other. Less obviously, Henley employs the photograph album that Babe peruses to establish that some "crimes" are no crimes after all. As Babe remarks, "the unhappy times" are just as much a part of "your life" as the happy ones and must be remembered "to keep an accurate record" (p. 59). The time of their mother's suicide that has haunted them can now provide a positive insight. After Babe twice attempts unsuccessfully—and comically—to kill herself (by, in rapid succession, hanging herself from the attic rafters and gassing herself in the oven), she understands why her mother killed not only herself but the cat as well; it was not to hurt the cat, which she "loved," but "'cause she was afraid of dying all alone" (p. 100). If their Granddaddy's intent was always "trying to make [them] happy" (p. 62), the MaGrath women realize that the true source of happiness comes from not being alone. In a final gesture of female support and bonding, Henley's sisters see their fear of living alone mitigated by their solidarity, however fragile, with one another.

In sharp contrast to *They Knew What They Wanted, Street Scene,* and *Crimes of the Heart,* Sidney Kingsley's prize winner for 1934, *Men in White,* stands as the only one of these plays which does not propose and accept a relationship of love as the ultimate answer and anodyne to unhappiness. In retrospect, it must have been the authenticity of the hospital scenes that made it a powerful experience for audiences and the first big success of the Group Theatre, for today it resembles nothing so much as the doctor and hospital TV soaps. Kingsley, whose play the advisory board chose without the drama jury's recommendation, attempted to garner for his work a kind of bogus scientific authority in the printed text when he included extensive footnotes on various diseases and vaccines, scientists, and medical procedures. Nevertheless, at the time of its original production, it did strike several critics as a major play and more: in *The Fervent Years,* Clurman recounts that "the notices, with a few exceptions, were breathtaking. Krutch called it 'a work of art.'"[10] Essentially an ensemble work, *Men* focuses on Dr. George Ferguson, completing a highly successful internship at a metropolitan hospital, and the conflict between further study in Vienna and then in the States under his mentor, Dr. Hochberg, or marriage to the wealthy Laura Hudson. The conflict, presented with the binary clarity of the morality play, is the familiar one between duty and responsibility on the one hand and love and money on the other. George must choose between medicine as an all-consuming vocation or simply as a profession. Both Hochberg and Laura want from George a total commitment to their particular way of life, which raises an ethical dilemma for him: in what does the good life reside? Is it in complete dedication and self-sacrifice or in following the "instinct to enjoy," to seek after immediate happiness?

Kingsley has sentimentalized George, making him a knight in white scrub suit. He is brilliant, willing to stand up and challenge incompetence, almost single-handedly righting wrongs. Yet he is human enough to fall in love and also to satisfy what Kingsley euphemistically calls his "impulse," when, out of loneliness and temporary rejection by Laura in one of her less understanding moments, he takes a student nurse to bed in his cell-like cubicle. Predictably, she gets pregnant from their one-night affair, yet conveniently dies as the result of a septic abortion so that George—though willing to do the right thing by her—will not have to marry her and thus ruin his career. But Laura, of course, discovers his unfaithfulness. Happiness, even the "impulsive" kind that Hochberg seems to sanction, exacts its price. A chastened Ferguson chooses his commitment to medicine; Laura, who sees her own selfishness, sends him off to "work hard" in the best American tradition. Whether they will someday get back together remains unresolved.

Many members of the Group Theatre evidently objected that Kingsley's work was insufficiently sociopolitical in its orientation, though it does touch on several then-current issues: marriage between Jew and gentile, and Germany's use of medicine for political purposes; abortion laws from the dark ages that preclude Barbara's receiving treatment at the hands of anyone but a butcher; economic needs that force hospitals to bow to their boards of trustees in matters of appointments to keep their charity wards open; and money as corrupting and destroying the doctors it touches—though lack of it during the Depression keeps sick people from receiving necessary medical treatment. In addition, a philosophical *angst* hangs over the play, as George almost despairs of the ability of medicine after Barbara's death.

Kingsley stages the central scene of his play, the ritualistic operating-room sequence, in the manner of the abstract expressionists, choreographing it as a kind of ballet, complete with minor characters who "move to and fro like so many pistons, efficiently, quickly, quietly—ghost-like automata."[11] This evidences a kind of beauty, but also a kind of inhuman precision, raising the question of whether George will not be somewhat lacking in the humanizing virtues—despite his considerateness and compassion—if he must deny himself married love in order to fulfill his vocation responsibly. No accommodation between devotion to duty and personal happiness is reached, nor is it more than slightly hinted that any ever easily could be.

In *Strange Interlude*, which in 1928 won for Eugene O'Neill his third Pulitzer for drama—and in 1985 enjoyed a successful New York revival (imported from England)—another man of science is among those who wrestle over the question of whether the urge towards personal happiness can ever serve as a satisfactory basis for an ethical or moral system. The novelty for the audience of breaking for dinner, changing into evening dress, and then returning for the second half of a nine-act play, together with the dramatist's technical innovation of stopping the action while characters reveal their thoughts in interior monologues, may, however, have obscured the play's real substance when it first opened. Through this technical device, O'Neill attempted to counter some of the limitations of drama as a literary form and bring to the stage the texture of the novel. *Strange Interlude* can, in fact, be called a stream-of-consciousness play, reflecting O'Neill's interest in and familiarity with Freudian psychology and analysis, as well as his understanding of what he termed "the special type of modern neurotic disintegrated soul."[12] Furthermore, he related the interior monologues to the use of masks in drama: seeing the rapid fluctuations between what a character says and does and what that character is thinking, either consciously or subconsciously, dramatizes how people constantly adjust and readjust the masks they wear to face both others and themselves. As O'Neill was among the first to admit, this device, which can prove technically cumbersome in production, is not totally successful; it is really revelatory only in the case of Charlie Marsden, the aging writer, for whom surface and substance radically diverge.

Nor can this device, by itself, camouflage the essentially melodramatic nature of the plot. Professor Leeds prevents his daughter Nina from marrying the man of her dreams, Gordon Shaw; after Gordon dies in the war, Nina debauches herself before marrying advertising man Sam Evans. When she learns from Sam's mother that mental illness runs in the family, she aborts their baby; later she conceives a child by Dr. Ned Darrell, names him Gordon, rears him as if he were hers and Sam's, and finally relinquishes her hold on her son so that he can marry Madeline after Sam's death. Nina herself finds peace and reconciliation at the end in a marriage "passed beyond desire" with the writer Marsden. Considerably aided by O'Neill's use of recurrent scenic images, the characterization and themes oftentimes manage, however, to rise above this plot. As characters assume different roles over the space of nine acts and almost three decades (Charlie, for instance, replaces Professor Leeds by acting as a surrogate father to Nina), they will occupy a piece of furniture located in the same position onstage as the parallel character occupied earlier. Or, in perhaps the most stunning visual icon in all of O'Neill, Nina appears triumphant at the close of act 6, surrounded by all her men, her multifarious roles as daughter, wife, mother, mistress all fulfilled, since she now possesses a father-figure in Charlie, a husband in Sam, a lover in Ned, and a son, baby Gordon, offstage.

Yet possession of other people as the means of achieving happiness proves a deceptive good; it is, along with what Darrell calls the "disease" of the "romantic imagination," the mistake that ruins more lives than any other. The professor's attempt to hang on to and control his daughter by forbidding her marriage to Gordon Shaw, for example, causes the initial rift between them and sends Nina in search of a Gordon-substitute. Her idealization of the father turns to hatred when he fails to sanction Gordon, since the father's denying the daughter the right to give "the gift" of herself means that she will lose her "happiness forever." But her "love" for the blond and virile Gordon was itself distorted by being overly romanticized, so much so that she fosters her fantasies by writing a biography of him as demigod. Having refused to go to bed with him before he went off to war, she felt a perverted sense of guilt that she then relieved through promiscuity with other soldiers. She now needs to be punished (as O'Neill characters often do) before she can forgive herself. Decrying the distant "modern science god" who is unknowing of suffering and needing to "believe in something," Nina would prefer a mother-god who understands pain and forgives rather than a father-god who exacts punishment. She initially defines "happiness" in totally nonaltruistic terms; it entails *not* thinking of the other, but only of the self. She marries Sam, therefore, not out of love for him, but only for the baby that he can give her, *her* baby, a little Gordon. Sam's mother, however, while sanctioning "being happy" as the only "good," insists on being other-directed in one's conduct; love demands "giving up"—though at this point she thinks solely of the impact of Nina's pregnancy upon her son. Darrell espouses the utilitarian view that happiness, which resides in accomplishing the greatest good for the greatest number, should be the norm for all human conduct. He echoes the chaotic times by arguing that all morality is relative, that man should not be constrained by scruples, and that "irrelevant moral ideas" be overthrown. But such an ethical system ultimately causes only suffering for those who live by it.

For his code of personal conduct, Darrell adopts a situational ethic that means not doing anything to hurt another person, and so he never reveals to Sam that Gordon is not his son. Because of this moral sensitivity, Darrell is rewarded with the satisfaction that comes from his work as a research physician, as well as by the success of his surrogate-son/ protégé, Preston. He comes finally to regret his earlier embrace of happiness as an ethical norm and, in a formulation of the evolutionary metaphor, to yearn for a return to the "sensible unicellular life that floats in the sea and never learned the cry for happiness."[13] Yet such a premoral condition cannot be an adequate response to modern man's dilemma. O'Neill, indeed, underlines the deficiency of the narrow scientism Darrell displays: Ned mistakenly thinks he can perform an action that possesses an ethical dimension—that is, conceiving a child with Nina—with the distanced stance and objectivity of a biological experiment.

Nina eventually acknowledges that because of her belief that one can be happy only by never putting another person before oneself she has, in a way, corrupted Darrell. Her fantasies have been destructive in that they have drowned other people. Yet she earns the peace of reconciliation and forgiveness from the father through Charlie's agency, as well as the tranquility that comes from living beyond passion, because she has grown from possessiveness to selflessness, from happiness for self to happiness for others, when she finally stops meddling in other people's lives as if she owned them. Knowing that it will make Sam happy and content in his last illness, she painfully sacrifices her son, Gordon, to Sam so that Sam can give him to Madeline in marriage. Her initial attitude towards Madeline paralleled that of the professor to the first Gordon, but she breaks that chain by releasing young Gordon from her hold; "sick of the fight for happiness" (p. 504), she renounces it. To do so is not a denial of life in O'Neill's terms, since there remains in him a deeply Puritan strain that demands the hard choice. Nina is now at peace, no longer suffering the pain of the mother—though that pain, ironically, will now be Madeline's to bear. The peace could not be achieved, however, until she first saw her obsession with Gordon for what it was: a product of the "romantic imagination" and thus a curse, a bringer of sadness rather than true happiness.

Oddly enough, the greatest measure of contentment and the least pain are proffered to Charlie Marsden, the effete artist who arrives at the knowledge that he has evaded his vocation and responsibility as an artist from fear of probing deeply lest he meet himself in his work. He grows from being a novelist of the "surface," lacking "the courage to write the truth" (p. 494), to the artist who finally "marries[s] the word to life" (p. 509), by writing their story, "the book of us" (p. 526) as they are living it. In helping Nina reach reconciliation with the father and bring her life to completion, Marsden reveals that the artist does not merely reflect life but affects it as well. The example of Marsden as writer adds a level other than the melodramatic to *Strange Interlude*. The creative act that illuminates life by seeing "it steadily and seeing it whole," the work of art that has the power to influence ethical and moral choice, and the decision to live for others rather than for self—and not simply for happiness—are the real avenues to release from the purgatorial interlude of suffering.

In these half-dozen works, the characters pursue happiness under a number of guises as a secular aim and virtue at a time when the traditional moral center either no longer holds or is inoperative for them. Most of these protagonists learn, finally, that happiness can be a valid and satisfying end only if it is a by-product of actively going out to another person with kindness and compassion. *You Can't Take It With You*, because of its nature as farce, prescinds from any subtle moral categorizing; it espouses a benign hedonism as a harmless antidote to the demoralization caused by depressed economic conditions and the paternalistic government of the time. By validating an affective ethic that sanctions the response of the heart over conventional moral systems, *They Knew What They Wanted* sets the keynote for the plays to come, especially for *Street Scene* in which humaneness is the chief virtue and for *Crimes of the Heart* with its emphasis on shared nurturing of the other person. Yet any ethic that elevates the heart into the final arbiter of the rightness or wrongness of an action, because it defies hard thought about difficult moral choices, is susceptible to being sentimentalized. Militating against the affective impulse is a determinism—either environmental (as in *Street Scene*) or hereditary (as in *Crimes of the Heart*)—that could be at least partially mitigated by more fluid social and sexual mores, as happens in *They Knew What They Wanted*.

Howard's play shares with Rice's a secondary focus on the tension between the city and the country. Rose's projected journey away from the urban life that stifles into some idyllically conceived countryside seems a rejection of any possibility for change within the system; while it might prove personally satisfying, her flight may be nothing more than an escapist response. *They Knew What They Wanted* defines the dichotomy between city and country less conventionally. Instead of remaining in the "garden" retreat, Joe actively chooses movement towards the city as a means of altering the social system—though within a few years the urban centers will prove inhospitable to the great mass of workers. Perhaps the undertone of *angst* in *Street Scene*, when Sam doubts any release from misery, rings somehow truer because more firmly grounded in the social reality than either Rose's or Joe's commitment to go out and change the world. In *Men in White*, George echoes that *angst*, though in his particular case it arises from an understanding of the limitations of science in the face of mortality. Kingsley's play and O'Neill's *Strange Interlude*, each with doctors as major characters, share in Krutch's perception that science can become a harsh and unfeeling god, both literally and metaphorically.

The characters' asides in *Interlude* do not disturb the boundary between stage and auditorium as might be expected. What appears to be a nonillusionistic technique really is not, since the interior monologues have the opposite intent of compensating for inherent limitations on characterization within drama by adapting a novelistic stream-of-consciousness to reveal the coexistence of the spoken and the thought. Nor, despite its fantastic happenings, does *You Can't Take It With You* play at all upon the audience's sense of being transported into a world of art or the imagination, just as neither the earliest (*They Knew What They Wanted*) nor the most recent (*Crimes of the Heart*) of these plays does anything to capitalize upon the theatre metaphor. The convention of the world as a stage does operate, albeit still in somewhat muted fashion, in both *Street Scene* with its minor characters acting as an onstage audience at the drama of others and *Men in White* with its operating room as theatre for a coldly stylized ballet. To the extent that it proposes an essential disjunction between the pursuit of individual happiness and a commitment to serving others, *Men in White* becomes a rather dour play, basically Puritan in its emphasis; personal contentment in a loving relationship seems inimical to the lot of those whose vocation, like that of the scientist/healer, is other-directed.

The most mature outlook on the ethic of happiness comes in *Strange Interlude*, and then in conjunction with a statement about the nature of art and the vocation of the artist. O'Neill's artist figure, Marsden, takes the raw material of experiential reality and imaginatively molds it into a higher truth that can illuminate the area of choice and serve as an ethical guide for Nina, prompting her to understand that the normal—because human—drive towards happiness cannot be simply self-directed. By thinking and acting in terms that transcend the self and the merely selfish, the self can finally achieve happiness and find fulfillment. Krutch detects a similarity between the goal of art and the goal of science, since both seek after the truth. For the artist, however, truth is subjective and pluralistic, whereas for the scientist it is objective and monistic (p. 103). Yet if the scientific perspective remains inadequate for providing a guide for human conduct, Krutch argues that to hope to discover "spiritual verities" through an escape into the arms of art might be just as futile, since a metaphysics based on fictions will lack "truths of reference" and so leave man adrift (pp. 156-157). Such a viewpoint is more pessimistic certainly than O'Neill's, which proposes that art alone in an age of uncertainty can lead man to ethical action, or than Kingsley's, which employs art (in the operating-room sequence) to examine and criticize the deficiencies of science. For these two playwrights, at least, fictions (Marsden's "book of us"; the sterile beauty of the operating-room regimen transformed almost into dance), though subjective and pluralistic, can still be revelatory of human values and conduct.

4

"Over There"— and Over Here

With such notable exceptions as Anderson and Stallings's *What Price Glory?*, Irwin Shaw's *Bury the Dead*, and David Rabe's *The Basic Training of Pavlo Hummel*, relatively few American dramas portray men at war or training for combat. As Shakespeare brought his second tetralogy on the War of the Roses to a close, he made explicit, in the prologue to *Henry V*, what must have been apparent to audiences all along: only their imaginative power, their capacity to "piece out [his] imperfections with [their] thoughts" (1.23), could compensate for the limitations imposed by the stage in dramatizing the arena of war. Modern playwrights usually handle only obliquely actions better suited to the broader canvas of the screen, with its unlimited spatial dimension. There exists, of course, a whole body of American film about war, particularly about World War II. As Bernard F. Dick demonstrates in *The Star-Spangled Screen*, these movies from the early 1930s through the mid-1950s not only reflect a changing attitude towards war but also helped to solidify opinion and unite Americans; these films, in fact, created a mythology of the war that was more "real" for moviegoing audiences than the historical events themselves. (Rabe reflects the continued hold of cinematic myth on the popular imagination in *Basic Training* when Pavlo, a Vietnam recruit, depends upon the B-movies served up by Hollywood to provide heroes as substitutes for the father he never knew as well as for a deluded sense of invulnerability in the face of war's power to kill.) In Dick's analysis, the early antifascist films that preyed on viewers' fears were seen as a war-mongering incitement at a time when the official public mood was one of neutrality and nonintervention. By the late 1930s, however, that mood had altered to one of preparedness and antipacifism, with characters—like Rick in *Casablanca*—eventually awakening to their patriotic responsibility; the attack on Pearl Harbor and the height of American involvement in the war effort generated scores of openly propagandistic films. It was, in Dick's words, "a 'people's war'" built upon "love of country and hatred of fascism" and "a refusal to remain passive"; though war itself as pictured in the films was "not a virtue" but rather "a job that must be done," courage and "valor," wherever they were exhibited among the Allies, were deemed "virtuous."[1] Only after the war does a revisionist critique of war's ultimate folly and futility set in—and even that takes time out for Korea. The early stages of this cycle, the movement from isolation to intervention, and the later period of revisionism are evidenced among the Pulitzer plays in *Idiot's Delight, There Shall Be No Night,* and *The Teahouse of the August Moon.*

Shakespeare's history plays, though about events that occurred a century or two before they were written, were produced in the decade after the defeat of the Armada and so helped glorify the nationalistic fervor of Elizabethan England. By no means unambiguously or uncritically celebrating the use of force, they nevertheless hold up nationalism as a desirable alternative to the factionalism of civil war. On the other hand, the Pulitzer dramas that focus on war almost invariably condemn an obsessive nationalism as a contributory cause and, once a nation has gone to war, a feeble justification for brutalities and a rationalization for zealously imposing its social values and political structures upon another. When men are reminded that they are citizens of a nation, they forget that they are also citizens of the world. And so the plays tend to be less nostalgic about the war and to have less a sense of reassurance springing from a victorious closure than the comparable movies do. But on two counts—the humanistic ideal of reason informed by the Western intellectual tradition as a guide to man's conscience and defense against backsliding into inhumanity, and the possibility of art as a moral force for educating mankind by interpreting the past—the ideology of these plays is more akin to that of Shakespeare's histories of civil strife than to America's films of a world at war.

Except for Richard Rodgers and Oscar Hammerstein's *South Pacific* (discussed in the next chapter), the only direct treatment among the Pulitzer dramas of America at war or as an occupation force occurs in John Patrick's *The Teahouse of the August Moon,* which he adapted from Vern Sneider's novel and which won the award over Robert Anderson's *Tea and Sympathy* in 1954. Although other Pulitzer plays employ narrators, Patrick's makes the most extensive use of a narrator in the Brechtian mode. In this charming fairy tale for adults, the narrator, Sakini, is both minor character and stage manager à la Wilder, heralding that the "play has begun" and interrupting the action for an intermission to "sip soothing cup of jasmine tea."[2] An interpreter for the occupation army on Okinawa, Sakini also functions as a bridge for the audience into an alien culture; as such, he calls into question the rectitude of imposing democracy from without. In the capsule history lesson contained in his verse prologue, Sakini judges the current United States occupation as only the latest in a pattern of successive "subjugations" over six centuries "by Chinese pirates...English missionaries...Japanese war lords...American marines" (p. 182). Sakini's tone, while mildly satiric, is not bitter; it is assuredly more good-natured and less cynical than it could have been had the play appeared in the Vietnam or post-Vietnam eras. The musicalization of *Teahouse* in the 1970–71 season (entitled *Lovely Ladies, Kind Gentlemen,* after the opening line of Sakini's narration) failed miserably, for example, managing a run of only sixteen performances. And Stephen Sondheim and John Weidman's *Pacific Overtures* (1976), a musical play which tackles East-West relations and explores the oriental concept of art in a manner similar to *Teahouse* (including, even, the use of modified Kabuki elements), ends on a decidedly discordant note underscoring how Japanese technology, a by-product of the nuclear age, comes back to haunt America.

Teahouse amusingly documents the attempts of the American military to introduce capitalism and democratic rule, even if to accomplish it means that "every one" of the natives must be shot, into a culture more interested in beauty than materialism and utility. Colonel Purdy, the stereotype of the bullying, barking, incompetent officer who lives strictly by the book because that is all he knows, errs in judgment when he sends a former humanities teacher, Captain Fisby, to implement the economic and social changes. Though in a pinch Fisby has enough perception, ingenuity, and good old American get-up-and-go to see the local sweet-potato brandy as a source of immense profit, he would much prefer to nurture the native crafts such as vase painting and sandal making for, as one of the artisans remarks, no one can "take pride in work of machine" (p. 191). Respecting the workers' instinctive understanding that the aesthetic sensibility must take precedence over more prosaic needs, Fisby allows them to construct an exquisitely simple teahouse rather than the school called for by the army manual. Now the ritual tea ceremony that embodies the serene Japanese way of life can be performed locally, and the old men need not go to their graves without ever having experienced it in its intended setting. The ambiance of Japan is further symbolized by the geisha, Lotus Blossom, who provides the love interest indispensable to comedy: at first rejecting her because he, in his cultural insularity, equates a geisha with a prostitute, Fisby later unselfishly renounces her because of the racial prejudice back in the States that would result in her rejection—an issue foregrounded earlier in *South Pacific* and later in Rabe's *Sticks and Bones.* But the American unreadiness to accept difference takes second place in *Teahouse* to America's failure to value art and beauty over commerce and utility, as well as its tendency to turn men into machines of production. The conquering heroes' orders to dismantle the teahouse symbolize these flaws; the sounds of its destruction disturb the audience in the same way that the ax blows felling the trees at the end of Chekhov's *Cherry Orchard* do.

Fisby embraces the oriental way of life characterized by the inner serenity that comes from contemplating and appreciating the sunset rather than always "getting and keeping"; from recognizing that it would be "wrong to... impose [his] way of life on [Lotus Blossom]"; from a "gracious acceptance" that leads to "peace with [himself] somewhere between [his] ambitions and [his] limitations" (p. 213). The play focuses as well on art and its ability to answer a deeper need in man, along with the sadness that this need does not seem an integral part of the American system to the same degree that it is part of the Japanese—though even the prosaic Purdy converts to poetry at the end of the play, once the town's financial stability is secure and he has saved face with Congress. Sakini explicitly becomes an illusionist at the play's close; after the teahouse is reassembled, he "snaps fingers and the August moon is magically turned on in the sky" (p. 215). But then he becomes Brechtian commentator: though he does not, like Prospero, abjure his magic, he does declare, "Our play has ended" (p. 216), sending the audience from the world of illusion that is the theatre back into the real world to "go home and ponder" what they have witnessed. Just as the Japanese enter the teahouse for a purifying and tranquilizing ceremony, the audience come to the theatre; yet neither can remain separated from the social community for long—and the values of the teahouse/theatre are meant to reinvigorate the world of everyday life. Sakini preaches that the "wisdom [that] makes life endurable" springs from the "pain [that] makes man think" (p. 216), which is a hard lesson only when any chance of communication between two cultures is obliterated by an excess of missionary spirit that renders the native culture totally subservient to the one the foreign conquerors impose upon it. Yet Patrick is a clever enough entertainer not to force difficult questions too emphatically upon his audience, but in so doing he risks allowing the more serious undercurrents to go undetected.

A similar tension between the two aims of the stage, to teach and to delight, faced Robert E. Sherwood in 1936. Sherwood, however, unlike Patrick, did not want entertainment to supercede education, openly fearing that *Idiot's Delight,* one of the best antiwar plays in American literature and one of the worthier Pulitzer winners, would be "accepted as a gagfest" when he intended "a burst of indignation."[3] Perhaps because war itself distorts the real world and disrupts the moral order into chaos, playwrights incline towards employing mixed modes when treating it. In the celebrated act 2 of *The Silver Tassie,* for example, O'Casey deserts realism for an expressionism filled with liturgical analogues to convey the absurdity of war. Shaw in *Bury the Dead* creates a surreal, phantasmagorical world (as Rabe in *Sticks and Bones* will) in which the dead soldiers refuse to lie down and be buried. Even Anderson and Stallings, in act 2 of *What Price Glory?*, most often praised for its realism, depend on the dream-like and nightmarish. So Sherwood is not alone when, in the cabaret style of *Idiot's Delight*, he veers wildly between opposite poles in style and tone, calling the work "completely American in that it represented a compound of blank pessimism and desperate optimism, of chaos and jazz."[4]

Idiot's Delight, which might be considered Sherwood's *Heartbreak House* touched by *Major Barbara*, earned him the first of three Pulitzers within less than a decade—a number equalled, and later surpassed posthumously, only by O'Neill. These three plays trace his journey (one that many intellectuals took in the 1920s and 1930s) from confirmed pacifism after World War I to interventionism with the rise of Adolf Hitler. Simultaneously, Sherwood undergoes a conversion from pessimism to faith, from his allegorical work, *The Petrified Forest*, which decries reason and technology gone mad, to a belief in democracy and Christianity as the hallmarks of civilization. But if Sherwood himself chooses to advance up the evolutionary ladder rather than retreat back down to the realm of the apes, his characters remain poised at that juncture. Sherwood, in *Delight* and again in *There Shall Be No Night* a few years later, introduces into American drama the "reverse" evolutionary metaphor that will appear again in such works as Williams's *Streetcar* and Albee's *Who's Afraid of Virginia Woolf?*; in the words of Thomas Mann quoted in the play, this descent is a "'spiritual backsliding to that dark and tortured age...a degradation painful and offensive to conceive.'"[5] Though the image may be Darwinian, these dramatists do not adopt a deterministic attitude, since mankind may choose either to ascend or descend the rungs on the evolutionary ladder.

The stage setting in *Idiot's Delight* itself indicates that most of the characters are on the verge of descending: a multilevel, Art Deco cocktail lounge styled after the "Fascist idea of being desperately modern—dynamic symmetry!" (p. 28) portends the spiritual atrophy and bankruptcy mankind slouches towards. Inciting this condition is the "virus" of "Chauvinistic nationalism!" That extreme nationalistic fervor turns the world into "a lunatic asylum" on the verge of war is conveyed (as it is in Jean Renoir's antiwar film of about the same time, *Grand Illusion*) through the setting and the languages spoken by the characters. The small resort hotel in what was once Austria but is now the north of Italy looks out on four countries whose traits are indistinguishable and whose boundaries are invisible—except that their governments have established artificial barriers, turning people into pawns of national states rather than into members of a world community; conquering armies even rub out inscriptions on tombstones and replace them with ones in their own language.

With characters representing several different nationalities, languages, and political ideologies (Italian, Austrian, German, French, English, and American), *Delight* furnishes a microcosm of attitudes towards war.

Nevertheless, even all of the characters who preach internationalism exhibit some flaw. Dr. Waldersee, although recognizing the "obscene nonsense" of war, lacks the courage to be a nonpolitical man of science whose patient is the whole human community rather than just his homeland. Before hostilities break out he says that the glory accruing to any cure for cancer he might discover belongs to Germany; and though he knows that returning to a Germany at battle will mean working on germ warfare, he still goes. Quillery, the radical French supporter of an international workers' revolution, espouses the non-nationalistic ideal; yet goaded into hatred by the war, he calls the enemy Italians "assassins!" and "toy soldiers," for which he is taken out and executed. Achille Weber, the munitions seller (a morally darker version of Shaw's Andrew Undershaft) is an internationalist, but of the wrong sort. Denying any ethical responsibility, this merchant of "the League of Schneider-Creusot, of Krupp, Skoda, Vickers and Du Pont. The League of Death!" (p. 50), rationalizes that he is simply an instrument of God, blaming war and death on those weak nations who must buy arms to create a false sense of superiority. His villainy extends, furthermore, to failing to vouch for Irene, the woman accompanying him, when she is questioned by the authorities.

Traveling on a League of Nations passport, Irene is the woman without a country or, more accurately, a citizen of every country and thus a positive symbol of statelessness, who knows that the only antidote to war is for individual soldiers to "refuse to fight." Throughout her life she always changed her nationality to fit the needs of the moment or her whims, taking on harmless disguises—masks that reflect her imagination. The artifice of the moment makes her what she is, the succession of masks makes her somebody rather than nobody. To adopt a mask is, however, a morally dangerous gesture, since a person's whole life can become a lie, as it has for Weber, to a lesser extent for Dr. Waldersee, and to a still lesser degree for Quillery.

After Weber deserts Irene, Harry Van, the American nightclub hoofer who apparently once spent a night with her and is now trouping through Europe with a bevy of chorus girls, chooses to remain even as the bombs fall. Van, the vaudeville entertainer, is Sherwood's master of ceremonies who effects the combination of "chaos and jazz" in a manner somewhat similar to that used later in *Cabaret*, a musical set in pre-Hitler Berlin. An entrepreneur and confidence man who expected to have his faith in man shaken, he has found it bolstered instead: "All my life I've been selling phony goods to people of meager intelligence and great faith. I suppose you'd think that would make me contemptuous of the human race? But—on the contrary—it has given *me* Faith" (p. 42). While he thinks of himself as "an optimist," Irene calls him a "naive...sentimental idealist," and he does at times seem to have walked out of the pages of William Saroyan. Yet he functions, too, as the dramatist's alter ego, convinced that after darkness "will come again the light of truth" (p. 45). He is a type of the secular saint, whose stage and real personalities are one and the same; recognized by Irene as an "artist," he can rescue this woman whose whole strength comes from the pose.

Irene voices most articulately the horror of war, what Leonardo da Vinci called "'bestial frenzy,'" when, Cassandra-like, she relates her prophetic daydream of what will happen to the English newlyweds: "his fine strong body...a mass of mashed flesh and bones—a smear of purple blood....the embryo from her womb...splattered against the face of a—dead bishop" (p. 63). Disillusioned by the meaninglessness of the conflict outside, she muses on a distant chairman-of-the-board godhead: "Poor, lonely old soul. Sitting up in Heaven with nothing to do but play solitaire. Poor, dead God. Playing Idiot's Delight. The game that never means anything, and never ends" (p. 62). Counterpointed against war is romance, both in the dances that distract them from the encroaching attacks and in Irene's salvation by Harry, who has "walked unafraid into the valley of the shadow—to aid and comfort a damsel in distress" (p. 105). The ironic finale, with Harry and Irene singing "Onward Christian Soldiers" as the bombs fall, has been widely criticized as sensational and melodramatic and as thwarting the audience's expectations for a happy ending. Essentially, it is an apocalyptic close, hinted at by the setting in the Hotel Monte Gabriele, named both for the Italian patriot Gabriele D'Annunzio and for the trumpeting angel. If the characters at the end of Shaw's *Heartbreak House* long for the return of the bombs as the only hope for excitement in their dull, rudderless existence, here Harry and Irene, two little people, do the only heroic thing still possible: they stand firm and face the onslaught.

By the time of *There Shall Be No Night* (the 1941 prize winner), Sherwood's pacifism and isolationism have given way, in the face of the Fascists and Nazis, to interventionism; yet he insisted that rather than "a denial" of *Delight,* the later play should actually be viewed as "a sequel." Abraham Lincoln, the hero of Sherwood's intervening Pulitzer play (discussed in chapter 6), acted as Sherwood's "tutor" in this change: "The development of Lincoln's attitude in the years before the Civil War paralleled the development of the attitude of the whole American people in the years before 1940. Lincoln knew that slavery was an evil, but considered war a greater evil" (pp. 140–41). What has not changed but has, paradoxically, even deepened is Sherwood's faith in mankind at a time when all experiential evidence points to the contrary. As in *Idiot's Delight,* a part of the stage setting symbolizes the moral bankruptcy threatening to overtake European civilization, of which America must see itself as the protector. Decorating the living room walls in the Finnish-American home of Dr. Kaarlo Valkonen and his American-born wife, Miranda, are a number of family portraits that provide a capsule history of the decline of America, "rugged heroism...developing into ruthless materialism...and then degenerating into [the] intellectual impotence and decay that eventuates in anarchy" (p. 159). In Sherwood's view, America can redeem itself from its downward spiral only by discovering a new energy and commitment. In Miranda's background, southern sensitivity met dour New England Puritanism; now, in Miranda, as well as in her and Kaarlo's son Eric, America meets the "rugged, honest, self-respecting, and civilized" Finnish (p. 165). In a recurrence of the evolutionary metaphor from *Delight*, the choice presents itself between using "mind" and "spirit" to rise "above the beasts" or becoming again "a witless ape" (p. 169) by returning to the forgetfulness of the ooze, the premoral and therefore prehuman condition that Lowell describes as man's tendency towards "the dark, downward and vegetating kingdom of the fish and reptile."[6]

Advance demands struggle against the threat posed by the German megalomaniac who "seeks to create a race of moral cretins whom science has rendered strong and germless in their bodies, but feeble and servile in their minds" (p. 167). Once again, the German race is represented by a doctor, Ziemssen, who stands opposite Valkonen. These men of science demonstrate the antithesis between the proper and the improper use of reason. Ziemssen, who knows well the threat the Nazis pose to men of intellect, still "admit[s] the necessity" for them to assert their power by reducing "inferior races" to "animals" (p. 231). Sherwood emphatically makes the other man of science his hero and *raisonneur*. Valkonen speaks with conviction of man's coming to "consciousness" about himself and the ethical dimension of his actions and of God being present in each person: "man will find the true name of God in...the mysteries of his own mind" (p. 289). When that occurs, "there shall," in the words from Revelation, "be no night." Man has, however, temporarily bypassed words and language—the outward sign of his reasoning faculty—as an antidote for brutality, and so the characters in the play are forced to respond by action. First Eric, who fights and dies along the Mannerheim line, but not until after marrying Kaatri, his fiancée and the mother of his unborn child (who embodies the hope of the future); then Kaarlo himself, who removes his Red Cross insignia and takes up the gun of a combatant, later to die; and finally Miranda. Although the Christmas tree stands decorated with its banner proclaiming "on earth, peace, good will to men" (p. 255), Sherwood underscores that the law of Christ's love and the taking up of arms are not in essence antithetical, that sacrifice may be necessary and can lead to resurrection; as Valkonen says: "The great leaders of the mind and spirit—Socrates, Christ, Lincoln—were all done to death that the full measure of their contribution to human experience might never be lost" (p. 312).

With Kaarlo's Uncle Waldemar, Miranda, like Mrs. Miniver, stays to protect her home as the Russians advance. Waldemar has been a prophet of despair, of the Apocalypse and the reign of the Antichrist, throughout the play, but as the curtain falls, he plays a Finnish folk tune, bringing "a kind of peace" to the house. Miranda's stand resembles that of Fanny Faralley and her son in Hellman's *Watch on the Rhine*, who know that their decision to support the anti-Nazi Kurt will cost them heavily. The existential toughness of the characters in *Night* is, in fact, cousin to that of Kurt, one of the demonstrably tragic figures in American drama, who must kill for the cause even though it goes against his conscience. (Although *Watch* received the Drama Critics Award, no Pulitzer was given in 1942, perhaps because *Rhine* was too similar to *Night*, which won the year before; though the drama jury voted Hellman a Pulitzer in 1959 for *Toys in the Attic*, the advisory board gave the nod instead to *Fiorello!*.) Despite all the deficiencies that the critics attribute to *There Shall Be No Night*—its propagandizing, its preachiness, its too easily won and therefore unconvincing optimism and hope—it remains distinctive among the Pulitzer plays and most drama, since it not only reflected prevailing opinion (which the generally conservative commercial theatre has always done), but actually helped shape and alter the opinions of Americans about entrance into the war.

Another family in fear awaits victimization by totalitarian forces in the 1956 prize play, *The Diary of Anne Frank*. Frances Goodrich and Albert Hackett's dramatization of one of the earliest, most widely known, and most universally loved examples of the literature of the Holocaust was as much an event as a play, and so when considering it, matters extraneous to the aesthetic one almost unavoidably arise. Goodrich and Hackett take passages directly from Anne Frank's book and use them to begin the play's scenes, moving gradually from narration to live action, thereby satisfying the audience's desire to see respected the integrity of the original. But the adapters choose not to begin with voice-over passages from their sources; instead, they create an original frame in which Mr. Otto Frank returns to the attic hideout after the war to re-experience the events, finding there the manuscript that Anne wrote before her arrest and eventual gassing. Frank acts as a mediator between the material and the audience as he relives the events in his mind's eye; if he can finally experience anew these wounds without despairing of the human condition, then perhaps the audience can too.

The *Diary* per se, and thus the play, does not center on the concentration camps themselves that hang as a threat over the Frank family and the millions of other Jews they represent; the audience, however, adds its knowledge of the camps to the play from the outside, increasing their tension and fear for these families. Goodrich and Hackett submerge the entire issue of race far beneath the surface for most of the play. True, when the Frank family tear the mandatory Stars of David—marks of Cain upon the innocent scapegoats—off their clothing once they are in hiding, the outline of the Star remains, an indelible mark because race is a birthright. Yet race is simultaneously, as Renoir suggests in *Grand Illusion,* an artificial divider employed as an excuse for brutalization. *Anne Frank* demonstrates how people not only can survive but also can transcend such efforts at dehumanization through linking their individual fates to the spirit of community that springs up between even absolute strangers in times of anxiety and fear—a point made earlier by *Night.* The play testifies to the inability of ever imprisoning the mind and the spirit—as Otto Frank tells Anne, "There are no walls, there are no bolts, no locks that anyone can put on your mind"[7]—while at the same time it demonstrates how the imposition of inhuman conditions on people can drive them towards inhuman actions. Destruction by victimization from without can be matched by self-generated victimization; as petty arguments and bickering break out, Frank warns, "We don't need the Nazis to destroy us. We're destroying ourselves" (p. 252).

Basically, however, *The Diary of Anne Frank* is a rite of passage play about the generational conflict in which youth attempts to salvage what is best from the older generation's values—its religious and societal mores and customs—while moving into the future free of cynicism and displaying self-sufficiency. As an adolescent whose extraordinary circumstances hasten her process of individuation, Anne faces several conflicts. First is the need to reach a truce with her mother. An ugly duckling compared to her older sister, Margot, Anne must belatedly resolve her excessive overdependence upon her father which would, if left unchecked, make her another Mrs. Van Daan, whose idolization of her father (symbolized by the fur coat she obsessively clutches) precludes any satisfactory emotional relationship with her husband. When Anne changes from a girl in whom the intellect is primary, as it is for her father, to one in whom— partly through her friendship with Peter—the emotions are released, then she can better understand her mother. This growth to a more intuitive acceptance of life accompanies the biological changes with the onset of menstruation that link her to all other life-giving creatures; though involving pain, it is a "miracle" as well, so that she "long[s] for the time when [she] shall feel that secret within [her] again" (p. 243). The second alteration is religious in nature. The traditional orthodox religion of the Jewish people is seen onstage in the celebration of Hanukkah, yet the religious rite does not interest Anne as much as the more universal ritual of gift giving that expresses her humanistic belief in the goodness of each towards each that comprises her only "religion." Finally, accompanying her growth as a daughter, as a woman, and as a moral creature comes her growth as a writer.

For Anne, writing a diary offers a means of gaining immortality (ironically, an immortality greater than any she could ever have guessed) by leaving something of herself behind. The act of artistic creation affords a means of handling fear and anguish, in much the same way that the audience, under Otto Frank's guidance, approach this play as an avenue for coming to terms with the horror of widespread inhumanity. The play functions not as a catharsis in the traditional sense but rather as a proof of the human spirit. Accompanying Frank on his visit to the upstairs room is Miep who, along with Mr. Kraler, helped the Franks and Van Daans throughout their period of hiding; they are outside sympathizers through whom the audience learn the need for involvement even at considerable personal risk. Miep is now pregnant, symbolic—as in *Night* and Thornton Wilder's *The Skin of Our Teeth*—of life beginning anew out of the wreckage of war. Suffering and death are "part of a great pattern" (p. 256) and possibly a prelude to resurrection and transcendence.

Bruno Bettelheim objects to the passivity that *Anne Frank* fosters among readers and theatergoers, arguing that it helps people rationalize away the Holocaust: "What is denied is the importance of accepting the gas chambers as real so that never again will they exist. If all men are basically good, if going on with intimate family living no matter what else is what is to be most admired, then indeed we can all go on with life as usual and forget about Auschwitz. Except that Anne Frank died because her parents could not get themselves to believe in Auschwitz. And her story found wide acclaim because for us too, it denies implicitly that Auschwitz ever existed."[8] The danger always exists that any play on war (or on race) might act to salve liberal consciences, making audiences feel morally smug because they feel sad. Bettelheim would probably react more favorably to Alain Resnais's short documentary film, *Night and Fog*, or to Miller's *After the Fall*, which employs the concentration camps as a symbol to argue that "no one they did not kill can be innocent again,"[9] a stance similar to Hellman's in *Watch on the Rhine*, where she proposes "For every man who lives without freedom, the rest of us must face the guilt."[10] Appropriately or not, *Diary* does not raise or foster feelings of universal guilt in its audiences; as most dramas of the 1950s do (with a few notable exceptions like Miller's *The Crucible*), it tends to calm rather than enrage. It is more a play of uplift than of anger.

Just as *The Diary of Anne Frank* is dramatized autobiography, Frank Gilroy's 1965 Pulitzer winner, *The Subject Was Roses*, has a basis in autobiographical material that would serve him again when he came to write his 1970 novel *Private*, which recounts a few of the same incidents. At base, *Roses* is a somewhat banal domestic drama whose characters and problems have long since become stereotypes. (Or has a long succession of American family problem plays simply created an archetypal pattern by now so familiar that original work in the genre is difficult?) *Roses* suffers as well from a lack of focus; it concerns partly a son's attempt to break away from his parents and partly the breaking apart of the parents' marriage. A step in the son's necessary separation involves going off to war (World War II) and coming home to confront the father who never had the opportunity to fight and thus never underwent that male rite of initiation; therefore, he feels unsure of himself as a man and lives a life of regret (a situation repeated with the father in Rabe's *Sticks and Bones*). *Roses* reveals less about the reality of war than about the myth of war and its centrality, not so much for the younger generation as for middle-aged men attempting to discover something in their past that would validate their existence in the eyes of their children (especially their sons), and substitute, in the absence of firm spiritual values, as a heritage to hand on.

Timmy, the homecoming soldier, hides the full effects of the war upon himself behind a certain reticence; as he ages he will come to a necessary, if distorted, accommodation with the experience. Maybe no other way exists to face what he was required to do and the feeling that he was not as heroic as he might have been. "The bravest thing" Timmy ever did in the war was to sleep "with [his] boots off";[11] "the smartest thing," for which he feels some shame, was to never volunteer for anything. He believes that his father would have been a better soldier, but John Cleary is not so sure of that. During the night, John looks longingly at Timmy's bemedaled army jacket, even furtively puts it on, plagued by the never-to-be-answered question of how he would have performed in the theatre of war. (Though submerged, the metaphor of war as a game adumbrates the drama.) Not having fought in the war becomes the barometer of John's entire existence: "I keep wondering what difference it might have made in my life" (p. 144). He fears he might not have been courageous, but he can never know; and not knowing if he would have failed is actually worse than if he in fact had. This perspective towards war as an opportunity for male bonding and a proving ground of machismo is a long way from the increasing outrage and cynicism of the Vietnam years when *Roses* appeared. Perhaps Gilroy can only be so oblivious of the skeptical attitudes then surfacing by setting his play in the personal and national past; yet there remains at least a subtle hint of the division between the older generation—who measure involvement in war by the clear-cut motivation behind America's entry into World War II—and the ever so slightly hinted-at hesitation of the young.

Although, as both Ibsen and Miller demonstrate in some of their best works, exposition may continue almost up to a play's resolution, Gilroy resorts late in *Roses* to long speeches that explain rather than dramatize. Those about John and Nettie's relationship indicate an uneasy match between the sensitive, romantic woman and the reserved, businesslike man. If present actions are any indication, John was always embarrassed over any open expression of feelings—a trait Timmy is developing as well. While John's feelings are usually repressed, a mean and petty anti-Semitism does at times surface. He is less likely to embrace his son than to demonstrate affection through indirection: playful sparring matches, shared jokes and limericks recited in place of curses, and the vaudeville routines "à la Smith and Dale" performed directly to the audience in an otherwise totally naturalistic play. Between himself and Nettie, physical contact has long been dead; his drinking has caused her to reject him, which has led in turn to his episodes of infidelity.

A private little war has always raged out of jealousy over the other's relationship with Timmy: John accuses his wife and son of an "alliance" against him; Nettie, as a non-Catholic, feels herself an outsider, though religion no longer forms a bond between father and son since Timmy, if he has not lost his faith, has left behind any formalized expression of it. Timmy has grown distant from his mother, too, forgetting that waffles were his favorite food and leaving the homecoming breakfast uneaten, a visual symbol for the lack of communion within the family. Yet because Nettie knows that she once had Timmy's affection, she can let him go more easily, though not without pain, realizing that she and John must solve their problems alone, without their son as ammunition. Thus it is the father/son relationship that dominates the play, John begging Timmy to stay for Nettie's sake—though really crying out for him to stay for his own—but finally demanding that Timmy leave. That happens, however, only after an embrace and exchange of "I love yous" that brings the father/son dynamic to completion in a way that the tension between husband and wife, because so long-standing now, can never be resolved. The drama is open-ended about whether the reawakened affectionate side of John will ever extend to Nettie, whether things will again be as they were for the few hours when she thought the roses came from John.

Timmy, likewise, remains an unfinished character at play's end; as the incipient writer he must leave the family behind. He goes without guilt, unlike Tom in *Glass Menagerie*, or recrimination, unlike Edmund in *Long Day's Journey into Night*. Unable to say who is to blame, he settles for the basically sentimental "no one is to blame." He comes home from the war, treated here with the obliquity common in American drama, only to leave—homecoming as leave-taking being, perhaps especially for the fledgling artist, a process of growth. But then, no one ever participates in or comes home from any war unchanged or intact. And John, denied the experience of the war, must always feel temporary about himself.

Considered chronologically, these Pulitzer plays about war reflect a shift in attitude parallel to that which Dick outlines in American film: from isolationism to interventionism to revisionism—but without an intermediate stop at the unadulterated heroics that the stage is incapable of containing. Except for isolated passages in *Idiot's Delight*, and fewer still in *There Shall Be No Night*, these five works do not bring the horror of war as it affects individuals prominently into focus. The majority of them are actually concerned with broader issues, the two by Sherwood—whose screenplay for *The Best Years of Our Lives* (1946), about the traumas soldiers face in readjusting to life back home, won him an Academy Award—even at some expense to the audience's involvement with the individual characters and their fates. In both *Delight* and *Night*, Western civilization, with its traditional values, comes under attack by the forces of "chaos and old night" that threaten to undermine everything that has contributed to mankind's advance. The antagonists are not only nazism and fascism and all other forms of totalitarianism, but all those who misuse and pervert man's reasoning faculty. Sherwood, as a Christian humanist, treasures reason rightly used, yet recognizes that it can be abused when distorted into a rationalism devoid of any moral dimension. Nevertheless, if Sherwood can conceive of instances when the man of peace must turn to force to preserve that peace, he does not probe the potential dangers in a nation's going to war with a missionary goal of converting others to its form of government or way of life by a misuse of power. The lengths to which a country should go in imposing its political system, however "right," upon the rest of the world, are scrutinized critically in *Teahouse of the August Moon*, where the satire is effected through Brechtian distancing devices far removed from Sherwood's emotional appeals. (Perhaps the most forceful comment in American drama on such misplaced zealotry appears in Kopit's *Indians*, which, by examining the exploitation of the native Americans at the hands of the federal government and the showmen/entrepreneurs, brilliantly indicts not only America's treatment of them but, by analogy, that of the blacks at home and the Southeast Asians abroad.) For Sherwood's characters, though, never is fighting a war part of a mystique, as it is for the men in *The Subject Was Roses*, where the battlefield becomes a proving ground.

Playing with the audience's awareness of itself, which perhaps tempers the content's sharp edge, occurs in all of these works with the exception of *There Shall Be No Night*. Even the otherwise realistic *Subject Was Roses* contains a brief vaudeville routine directed at the audience, perhaps reminding them nostalgically of an earlier time and preventing too close a scrutiny of the way in which perpetuating the myth of manhood through soldiering may actually help perpetuate war itself. In *Idiot's Delight*, the stage is clearly a stage on which the old hoofer Harry Van directs his chorus line for an onstage audience who are the viewers' representatives. Yet Sherwood's "artist" is a man who refuses to escape from the responsibility to live with the reality of war—without despairing of the individual's capacity for goodness. In *Teahouse of the August Moon,* the teahouse becomes a kind of theatre within the theatre or a stage upon the stage: it works its magic upon those who enter it in the same manner that the narrator/artist/illusionist plays upon the audience, pulling them momentarily away from a life driven by pragmatism and technology into the serene world of beauty and art. *The Diary of Anne Frank* employs, in effect, a dual narrator: the narrator of the outer frame (Otto Frank) is a moral chorus who acts as a critic/interpreter of the inner narrator (Anne herself); he imposes himself between the theatre audience and their initial response, urging them to adopt a broader perspective that would see the work of art (the *Diary*) as a palliative that can somehow help assuage the horror of the extermination camps. This strategy of narration within narration keeps that reality, already palpable only through the knowledge that an audience brings with it to the theatre, somewhat further removed and at bay. By their techniques of mythicizing (*Roses*) and distancing (*Teahouse* and *Diary*), these works implicitly suggest that theatergoers can bear only so much of the truth about war. The apocalyptic moment that ends *Idiot's Delight* remains the most resonant.

The Fifth Horseman of the Apocalypse— Race

It would be over fifty years after the establishment of the Pulitzers and well over forty years after the first Broadway production of a work by a black writer (Garland Anderson's *Appearances* in 1925) before a black playwright would receive the drama award. Racial issues, however, not only surface in but dominate a number of American plays from the mid-nineteenth century on, including such well-known ones as George Aiken's adaptation of *Uncle Tom's Cabin* (1852), Dion Boucicault's *The Octoroon* (1859), Edward Sheldon's "The Nigger" (1909), O'Neill's *All God's Chillun Got Wings* (1926), Langston Hughes's *Mulatto* (1935), and Louis Peterson's *Take a Giant Step* (1953). In her study *Negro Playwrights in the American Theatre 1925–1959*, Doris Abramson argues that the earliest plays by black authors—*The Escape; or a Leap for Freedom* (1858) by William Wells Brown and *Caleb, the Degenerate* (1903) by Joseph S. Cotter—inaugurate the "two strains," respectively, of "protest against...the status quo" and of "acceptance of the status quo" in works "directed more against the attitude of [the blacks] than against white society" that will continue well into the twentieth century.[1] Abramson's book also makes clear the artistic concessions and compromises that playwrights made in treating the volatile issue of race so that their works would be palatable to commercial theatergoers.

Central to a consideration of any protest drama is, of course, the question of audience. If the protest is directed against the political and social values of the bourgeois establishment who make up, in large part, the audience of the commercial Broadway theatre, then it will likely be guarded and muted, only mildly reproving. The first two plays discussed in this chapter—one having to do with the cultural and racial differences between Americans and Polynesians, the other with anti-Jewish (and in some senses anti-intellectual) sentiment—are cases in point: despite their considerable protest against these forms of racism and prejudice, it is difficult to dispel the notion that either *South Pacific* or *Talley's Folly* is anything more than *just* theatre and theatre as an escapist withdrawal into a kind of fantasyland at that. Both works employ stage space and even the theatre metaphor in a very similar fashion: the characters retreat from society—in the first instance to an island, in the second to a boathouse—in the same way that the audience come into the theatre. In each, the theatre is where the audience go to dream, where the unlikely comes to pass; the romance will be remembered, while the reality will be filed away. What occurs on that island, or in that boathouse—that is, in the theatre—seems remote from the world outside, and so the connection between art and life is not forced home in any astringent manner. It is there for the taking or the leaving.

When it came time for the 1950 awards, the drama jury recommended Gian Carlo Menotti's "opera" *The Consul*—which received the music prize instead. The advisory board, ignoring the jury's selection, chose Richard Rodgers and Oscar Hammerstein's *South Pacific,* based on James Michener's *Tales of the South Pacific,* winner of the 1948 Pulitzer for fiction. (It especially pleased Rodgers that he as composer shared as an equal contributor in the award, since George Gershwin's name had not appeared on the citation for *Of Thee I Sing* eighteen years before.) Somewhat less Pollyanna-ish than the majority of musicals that preceded it, *South Pacific* boasts a more than usually full plot. Drawing mainly on three Michener stories, "Our Heroine," "Fo' Dolla," and "The Remittance Man (The Cave)," with a lesser debt to two others, "Dry Rot" and "A Boar's Tooth," *South Pacific* charted new territory for the musical: because neither the main plot concerning the French planter Emile DeBecque and the Navy nurse Nellie Forbush nor the subplot (really a double plot because it parallels and comments upon the other so neatly) between the American Lieutenant Cable and the Polynesian girl Liat is comic, a third plot strand involving Luther Billis and Bloody Mary was added, as Rodgers notes, for "comic leavening."[2] Furthermore, the show lacks extended dance routines, the only one of Rodgers and Hammerstein's classic musicals of the late 1940s and early 1950s not to include a ballet sequence.

South Pacific explores two major concerns: the tension between isolation and commitment in personal affairs and politics and the racial prejudice between cultures thrown together by war—the latter the subject two decades later of Rabe's much angrier *Sticks and Bones.* The first concern revolves around the pull between public and private duty, a popular motif before the war—and in Sherwood's plays—but one that by the late 1940s had lost some of its social edge. Tied in with this is an emphasis on love as a means of overcoming the separateness and estrangement endemic to the human condition. As the lyric to the haunting "Bali Hai" says, "Mos' people live on a lonely island, / Lost in de middle of a foggy sea," longing for someplace where their special "hopes" and "dreams" might live.[3] But that searched-for place might, significantly, be only another "island," romantic and dreamlike, since love between different races evidently cannot exist within the framework of the advanced social structure called civilization.

This concern about racial hatred and whether it is born into a person or generated through training and environmental attitudes seems to receive, Rodger's disclaimer against intending any "propagandistic message" notwithstanding, the major emphasis. Almost twenty years before *South Pacific*, Jerome Kern, Hammerstein, and Edna Ferber treated the subject of miscegenation in *Show Boat*, which might justifiably be called the first modern musical play; in *South Pacific*, however, the races are not black and white but Caucasian and Oriental. The racial issue, which appears in both major plot lines, is encapsulated in Cable's act 2 song, "You've Got to Be Taught," which, contrary to Nellie's belief that her racial attitudes are emotional predispositions born in her, proposes that these are acquired hates and fears inculcated into the children: "It's not born in you. It happens *after* you're born" (p. 346). This song constitutes the thematic center of the play.

Emile, the fugitive running away from a past in which he killed a man who tried to corrupt and take over a town, and Nellie, the corny," cock-eyed optimist" (as she dubs herself in a lyric indicative of Hammerstein's consistently hopeful philosophy) who is running towards something, contrast with one another. If Emile once chose active involvement while the rest of the world just sat by and watched (is the man he killed to be seen as a symbol for Hitler or Benito Mussolini?), he now opts for savoring the sweetness of life with Nellie rather than risk losing her in a show of patriotic heroics. The hero and heroine's falling in love at first sight on an "enchanted evening" is as predictable and conventional as in most musicals (a truly unsentimental view of love and marriage will not come in a musical until almost a quarter century later with Sondheim and George Furth's *Company*). The dramatic "Twin Soliloquies," with some of their lyrics taken directly from Michener's words, help make the too-sudden love more plausible and effect suspension of disbelief by openly admitting the artificiality and even ritualizing it through rhyme. Later, the Thanksgiving Follies segment employs the show-within-the-show, casting the audience in the role of American troops watching a musicale, thus furthering the breakdown of the barrier between auditorium and stage begun when Bloody Mary addresses the audience as customers for her exotic wares.

When Nellie runs off after learning that Emile had two children by his Polynesian wife, which momentarily destroys any chance that she could still consider marrying him, Emile decides to accompany Cable on a dangerous reconnaissance mission; he involves himself not from any sense of patriotism, but only from a feeling of having nothing left to live for. Cable dies, but his "springtime" love for Liat has already been cut short by the realization that he could never cross the racial prohibition against intermarriage except on an island where spells are cast and dreams come true—in the theatre. Even with his death, the war as pictured here is hardly realistic, seen instead through the nearsighted lenses of postwar euphoria with Billis as guide: exotic locales and customs, get-rich-quick schemes with the natives (as in *Teahouse*), and clowning around and sexual high jinks with the nurses. The unhappy ending of the subplot renders Emile's return and reunion with a chastened and wiser Nellie indispensable for the musical comedy audience. Yet if *South Pacific* makes no very substantial statement about war, or even about love, it does make a provocative one about racial attitudes and prejudices: to see them as *learned* responses implies that someday they might be unlearned and eradicated.

Given the strain of anti-Semitism that continues to exist just under the surface of American society, as evidenced in its most pronounced form by the renewed stirrings of the neo-Nazis in the late 1970s, it is perhaps not surprising to find Lanford Wilson exploring the issue in his 1980 prize play. Set on July 4, 1944, *Talley's Folly* is a slight, sentimental effort, somewhat redeemed by its endearing and engaging central couple: Matt Friedman, a liberal in his early forties, and Sally Talley, a nurse headed for self-imposed spinsterhood, who are misfits in the real world but, finally, fit together almost too neatly by the prestidigitation of some mischievous angel or crazy Providence. As misfits fearing the hurt of rejection, the egg serves as their overriding symbol: "Crack our shells, never be any use again. . . . individuals. We had to keep separate, private."[4] Wilson disguises the slightness of his play in two ways: by the paranoid Matt's Jewish comedy routines (including Bogart imitations and farcical pratfalls) that Matt uses as ploys to cover his own vulnerability and keep cynicism at bay and by the Wilder-like frame of Matt as narrator/stage manager/central character addressing the audience. The latter device, rather than apologize for, actually calls attention to the saccharine, fairytale nature of the play. Here the nonrepresentational form is not integral to the content; rather, it is a clever ploy. What audience, warned beforehand not to expect more than its author is prepared to deliver, could fail to like a play that wears its heart so openly and unashamedly upon its sleeve?

Folly is, essentially, a play of character revealed largely through exposition and some lengthy monologues. Matt, because of the history of his wandering family, considers himself non-nationalistic and feels little allegiance to any political cause or "ism," distrusting them all because "in no time at all you start defending isms like they were something tangible" (p. 46). When he tells Sally the tale of his past—of a Prussian father and Ukranian mother "indefinitely detained" by the Germans in World War I, of a Latvian sister tortured by the French so that their father would divulge information he did not have, and of himself, born in Lithuania and arriving as a refugee with his uncle and family from Norway via Caracas—he distances the story by narrating it in the third person, almost as if it were a parable or folk tale. Only unconsciously does he slip into the confessional, first person "I." Although he escaped the draft because of his age, he is not unaffected by the war (which governments deliberately prolong, he thinks, for economic stability). Since the way of the world for Matt has always been that "life was war, war was life" and since he feels uncertain whether there will even be a time after this war, he refuses to "bring into this world another child to be killed for political purposes" (p. 40), and so he hesitates to marry Sally. In one of the running gags expressing his belief that "the car" (America) "is out of gas" (hope) (p. 50), he foreshadows the emotional and physical aftershock of Vietnam that will be felt by the characters in Wilson's sequel, *Fifth of July*, which occurs thirty years later.

For herself, Sally yearns on this Independence Day to break free from a restrictive family that is antiliberal, anti-Semitic, and anti-German—and so anti-Matt. Yet political, religious, and racial intolerance are not the only things preventing her marriage. She was engaged once before to her high school sweetheart and fellow "golden" child, and their marriage portended a merger of the two families. But her father committed suicide in the Depression, and—in the secret the audience waits to have revealed—an illness left Sally sterile. Once her misconception that Matt was only *saying* he would never father a child so as to spare her the burden of not being able to give him one is cleared up, then these two, made for each other, can come together. Such a resolution has been inevitable all along, and if Wilson equates himself with the Providence who through sleight-of-hand finally brings them together, he delays that union until the last possible moment.

The "folly" of the play's title and the setting of the action is a boathouse that Sally's Uncle Everett, a free spirit like Matt, constructed in place of the gazebo that he had hoped to build. For Sally, it is a place of escape, of "magic." Matt and Sally leave this place to return to a family and a community unprepared to accept them, to one which will ostracize them, just as Matt, the stage manager again at the end, sends the audience out from the theatre exactly ninety-seven minutes later and back into their imperfect world where the only certain value seems to be love on a very selective and limited basis. A dissonance exists between what Matt calls the "waltz" or "valentine" of this "once upon a time" bauble the audience has been watching and the prejudice that pervades the world. Maybe only art, the play, can make that reality bearable or lead the way to a change.

Certain dramas written by black authors in the 1950s and 1960s might well have been honored with the Pulitzer, for example, Lorraine Hansberry's *A Raisin in the Sun* or LeRoi Jones's *Dutchman*, which both explore, in Jones's words, "the difficulty of becoming a man in America."[5] If Hansberry upsets many among a black audience by not questioning critically enough whether the dream that her protagonist pursues has been irreparably tainted by white values, she does examine the ethic that equates "being somebody" with material success while urging a new generation of black men to achieve dignity by coming into their own as husbands and fathers. As Clinton Oliver suggests, however, *Raisin*, though written by a black, is intended as "bourgeois or middle class drama" and so "is essentially integrationist." Yet he is quick to deem that "an oversimplification. The segregation of the Negro from the mainstream of American life has made his art necessarily a reflection of this fact, and is therefore in its profoundest aspects, separatist"[6]—as *Dutchman* more obviously approximates. If Jones annoys many in an establishment audience by his insistence that white society has emasculated the black man, at the same time he still emphasizes how an assimilationist stance by blacks subverts selfhood; the blacks' justifiable hatred and impulse towards violence might even be seen as channeled into and sublimated in artistic creation. Before 1970, however, the two plays focusing on black/white issues that won the drama Pulitzer were both written by whites.

Paul Green's *In Abraham's Bosom*, the first off-Broadway and the third regional drama to win the Pulitzer (for 1927), is, more importantly, the first specifically Southern play and the first about the black experience to be honored. Green (who later collaborated with Richard Wright on the dramatization of *Native Son*), adapted *Abraham's Bosom*, which covers a period of eighteen years beginning in the 1880s, from three of his one-act plays, accounting for the looseness of its structure and abundance of material and detail. The looseness is justified partly by the chronicle nature of the play and mitigated further by patterning the work as one man's odyssey towards selfhood. Moreover, an impressive, heightened rhetoric, appropriate because historical and biblical myths overlay the action, helps direct attention away from the structural flaws. Even though the Abraham whom Green alludes to in his title (taken from a well-known Negro spiritual) is the Old Testament patriarch, the mainly white audience might well connect the self-taught Abe McCrannie's efforts to educate and thus emancipate his people with those of Lincoln. McCrannie gives his son the name Douglas, evidently in honor of Frederick Douglass, the freed slave turned abolitionist and orator whom McCrannie himself emulates and may even be partly modelled after. That Douglas fails so miserably in living up to his namesake and in being the obedient son that Isaac was to Abraham, or like Moses in delivering his people out of the wilderness, are only a few of the play's multiple tragic ironies. Along with the patterning of fathers and sons, the archetypal antagonism between Cain and Abel underpins the work. As the mulatto McCrannie kills his white half-brother, Lonnie, the moral categories of good and evil become confused with the racial coloration. Finally, as frequently happens in American literature, the white/good and black/evil stereotypes are inverted and their validity questioned.

An action Abe performed two years before the play opens began his troubles; he buried a black man lynched for attacking a white woman and was saved from the angry mob only by the intercession of his father, the Colonel, who, though inwardly proud of Abe's strength and intelligence, must respond to his son in public in the way society demands that its leaders act towards blacks. So when Abe retaliates against the jealous Lonnie for striking him, the Colonel whips Abe, calls him a slave, and banishes him. The action picks up in Abe's two-room cabin in the springtime three years later; adorning the walls is a calendar picturing a slave leaving his chains with the caption, "'We Are Rising,'"[7] which foreshadows the aspiring Abe's own ascendency. His wife, Goldie, has just given birth to their third child—and first to survive—a son; and the Colonel, praising Abe's perseverance in contrast to Lonnie's laziness, gives Abe the house and land, as well as permission to teach at the black school. But in this play where the mood is a seasonal, shifting sistole and diastole of joy and grief, the winter—with the ragged field showing through the window—finds Abe beleaguered by the angry parents for having beaten one of the recalcitrant youths. Fifteen years later, on a dying winter day in Durham, Abe is devoid of funds and of any hope for his son; breaking the bond of kinship with Douglas, he even demands that the boy change his name. Instead of the Douglas/Abe relationship mirroring that of Abe and the Colonel, it more closely repeats the Lonnie/Colonel pattern. Deciding that their time in the urban hell has been a dark night of the soul, they return to the country and, close to the soil, make a new beginning. When Lonnie steals his crop and threatens him, Abe kills Lonnie in self-defense. Seeing himself as another Cain, deserted by God, Abe comes close to despair; stones are pelted through his window, and he is finally shot down like a dog.

In killing Lonnie, Abe kills not only his half-brother but tries to exorcise the white side of himself that has always existed so precariously with the black. Abe is a divided self, a constant struggle ensuing between his intellectual aspirations and his instinctive emotional drives; as one of the minor black characters analyzes it, his "nigger" heart lives in opposition to his "white" head. Acts 5 and 6, during which Abe kills Lonnie, seem indebted in their psychological use of stage setting to two of O'Neill's plays which feature blacks, *All God's Chillun* and *The Emperor Jones*. At one point, great leaping shadows that expressionistically objectify Abe's inner turmoil fill the cabin; later, when Abe is pursued in the moonlight, the trappings of civilization, such as learning and speech, fall away from him just as Jones sheds them in the forest. After killing Lonnie, Abe senses his spirit in the wind and sees the tree branches as menacing hands; he hallucinates, envisioning a lynching, ghosts and haunts, and finally a young Negress and a dandified white man coupling like "hawgs." It is Abe's vision of the primal scene, and the child they conceive is himself. This contributes to the impression of Abe as a victim of his birth, who seems in the evil he does mainly to *react* to outside stimuli rather than to act, making him less tragic a figure than Green evidently intended he would be.

No matter how sympathetic an audience might be to Abe today, the play is not only a pessimistic and unlightened examination of the racial question, but even a reactionary one. Certain of its ideas do retain their viability: violence is not the solution; the urban ghettos are as enslaving as the cotton fields. On at least one point—the necessity for breaking down the idea of God as exclusively white—the play was even prophetic. Abe moves, in fact, from a belief that black oppression means a white God rules the universe to a recognition that God encompasses both black and white. But the work's central emphasis, voiced by Abe himself, clearly places the burden on the black man for his own lot: it is not white society that must change, but the black man who will rise only when he has first freed his mind through education. In Green's amelioristic approach, blacks are not yet ready to be the equals of whites—a viewpoint that may have made the play palatable to audiences of the 1920s but which renders moot any question of reviving the work today. Green, along with Abe and the minor black choral figures who reject Abe's way and opt instead for maintaining the status quo with the whites as superior, carefully prevents the whites in the audience from feeling guilty, even makes them feel complacent, which severely vitiates any grandeur the play possesses in characterization and language. Two Pulitzer plays on the racial issue from the late 1960s do, however, distribute the blame more equitably.

For over two decades now, the center of original theatrical activity in America has been shifting from on Broadway to off, even to the regional theatres, and a number of the more recent Pulitzer plays, like Howard

Sackler's *The Great White Hope*, which won the award in 1969 but first opened at Washington's Arena Stage in 1960, reflect this trend. *White Hope* covers roughly the same time period in American history as *In Abraham's Bosom* and falls even more clearly into the chronicle-cum-tragedy form than does Green's work. But it owes just as much, as Gerald Weales notes,[8] to the Brechtian epic theatre for its episodic structure, its style that blends song with dialogue, and its social commitment, though it does not depend on estrangement devises to stimulate an intellectual reaction at the expense of emotional involvement. Although several earlier American plays demonstrate some dependence on Brechtian techniques, Sackler's is so far the only winner wholly in the neo-Brechtian mode.

As a chronicle-cum-tragedy, Sackler's work details the desperate attempts of the white establishment, reaching even to the White House, to find a "great white hope" capable of defeating the black heavyweight boxing champion, Jack Jefferson, a thinly disguised portrait of Jack Johnson. As if his race were not embarrassment enough to white strangleholds of power and authority, the married Jefferson further fuels the hatred by openly living with his white mistress, Ellie, eventually violating the law by taking her across the state line. Yet the conflict becomes one not simply of law versus love, but of the necessity to sacrifice personal integrity to the public role that America thrusts upon her culture heroes; for the white Kid who finally defeats Jack is as much a martyr to racial bigotry as is Jack: "his smashed and reddened face . . . barely visible" as he is borne out through the jubilant crowd, he is dehumanized by being turned into an object, a parody of "the lifelike wooden saints in Catholic processions."[9]

His determination to define his life on his own terms makes Jack, hounded out of country after country, reduced to playing Uncle Tom to Ellie's Little Eva on the cafe circuit in Budapest and even to selling his gloves to survive, less the victim (as Abe is) and more the tragic sufferer, Promethean in his defiance of established codes. What topples him is not only his freely chosen burden of Ellie but also the unsought burden of being manipulated by his own race—most of whom long either to be assimilated into white society or kept in their lowly place. Despite his wanting to fight only for himself and not to deliver the black race, others force a Messianic role upon him until the gold belt becomes his albatross: "Ah'm stuck widdit, see, a hunk of junky hardware, but it don't let go" (p. 137). If the majority of blacks quickly lionize him, some who are making inroads into the white power structure hasten to vilify him for fear that their own standing will be jeopardized, while others want nothing more than to remain subservient, like his mother who "tried to learn him like you gotta learn a culled boy" (p. 75). So Sackler's play is a two-edged sword, cutting at both blacks and whites, as Jones does in *Dutchman*.

Sackler never adequately dramatizes the relationship between Ellie and Jack, and yet on its outcome hinge the final choices that determine

Jack's heroism. The same skepticism about the option of interracial marriage as a step towards integration pervades *White Hope* as underlies Green's drama. Ellie claims him to be kind and sensitive, yet the audience never sees this—unless the embarrassing sexual banter in the cabin is to be accepted as proof; when Jack's resentment boils over, he takes it out on her, forcing her to leave, which leads to her suicide. After her body is brought in, Jefferson decides on retaliation against what "they" have done; he refuses to throw the fight and will do his best to triumph. In the process, he endures a terrible battering, finally securing his freedom from control and his sense of dignity.

In place of depth, Sackler provides expansiveness through the panoply and pageantry of the chronicle form to which are added blackouts—with sound effects used as transitions or bridges as they would be in radio or film—and spirituals, blues, and pop tunes to punctuate the short scenes. Frequently, characters interrupt their longer speeches with single lines of direct address, further breaking the illusion of reality and establishing this as a convention, so that the five long speeches—three directed to the whites in the audience and two to the blacks—are prepared for. In the first of the three addressed to whites, Cap'n Dan, a former champion turned referee, declares that having a black wear the heavyweight crown is "like the world's got a shadow across it" (p. 42). In the second, Ellie's mother reiterates the numerous stereotypical connotations of the word *black*— "the dark to be afraid of, pitch black, black as dirt, the black hole and the black pit, what's burned or stained or cursed or hideous, poison and spite and the waste from your body and the horrors crawling up into your mind" (p. 135)—demonstrating how language can be used to foster and support prejudice, corrupting its original function. Just as Green takes pains not to annoy his white audience, Sackler allows the liberals to feel self-satisified and morally superior, while at the same time playing to the white silent majority, as when he allows Dixon to echo their fears: "Give it some thought next time you're alone on the streets at night" (p. 111). The Brechtian form, however, demands less ambiguity and a clearer demarcation between heroes and villains and a more consistent social philosophy than the fence-straddling for the commercial theatre apparent here.

Two speeches addressed to the probably few blacks in the audience create additional difficulties. The first, by a character named Scipio who is totally extraneous to the play's action, speaks out for black pride— taunting the blacks by asking, "How white you wanna be?" (p. 71)—and holds up Jefferson as an example of selling out to the white value structure in a new brand of slavery. He urges them to take pride in their black civilization and culture: "Time again to make us a big new wise proud dark man's world—again!" (p. 72). The second black monologuist and final commentator is Jack's estranged wife, Clara, motivated by personal jealousy and vengeance against Jack for having turned his back on black women and succumbed to the white woman's mystique of black male sexuality. Costuming her in a garment stained by blood and excrement makes her appearance unnecessarily sensational. But then Sackler depends on broad strokes and effects throughout rather than on subtlety to propel his play, which is as much shadowboxing as the real thing.

Even before Green wrote *In Abraham's Bosom*, authors were beginning to formulate an aesthetic for a black drama that would address itself largely to a black audience. In his 1925 essay called "Play-writing," Mark Seyboldt, while granting that black playwrights must continue to be aware of "two different audiences," one "'used to theatre going'" and the other not, urged them to be "'mainly interested in the second audience; we want colored folk to add the new diversion of drama to their lives. . . . It will stimulate and broaden cramped lives.'"[10] By the following year, 1926, in a manifesto written for the Krigwa Players' Little Negro Theatre in Harlem, W. E. B. DuBois was arguing that "'The plays of a real Negro theatre must be: 1. *About us*. . . . 2. *By us*. . . . 3. *For us*. That is the Negro theatre must cater primarily to Negro audiences. . . . 4. *Near us*.'"[11] By the late 1960s, the notion not just of two audiences but of two Americas had become a sad fact of American society, and the Black Arts Movement had linked itself inextricably with, and become an instrument and expression of, Black Power—an understandable alliance for the drama since, as Larry Neal asserts, "theatre is potentially the most social of all the arts."[12] Adopting Frantz Fanon's belief in the inability of "acquir[ing] the oppressor's power by acquiring his symbols," Neal proposes that "a 'black aesthetic'" must replace "the Western aesthetic [that] has run its course" as a viable "cultural sensibility": "The motive behind the Black aesthetic is the destruction of. . .white ways of looking at the world. The new aesthetic is mostly predicated on an Ethics which asks the question: whose vision of the world is finally more meaningful, ours or the white oppressors?" (pp. 29–30). Though neither seems addressed to an exclusively black audience, the two plays by blacks that have won the Pulitzer, perhaps especially the first, participate in the agenda that Neal envisions for black drama.

Charles Gordone, the first of only two blacks thus far to win the Pulitzer for drama, frames the action of his "Black Black comedy" and 1970 award play, *No Place to Be Somebody*, by employing a nonrealistic technique. The frame hints that the entire play may be occurring in the mind of the apocalyptically named apprentice playwright, Gabe Gabriel—may, in fact, be the play he is writing. The nonillusionistic devices, including long narrative passages and poems, function more satisfactorily than the similar ones in *White Hope* because Gordone establishes the illusion-breaking conventions earlier and employs them consistently. *No*

Place departs from the traditions of the barroom drama in America (evident in such plays as Saroyan's *The Time of Your Life*, O'Neill's *The Iceman Cometh*, and Jack Gelber's *The Connection*) in that although some of the bar's habituees gravitate to it as a protective womb or source of intoxicating illusions or forgetfulness, it is not, finally, a haven of safety and security. It becomes, instead, a testing ground for people's perception of race and the black movement.

The rather cluttered melodramatic action, reminiscent of a grade-B gangster movie, can be dealt with quickly; it is important mainly for the effect that it—real or imagined or both—has upon the light-skinned Gabe and, by extension, the black race in general, in the change from nonviolence to violence. Since the events are melodramatic, Gabe can participate in actions which, lacking subtlety, ambivalence, and ambiguity, force reactions that reveal his progression. Gabe writes his play in a bar owned by Johnny Williams, a black pimp intent on leading a Black Mafia, who equates respect for the law with the white way. In his stable are two black (Evie and Cora) prostitutes and one white (Dee). Frequenters of the establishment include Shanty, a hypster white drummer who dreams of winning Cora through his music, which supposedly proves he has as much soul as any black; and Melvin, a black dancer. Arriving at the bar after a long absence in prison is Sweets Crane, a reformed black racketeer and Johnny's surrogate father. Sweets, challenging Uncle Tomism, regrets that Johnny has aped his "bad points" and expresses disdain "for giving Johnny the worst sickness of all: the Charley fever."[13] Coming into the bar for the first time are two whites, Mary Lou (daughter of Judge Bolton) and Ellen, both civil rights picketers. The judge, it happens, has risen to office by acquitting two Italian mobsters on charges of bribery and murder, and Mary Lou willingly turns over a file incriminating him to Johnny. Dee, jealous of Johnny's attention towards Mary Lou, degrades herself by putting on black face and ultimately commits suicide. Sweets, after willing everything to Johnny provided he reform, knifes Mafucci and is himself killed in an altercation over the files. Johnny taunts Gabe, who has "no stomach" for this personal war against whites and refuses to hand over the information, with being a "lousy, yellow, screamin' faggot coward" (p. 113) and threatens to kill him. In a pattern that closely repeats the action of Albee's *The Zoo Story*, Johnny drives Gabe to kill him so that Gabe can no longer be the uninvolved, nonviolent observer, the passive commentator who speaks through words rather than actions.

Gabe addresses the audience directly in three of his poems. The first is a satiric work about a Whitmanesque speaker at a civil rights protest rally who tries to embrace all blacks, pleading for solidarity rather than violence, but receives no response. The second narrates a fable about blacks who move into the white world, go unaccepted, and finally return to the black world, only to find rejection there as well. This poem, which begins with Gabe intoning the old Protestant hymn, "Whiter Than Snow," underscores (like Mrs. Bachman's monologue in *White Hope*) and simultaneously undercuts the stereotypical association of whiteness with moral rightness and purity. Gabe's final verse insists, "There's mo' to bein' black than meets the / Eye" (p. 79), yet it ultimately defines blacks by the same stereotypes that they themselves help the whites to perpetuate. Gabe symbolizes his own prescience as black poet and suggests the violent course of action he will follow through the mock communion in which he eats a gun and drinks a Molotov cocktail.

Just as Sackler introduced Scipio, the black militant, Gordone brings on an equally unprepared-for character named Machine Dog, dressed in a military uniform and given to Nazi-like salutes. Whether he exists only in Johnny's imagination, or only as a tempter in Gabe's mind, is not clear; what is clear is that Machine Dog serves as a kind of *deus ex machina* (perhaps that wryly accounts for his name), delivering an edict canonizing Johnny as a heroic martyr for his people. His revivalist monologue delivered immediately after Gabe kills Johnny is rhetorically confusing and probably an obfuscation for an audience in the theatre, though it appears to be a series of charges against the blacks for failing to aid the revolutionaries.

In the epilogue, Gabe appears one last time, now dressed in a new role as a woman in mourning, to utter a jeremiad in biblical phraseology that recalls the prologue. Contrary to Walter Kerr's belief that the "Epilogue" is "false to the play's tone...too thin and obvious in its humor for the weightiness of the text as a whole and should...be dropped,"[14] it marks the essential end-product of Gabe's development. Appropriately dressed in the widow's weeds that had become so familiar an American sight by the end of the 1960s, Gabe—and through him, Gordone—mourns the years of dehumanization and degradation that the people have allowed themselves to suffer, mourning, too, the end of nonviolence as a solution for himself and for his race. The play's title suggests that finding and living by one's own proper identity is a near impossibility for the blacks in this society, that there is, literally, "no place" for them "to be somebody" except by aping Charley's ways, which ironically only renders each of them even more of a "nobody." The epilogue rounds out the play thematically by suggesting the frightening impasse at which the struggle for racial equality has arrived.

With *A Soldier's Play*, Charles Fuller became in 1982 the second black to win the drama Pulitzer. His play, which mixes yet finally transcends two perennially popular forms, the whodunit and the courtroom melodrama, is acted out on a nonrealistic set in the shape of a "horseshoe-like half circle" resembling a courtroom. It opens with a tantalizingly incomplete reenactment of the 1944 murder of a black tech sergeant, Vernon C. Waters, near an army base in a small Southern town; by the time it ends with a complete reenactment of Waters's death, suspicion has shifted from the Klan, to two white officers, and finally to the two guilty black soldiers. In its overall physical conception of the setting and its fluid, cinematic shifting between present and past, Fuller's work recalls Peter Shaffer's *Equus,* also an investigation of sorts, albeit a psychiatric one. During the criminal investigation, testimony about the past is not simply recited but is acted out (again as in *Equus*), the audience sometimes viewing the past within the past. Because of the courtroom setting, the audience become implicated in the action as spectators at the inquiry and even as a tribunal or jury assessing guilt and innocence. When the killers are revealed, however, the complex question of guilt still resonates.

Capt. Richard Davenport, dispatched from Washington to conduct the investigation, functions as the play's most obvious narrator, establishing the time frame as he probes the witnesses. But as these witnesses testify, they, too, become narrators, helping to distance the theatre audience, as Brecht does, and permitting it to analyze the events with a degree of objectivity. The white company commander, Capt. Charles Taylor, has been so acculturated with the stereotypical white-as-master/black-as-servant division that he finds it difficult to accept Davenport's authority, especially before he learns that he has been betrayed by the white superiors who have tied his hands out of fear the scandal will spread. Yet Davenport, who has always tried to be a source of pride for his fellow blacks, ultimately wins Taylor's support and respect because he is "not your yesserin' colored boy."[15] That Taylor attains this new attitude because of Davenport's conduct and despite his skin color is one of the positive notes in an otherwise pessimistic play, and it is signalled by Davenport's finally shedding the tinted glasses he has hidden behind. But Davenport's awareness, expressed in his preachy summation, that "the madness of race in America" (p. 84) has made blacks as well as whites small of heart counterbalances Taylor's growth.

Waters, under the tutelage of his "Daddy," came to regard the army as the only avenue open to blacks for entrance into the white power structure. He became, though, as racist as any white, psychotically obsessed in his preaching against "lazy, shiftless Negroes." Peterson, one of the black soldiers, hints at the analogy between Waters and Hitler; Waters, indeed, developed his own version of the Nazi plan for a master race by campaigning to eradicate certain kinds of blacks he despised. One of these, the gentle musician C. J. Memphis, embodied for Waters all the worst features of the "cotton-picker, singin' the Blues, bowin' and scrapin'— smilin' in everybody's face" black (p. 55). So the megalomaniac Waters, like Lula who represents white society in Jones's *Dutchman,* goaded C. J. into reacting against him, only to break him—a pattern of action that (again like Lula) he had successfully followed elsewhere. C. J. commits suicide in prison, prompting Peterson's eventual vengeance against Waters. Waters, attempting to gain an entree into white authority structures by hating his own race, redefined himself in terms that masked his true identity. Because he tries to deny his brotherhood with other members of his race, Waters reverts when drunk to an animalistic black every bit as stereotypical and onerous as the shuffling Uncle Toms he has goaded to death. His futility at the point of his own death resides in his recognition that those in power who successfully connive to have him do their dirty work for them "still hate [him]" (pp. 4, 82). By repressing his racial identity, he has enslaved himself.

As important to the total impact of the play as Waters's and Davenport's attempts—the first despicable, the second admirable—at discovering a social role that can mesh with a private role without any concomitant loss of integrity, are the modes of response of the minor characters. In his handling of them, Fuller is at his most subtle and complex. At opposite sides of the stage hang two pictures: one of FDR in Taylor's office; a second of "Joe Lewis in an Army uniform" above the words "We'll Win Because We're on God's Side" (p. 3) in the soldiers' barracks. The portrait of FDR serves as a reminder that the avenue of political action was largely closed to blacks, despite the generally liberal stance of the Roosevelt years, and would remain closed to them for two more decades. The poster of Louis suggests that the way to success most available to blacks was—and this remained true for a long time afterwards—sports; in fact, the black soldiers segregated in this barracks are being exploited for their success in the Negro Baseball League. They yearn to fight in the war against Hitler and the Japanese, but they fail to see any connection between Hitler's oppression of the Jewish people and white oppression of blacks, and between themselves as victims of American racism and the Japanese in America as victims during World War II. They want only to be called up into the game of war (certainly one of the connotations of the title *Soldier's Play*) and are elated when they finally receive equal treatment and are shipped out—though they do not understand the hypocrisy of America's missionary zeal abroad when coupled with its moral astigmatism over racism at home. Ironically, the entire squadron, black soldiers and white officers, die almost as soon as they see action. Fuller's drama is thus more radical and subversive than at first appears, taking a stand against all power structures that abuse people by too narrowly defining their roles or by inculcating distorted values. Certainly in Fuller's America both sides, black and white, are guilty, and both sides lose. Fuller arraigns both society as a whole and his specific audience who, unless they actively protest the status quo, are tacitly furthering it.

Not until Gordone's *No Place to Be Somebody*, which premiered at Joseph Papp's Public Theatre, and Fuller's *Soldier's Play*, first produced by the Negro Ensemble Company, are there Pulitzer plays about the black experience that do not bow to commercialism, partly—maybe even primarily—because they were addressed to a black audience as well as to a white. In *Abraham's Bosom* and *The Great White Hope*, written by whites with an almost exclusively white audience in mind, both sacrifice some of their dramatic consistency and integrity to make their material palatable to paying customers; they both insist on straddling the fence, critical of the manner in which blacks have been oppressed and yet careful not to make whites feel too guilty or uncomfortable. *No Place*, the most theatrically complex of all these works, and *Soldier's Play* both rely on conventional, easily recognizable forms—the gangster movie in the first, the courtroom melodrama in the second—used in unconventional ways to dramatize the dilemma blacks face in a white society: how to discover a black identity that is not defined by a white power structure and value system and so is no better than what it attempts to change or replace. Yet blacks in these plays who try to goad their fellow blacks out of complacency risk becoming as oppressive as their own oppressors. As one of the characters in August Wilson's recent *Ma Rainey's Black Bottom*, about racism and rage in Chicago in the 1920s, sums up the problem, "As long as the colored man look [sic] to white folks to put the crown on what he say. . . as long as he looks to white folks for approval. . . then he ain't never gonna find out who he is and what he's about."[16] One of the most pernicious cultural inheritances—and one, ironically, fostered and sustained by literary symbolism—which these playwrights as far back as Green have attempted to expose, is the antithetical way of perceiving experience that sees white as synonymous with right and good and black as synonymous with wrong and evil. This mind-set is now so ingrained in the consciousness (and racial unconscious) that to alter it will demand, Sackler and Gordone and Fuller know, a change not only in their audience's way of thinking but also in their very habit of being.

Five of the six Pulitzer dramas that examine the racial issue break, to a greater or lesser extent, the confines of strict realism. *Soldier's Play*, *No Place to Be Somebody*, and *Great White Hope*, by employing Brechtian distancing devices, all preach directly to an audience aware that they are watching a play. The stage in the last two even becomes at times a lectern or platform, except that the messages sent are occasionally confusing and/or obscure, probably because of uncertainty about the nature of the audience in a volatile and unstable time. *South Pacific*—which at one point casts the theatergoers in the role of American troops enjoying a musicale-within-the-musical—and *Talley's Folly* force their audiences to think about the experience of going to the theatre, intimating that only in a place of romance and illusion removed from the real world (the island Bali Hai, Uncle Everett's boathouse) can racial differences be ignored and overcome in love relationships. Yet both are only gently corrective of civilization's failure, with the playwrights' intention to entertain remaining preeminent. It might even be that the theatre metaphor itself in each of these works, because it emphasizes the illusionary nature of what happens up on the stage, acutally helps shield the audience from the racial issues; both of them, to extend Matt's categorization of *Folly*, might well be called "valentines" sent to their audiences. *Folly*, however, more so than *South Pacific*, adopts the paradigm of sending its audience back out into society to face and maybe to solve the problem, a strategy that *White Hope* and *No Place* and, to a lesser degree, *Soldier's Play* follow as well. Most prominently in *Soldier's Play*, the stage of the action moves out into the audience as they watch the play; they become aware of themselves as a jury weighing the evidence and passing moral judgment on the American political and military system as the radical protestors have always done.

6

The Political Animal

In his history plays, Shakespeare attempts to define the qualities of the good king, proposing a relationship between the health of the body politic and the moral nature of its rulers. This link was not original with the Renaissance; anthropological studies reveal that ancient societies knew "the king must die" so that the wasteland could be made fertile. Shakespeare's perspective is further characterized, however, by the suspicion he casts upon the ability of the ruler to maintain his personal integrity when it inevitably comes into conflict with his position of power. This question of the relationship between a ruler's personal moral integrity and the exercise of political authority pervades the Pulitzer prizewinning dramas about presidents and mayors and members of Congress, though these dramatists' points of view about the political system's effect upon its elected rulers are generally less skeptical and more sanguine than Shakespeare's. Although audiences much loved the two plays among this group that feature a revered historical figure as their subject—Lincoln and LaGuardia—taken as a whole these political plays are the least substantive of all the Pulitzer dramas, lacking much theorizing about history and the political man, such as readers and viewers continue to receive from Shakespeare's chronicle plays.

What may, in part, account for the relatively unchallenging nature of these works—from both a dramaturgical and an ideological perspective—is the playwrights' hesitancy to criticize the audience/electorate too openly for the lack of wisdom exhibited by the rulers it elects, perhaps out of fear that such criticism would be seen as directed against the democratic system itself. Yet at least the first three plays to be discussed here implicitly espouse a notion of the electorate not unlike that found in the writings of Alexis de Tocqueville and John Stuart Mill, both of whom, while prizing individual conscience and character, sensed that majority rule may mean that mediocrity rules. Tocqueville, who seems to have taken over from religious thought into political philosophy the belief in an "inner light" that guides the individual, knows that the majority opinion may be intolerant of the minority viewpoint in its midst, enforcing conformity rather than independence in thought and action. As he writes in *Democracy in America,* "What is a majority, in its collective capacity, if not an individual with opinions, and usually with interests, contrary to those of another individual, called the minority?"[1] Mill goes further in his suspicion that collective rule by the majority tends to level everything down to a kind of uniformity, an average that prevents the exceptional from flowering except when a society is willing to counter this by permitting and nurturing an indispensable aristocracy of thought and character: "No government by a democracy or a numerous aristocracy, either in its political acts or in the opinions, qualities, and tone of mind which it fosters, ever did or could rise above mediocrity, except in so far as the Many have let themselves be guided (which in their best times they have always done) by the counsels and influence of a more highly gifted and instructed One or Few."[2] For most of the playwrights here, this expressed need for exceptional persons to lead society inevitably conflicts with their preception of the audience's predisposition against even righteous individuals who appear to reject the wisdom and will of the collective majority. This timidity in making the audience examine its potential flaws as a citizenry finally constricts the forcefulness of many of these political dramas.

Of Thee I Sing, one of the earliest important American musicals and the first of only a half-dozen to win the Pulitzer, must have seemed at least a quirky and at best a daring and rebellious choice for the prize in 1932, since it received the honor over a number of serious dramas, including O'Neill's *Mourning Becomes Electra.* (At that time, no provision was made for composers to share in the drama award, so the citation named librettists George Kaufman and Morrie Ryskind along with Ira Gershwin who contributed the perky and biting lyrics, but not his brother George Gershwin who wrote the music.) Kaufman and Ryskind's farcical book moves in broad strokes, much like a political comic strip. The nature of *Of Thee I Sing* as an irreverent lampoon can best be seen in the still amusing treatment of the much-maligned and joked-about vice-president, Alexander Throttlebottom; his very name, naturally, occasions malapropisms galore—including "Gottabottle," "Bottlethrottle," and "Teitelbaum." A "hermit" before the kingmaker Fulton picked his name out of a hat to serve as John P. Wintergreen's running mate, Throttlebottom poses a distinct liability to the ticket, sure to precipitate a loss if anyone as much as sets eyes on him. After the ticket wins, he intends to resign so that his mother will not be embarrassed, he loses his pass to the inauguration, he can only gain entrance to the White House by joining a tour, and he cannot obtain a library card because he lacks the necessary references. He is so totally inept that when he does preside over the Senate (confusing the senators with the ball team), he institutes a musical roll call, pays tribute to Paul Revere's long-dead horse Jenny, and fills up his time knitting baby clothes. Yet his historic function—to assume the duties the president cannot in times of incapacitation—and his dramatic role dovetail when he unexpectedly realizes, before anyone else, the solution to the president's romantic difficulties: Throttlebottom can be the essential fourth party who "squares the triangle" by marrying the president's cast-off girl, thus allowing a resolution to the love plot.

Wintergreen, lacking a platform on which to run, takes the unsolicited advice of a hotel chambermaid and runs on "love," complete with a beauty contest to find a Miss White House to become the First Lady. The national committee picks Diana Devereux, a dumb blond sexpot, whom they later try to legitimatize through claiming that she is the "illegitimate daughter / Of an illegitimate son / Of an illegitimate nephew / Of Napoleon."[3] But Wintergreen's heart goes to Mary Turner, famous for her corn muffins made without corn. Diana claims such breach of promise is a "communistic plot," but the Supreme Court justices, after going into a football huddle, decide in Mary's favor because she is pregnant and so "posterity is just around the corner" (p. 737)—the closest reference to the raging Depression in this piece of escapist fluff.

While this outcome satisfies the demands of the musical comedy audience for a happy union between hero and heroine, it fails to conclude logically the sequence of political satire; it can, moreover, only uphold the inner logic demanded of farce if it is taken as a satiric jab at the audience's own desire for a romantic ending. Wintergreen is, though, a far cry from the typical hero; that Kaufman and Ryskind paint him so darkly at the beginning makes the later shift to greater sympathy implausible. Wintergreen nominated himself as presidential candidate, but not until the sixty-third ballot, and will play dirty in order to force himself down the populace's throats; and only his "delicate condition" as an expectant father prevents his impeachment once elected. Even in these premediamad days, image supercedes issues, although they, too, lack substance: a dearth of Chanel No. 5, bringing back black cotton stockings, and changing the name of the Virgin Islands since the connotations prove bad for trade. *Of Thee I Sing* seems, finally, despite its fun, to have a critical attitude towards the majority hidden beneath its good-natured face: if the electorate is so blind and allows itself to be manipulated by a do-nothing administration, then maybe it gets the rulers—and "heroes"—it deserves.

Perhaps *Of Thee I Sing* does well not to have a hero, since the next year in *Both Your Houses,* Maxwell Anderson cannot resist making his hero too good to be convincing, although the playwright intends that his ideas take precedence over character credibility. Anderson, author of such works as *Winterset* and *Elizabeth the Queen,* stands as virtually the sole poetic dramatist in the American theatre, yet he won the 1934 Pulitzer for a prose play; ironically, he considers *Houses* "by all odds his worst" offering.[4] Essentially a polemical tract parading as political satire, it follows the career of a United States congressman. The transparency of the play's moral conflicts is thrust at the audience through the too-schematic name symbolism. The naive hero-writ-large is named Alan McClean; he is surrounded by a tainted politician named Simon Gray and a wise old politico totally without guile named Solomon (what else?) Fitzmaurice. Although the play boasts a refreshing turn in that the guy does not get the girl—in this instance the daughter of his foe—Alan's idealism is never challenged; because he never finds himself truly on the defensive, there is little internal conflict or possibility for growth. What exists in abundance is authorial commentary, including an unexpected dose of cynicism about the democratic system that faces its greatest challenge because of a disinterested and apathetic electorate—a criticism Anderson can afford to make more explicitly, albeit more heavy-handedly, than Kaufman and Ryskind could within the scope of an entertainment.

Alan arrives in Washington a political neophyte, wide-eyed and uncompromising. Son of a newspaperman, wearer of mail-order clothes, and devotee of Thomas Jefferson, he lost his college job because of his social commitment and now, like an earlier-day Ralph Nader, even has his own election investigated for possible abuse. Assigned to the appropriations committee, he discovers that all the other members are out to get something for themselves and their constituents by tacking amendments onto a bill for a dam. Alan's instinct to hate the system but maintain faith in the citizenry seems confirmed by the facts at this point. Solomon, as Anderson's *raisonneur*, does not, however, hold such a complimentary view of the voters; a former radical who is frank about his own motives and about the evils that daily creep into the American system—for example, using taxpayers' money for patrolling the Canadian border to prevent an invasion of Japanese beetles from the Southwest—he counsels Alan that reform is not possible. Better to concentrate on the individual virtue of being fully humane, which in this instance pragmatically means not revealing the former corruption of Senator Gray that would now wreck his life. When one considers the magnitude of the evil (Warren G. Harding was nothing, supposedly, compared to this), the Messianic fervor of youth must naturally buckle under. Alan decides to undermine the system by arranging to have so many extra appropriations tacked onto the bill that it will surely invite a presidential veto. Since the vote is strong enough, however, to override the veto, his scheme backfires. Consequently, Alan has accomplished more harm than good; inadvertently he has taught his unethical colleagues a tactic that will mean even bigger expenditures in the future.

Rationalizing that even honest people are corrupt and that honesty is perhaps impossible under the American system, Gray plays the devil's advocate who receives a partial nod from Anderson. For Anderson hints that something negative infests the very core of the process, some choice made long ago that is partially responsible: the pragmatic robber barons, embodiments of the height of capitalistic enterprise, showed that graft could guarantee prosperity. Yet the voters themselves have a great faith in the promise of the democratic system, and Anderson follows Tocqueville and Mill in suggesting that they must be awakened out of their mediocrity: Solomon claims "no word" or "figure of speech [can] express the complete and illimitable ignorance and incompetence of the voting population."[5] Anderson's "Don Quixote" finally realizes that, far from perfect, this is perhaps not even the best method of government and that revolution is long overdue. But neither the ignorant and incompetent voters nor the Congress appear likely to take action to change things. Maybe Anderson is actually warning against allowing an attitude to develop that will make the country susceptible to precisely what was beginning to occur in Germany, where a sleeping, apathetic people were awaking to find that the monster in their nightmares was real and that they themselves had helped to create it.

If *Both Your Houses* focuses on politicians already in positions of power, *State of the Union*—loosely based on Wendell Willkie's campaign and the prizewinner for 1946—details that rise to power. The emphases in the two works are, nevertheless, virtually identical, though *Union*, more comedic, hits less bullishly. As the coauthors Howard Lindsay and Russel Crouse comment, they desired "'to stir the conscience of the individual citizen . . . to say certain things but to do so amusingly.'"[6] *Union*, like *Houses*, is basically an actionless play, though with a slightly less idealized hero who ends, however, in essentially the same stance as Alan. The playwrights siphon off their indignation through Mary, the candidate's wife, just as Anderson does through his character Solomon. Both plays, too, involve questions of ambition versus integrity, of public morality versus personal relationships. The word *union* in Lindsay and Crouse's title combines a political with a private connotation; the third point in the triangle involving Mary and Grant Matthews is sometimes the political game yet is just as often the other woman, the big-city newspaper publisher Kay Thorndike. In fact, the romantic relationship becomes almost more central than the political conflict in this comedy of manners that only rarely reaches the high level of epigrammatic wit characteristic of the form; about the best the authors seem able to muster are quips such as, "Politics makes strange bedfellows" or "Our personal relations are strictly political."[7]

State of the Union examines the role of the woman behind the political figure. Kay builds up Grant's self-confidence, while Mary—who bemoans the fate of the politician's wife long before it became fashionable to do so—sees her primary function as keeping Grant's ego in check, her worst days being those when he falls prey to the "big man" complex. For Grant is another "Sir Galahad," totally untutored in the seamier side of political reality, determined to campaign and win while remaining morally unscathed. Such a "streak of decency" can be a burden since, for the man of conscience, every decision becomes a moral choice. Politics, which initially seems to keep Grant and Mary apart, ironically brings them closer together as she senses the return of the idealistic boy she wistfully recalls from their honeymoon days. If the campaign turns back the clock on a marriage gone stale, it also forces them to confront large ethical issues. Grant is an unassuming and yet charismatic figure, not as pure as Alan (he vaguely admits to having paid hush money in the past), but one who continues to have faith in the American people and insists on appealing to their best rather than their worst instincts—refusing, for example, to trade on the emerging Cold War hatred against the Russians. What does surprise him is the cynicism of the political giants who take advantage of the "lazy...ignorant...prejudiced" people. These lawmakers tend to view politics as a game, and it is in such "political" plays as *Of Thee I Sing* and *State of the Union* that the game metaphor so prevalent in political rhetoric of the 1960s and 1970s first enters American drama. As James Conover, the kingmaker, remarks in one of the more obvious expressions of this metaphor: "In this country, we play politics and to play politics you have to play ball" (p. 222). Grant, finally, refuses to cooperate, deciding that he cannot be a candidate on anyone's terms but his own; instead he will be a gadfly from the sidelines—a resolution identical to the one reached by the former political candidate in Robert Anderson's *Come Marching Home* from the same season. In assuming this role of watchdog, Grant does only what every good citizen must: there can be no such thing as an apolitical stance within a truly democratic society.

Fiorello! (the 1960 Pulitzer winner) raises the identical question asked by the other prize plays discussed so far in this chapter: namely, is it possible for the public servant to retain his high ideals and moral values and still succeed politically? The play answers the question uncharacteristically, however, by providing a resoundingly affirmative response in the person of the title character. Since this musical appeared at the tag end of an age of relative stability and optimism—after the second World War and the Korean conflict and in a nation led by a popular and revered hero—it is not surprising that it dwells on a man who was one of America's best-loved politicos rather than on the issues. Selected by the advisory board and not the choice of the drama jury (which gave its nod to Hellman's *Toys in the Attic*), *Fiorello!* can in no way be considered a landmark American musical; rather, it is an old-fashioned, if thoroughly professional show with a score by composer Jerry Bock and lyricist Sheldon Harnick—later of *Fiddler on the Roof* fame—and a book by George Abbott and Jerome Weidman.

The man affectionately known as "the Little Flower" first appears, in a frame that inexplicably occurs only at the beginning, reading the comics over the radio to his adoring constituents. If he possesses an ingratiating political style, complete with theatrical props and costume, he evidences as well a real empathy and concern for the common people. His enemy and theirs is the Establishment: the exploiters who murdered his father during the Spanish-American War, the owners of the sweatshops who take advantage of women workers, and the ward bosses of Tammany Hall. But amidst the corruption of the political machine and even of the courts, as exposed in the memorably satiric number, "A Little Tin Box," Fiorello remains totally incorruptible, always "on the side of the angels."[8] Along with this incorruptibility runs a strain, however slight, of self-righteousness; his aide Ben warns him against being totally uncompromising and falling prey to the great-man syndrome or, worse still, to self-aggrandizement. For Fiorello, without any power base except the people, must merchandise himself through the media, as later politicians will become masters at doing. If Fiorello as showman capitalizes on the theatrical aspect endemic to politics, that remains preferable to reducing politics to a game (as described in the lyric "Politics and Poker") in which "usually you can stack the deck!" (p. 26). Fiorello, nevertheless, stands by his principles: he is independent, anti-isolationist—he even enlists in the Army—slightly Marxist in his economic theory of money as the root of all evil, and tentatively revolutionary in his insistence on placing the individual citizen over and above the law.

Like virtually every musical, *Fiorello!* involves a love triangle and includes a comic subplot. The latter, between Dora and Floyd, a policeman turned sewage treatment entrepreneur, underlines the corruption of Tammany Hall, which Floyd finds synonymous with "tyranny" because it runs on patronage and protection. In the main love plot, Fiorello first marries Thea, a political activist, realist, and something of a New Woman; after her death, he marries his secretary Marie, a confirmed romanticist. Thea first attracts Fiorello because she is the underdog, spokeswoman for the put-upon garment workers; he associates her courage in standing up against those who say women should stay in their place and in sacrificing herself for a cause with that of "Joan of Arc," just as she regards his commitment to causes as the actions of a "Sir Galahad." If Thea is the public person, Marie is the private one for whom the laws of love and family reign supreme and for whom marriage is the only role; she would "outlaw bachelorhood," "rid the country / Of contempt of courtship" (p. 50), and "marry the very next man who asks [her]" (p. 33) before it becomes too late. This elegiac tone pervades Thea's song, "Til Tomorrow," which ritualizes the passing of time in a foreboding way. When Thea dies, Fiorello has just been defeated in his bid for mayor, so his political and personal misfortunes mesh. He must pick himself up and begin anew, through hard work and determination. Marie forces him to take hold, in her traditional role as the woman behind the man, and he emerges victorious.

Not all American musicals express an elemental faith in America and American savvy and self-reliance, but *Fiorello!* assuredly does, for it looks back nostalgically at a period of war and Depression and suggests that these can be overcome. It remains a too sanguine and sentimental look, though, with the tension between public and private morality never translating into a real conflict for the central figure.

The pattern of two very different women and their impact upon a public figure from *Fiorello!* and *State of the Union* appears even earlier in Robert E. Sherwood's *Abe Lincoln in Illinois,* which won the 1939 Pulitzer. Sherwood reportedly admired John Drinkwater's *Abraham Lincoln,* which (complete with verse prologues) premiered in New York in 1919 and began where Sherwood's would leave off, with President-elect Lincoln preparing to leave Springfield for Washington. Had Drinkwater been American rather than British, his work would probably have won the prize over O'Neill's *Beyond the Horizon;* the advisory board, in fact, issued a statement "record[ing] their high appreciation" of Drinkwater's play and "regret[ting] that by reason of its foreign authorship, [it] was not eligible for consideration."[9] Sherwood's main source, however, was Carl Sandburg's *Abraham Lincoln: The Prairie Years* (1926)—itself disqualified from consideration for the history award because of a prohibition then in effect against honoring books about Washington and Lincoln—with a lesser debt to works by William H. Herndon, Nathaniel Wright Stephenson, and Albert J. Beveridge, as well as to Lincoln's own writings.

The action of Sherwood's episodic but economically handled chronicle play is less important than the characterization of Abe, which reveals a psychological complexity missing from the portraits in the other "political" plays, making the work most compelling in those scenes that attend to Abe's inner life. Sherwood's Abe is a Hamlet-like creature: rootless, and so thrown back on the elemental influences in his life; a loner with a low opinion of himself; melancholic and misanthropic, yet, like Swift, someone who "likes people one-by-one, but not in crowds, mobs, or armies."[10] His virtues arise from and are inextricably bound up with his frailties and flaws. John Keat's poem, "On Death," which Abe reads aloud at the end of scene 1, serves as a leitmotif for the work; not only does it establish a somber tone that presages the deaths of Ann Rutledge and (outside the play) of Abe himself, but it also relates as well to Abe's instinctive desire to retreat from the burdens of public life and succumb to a death wish. His political leanings, in fact, are not towards withdrawing but from never entering the arena in the first place. Abe seems at times more than half in love, even obsessed, with easeful death; oftentimes he gloomily repeats the phrase, "If I live. . . ." Yet since Keats firmly places his emphasis on awakening from "a life of woe" that "is but a dream" to immortality, man's "future doom" will actually be a respite from pain and a dying in order to rise. Part of Abe's immortality, that he could only vaguely have guessed at, comes from the process whereby his life enters the realm of myth. To win Ann, who frees his emotional or romantic side, would have made a reality of all that Abe read about in books of poetry; she helps him have faith in the beauty and purity of people and solidifies his belief in God. She would have distracted him, however, from the call to duty and so not have been a positive influence on his political career. The sketchily characterized Mary Todd, a disillusioned and mentally unstable woman, exerts just the opposite influence; she succeeds in being the shaping force behind Abe's life, not so much directing his ambition as instilling it. But a gulf exists between them, her emotional reticence matching his own. Winning the highest office in the land does not guarantee contentment; in fact, duty and personal happiness seem incompatible. That it is Mary, and not Ann, who is temperamentally more suited to becoming a president's wife only underscores this.

In writing about Abe, Sherwood pens his own intellectual and spiritual autobiography, and a biography of the nation as well. As he remarks, "Lincoln's life. . .was a work of art, forming a veritable allegory of the growth of the democratic spirit."[11] Abe as the common man is also Everyman, the protagonist of a morality play; there is, he admits, a civil war "going on inside [him] all the time. Both sides are right and both are wrong and equal in strength" (p. 326), since the struggle is between two imperatives, a hatred of force (war) and an equally intense hatred of slavery (life under dictatorship). Abe's private battle reflects the public one in 1938, mirroring for the audience not so much the Civil War as the trial facing the American people on the eve of World War II. Sherwood employs the history play for a traditional purpose: to present the past as lesson for the present. As much as Americans in 1938 hate war, they must hate even more the threat to humanity's freedom posed by the Nazi tyranny. Man, like Abe, "cannot go on to the end of [his] days avoiding the clutch of his own conscience" (p. 325); he must decide that a "wrong" law "must be changed, if not by moral protest, then by Force!"—and that "some ideals are *worth* dying for" (p. 333). Lincoln, "who is against slavery, but even more opposed to going to war," must declare war; by doing so, however, he becomes a timeless model for the audience, in the same way that he inspired Sherwood to understand that "a natural, intellectual, and moral world must be cultivated" (p. 353). Sherwood underscores Abe's role as an example for all seasons when the crowd at play's end bids Lincoln farewell by singing the chorus from "The Battle Hymn of the Republic," interpolating a line from the earlier "John Brown's Body," which, significantly, has its source in a Negro spiritual: "His soul goes marching on" (p. 353). This apotheosizes Abe, confirming his place on the level of ahistorical myth.

This group of Pulitzer plays seems not to look too hard or too critically at the conduct of America's leaders. Given the almost inevitable conflict between maintaining private integrity while wielding public power, these playwrights could potentially have drawn protagonists open to tragedy, but only Sherwood's Abe, forced to choose between two morally good objectives—union and an end to slavery—approaches that possibility. If Abe is a secular saint, he is a troubled one; public service not only exacts the price of personal happiness, but to follow one's conscience in the political arena means waging a war within oneself. Perhaps partly because of the play's facticity and because of what an audience cannot help but bring to it, Abe's battle seems compelling in a way that the heroes' conflicts in *Both Your Houses* and *State of the Union* do not. With their idealists under fire for their integrity, those two plays bear a relationship to works such as the populist filmmaker Frank Capra's *Mr. Smith Goes to Washington*. They offer their audiences the comfortable facade that they are doing some hard, sophisticated thinking about complex issues and that the "other man" is the guilty one while they are "on the side of the angels." These are not, however, serious social problem plays. They cater to the vague discontent everyone experiences with any imperfect—because human—political system. Although they may mildly criticize the system, especially the corrupt, or at least morally compromised, power brokers, they might also, albeit unintentionally, help to buoy up the status quo, creating an even more deeply rooted and insidious complacency among an audience generally disinclined to admit that what Tocqueville and Mill feared about the majority within a democracy might be true. Furthermore, the naiveté of the hero in *Both Your Houses* is hardly less unappealing than his near perfection, and the self-righteous attitude Anderson assumes towards his audience results in a rather dour play. *State of the Union*, of course, appeared in the aftermath of one of America's greatest victories, during a period of national euphoria when any questioning of the system's goodness was not yet in fashion; but such uncritical acceptance fed directly into the tyrannical rejection of the least ideological difference during the Joseph McCarthy years.

Of Thee I Sing, with its government that trivializes the issues and depends solely on image—and is permitted to do so by the gullibility of an unenlightened electorate—might have been the *Doonesbury* of the Depression; instead, it offers little except the escapist medicine of laughing the country's troubles away. *Fiorello!*, too, though bright and snappy, is little more than an exercise in nostalgia for a simpler time, as if its writers intuitively sensed that political and social turmoil were just around the corner and that theatergoers would not want to confront those in their entertainment. In *Fiorello!, State of the Union,* and *Both Your Houses,* moral principles comfortably survive, if they do not completely triumph. Sherwood alone dares to leave his audience with the darker possibility that the leaders of the nation and her citizens might indeed have diminished since the days of the Declaration. As Abe states the challenge: "We gained democracy, and now there is the question of whether it is fit to survive. Perhaps we have come to the dreadful day of awakening, and the dream is ended" (p. 352). That these "political" Pulitzer plays generally lack the technical variety and virtuosity of so much of the best American drama may help account for their thinness. Their authors' unwillingness to question the spectators' traditional aesthetic assumptions about how drama works, to break down the invisible barrier between stage and auditorium, characters and audience, mirrors their hesitation to challenge—as Tocqueville and Mill were not afraid of doing—the spectators' long-held but probably unexamined political views. Unadventuresome techniques and timidity in ideas are, for these Pulitzers at least, two sides of the same coin.

Whatever Happened to the American Dream?

At the close of F. Scott Fitzgerald's *The Great Gatsby*, the narrator, Nick Carraway, stops by Gatsby's house for a last look before returning from the East to the Midwest. His mind roams to "the old island here that flowered once for Dutch sailors' eyes—a fresh green breast of the new world. . . . man must have held his breath in the presence of this continent. . . face to face for the last time in history with something commensurate to his capacity to wonder."[1] The American continent seemed to promise a second chance for humanity; Adam fell from grace, was expelled from the Garden, but sought redemption in a new world. As Frederic Carpenter had discerned, however, an ambiguity complicates the American myth: In one version, the American Adam "lived, free and innocent and uncultured, in the isolated wildness," falling "from grace" in the face of "the evils of industrialism" which destroy the new Eden: he descended from "idealism" to "disillusionment." In a second version, "industrialism closed 'the frontier' and built cities 'in the garden,' without destroying the idealism." These two paradigms ask, in short, whether "paradise [is] hopelessly lost," or if it can "ultimately. . . be regained"?[2]

The two American plays actually bearing the title "The American Dream" both exemplify the first of these interpretations. George O'Neil's *American Dream* (1933) chronicles the decline of the Pingree family over a period of three centuries. In 1650, the first Daniel Pingree leaves his cabin and the clutches of his vengeful father to venture into the wilderness, "the place of fulfillment—an Eden, if you will, waiting for the return of the redeemed exile—the wise Adam."[3] In 1849, another Daniel, totally without fear of God, escapes the conditions of the mills to seek his fortune of "endless promise on the frontier" (p. 71). In 1933, a third Daniel, a disillusioned writer and former idealist who believes "there's nothing to give a damn about!" (p. 156), commits suicide over the vapid materialism of his social class that exploits the poor to gain wealth, his blood splattering the angel figurehead from the ship that had originally brought the family to the new world. Since the only remaining "frontier is. . . in men's minds" (p. 99), Daniel knows that the answer to materialism rests with art and the artist, here in the person of the black poet Carver. In the second and more widely known of these plays, Albee's *The American Dream* (1961), not even the antidote of art remains. Here the family is askew: the older generation, in the person of Grandma who values the past, is sent packing as the emasculating Mommy rules the household. The American Dream is personified by a blond, muscle-bound, aspiring actor, "Cleancut, midwest farm boy type, almost insultingly good-looking in a typically American way,"[4] yet spiritually and emotionally empty within. When Mommy mutilated his twin, he too, "suffered losses. . . . A fall from grace" that left him "unable to love": "[He] no longer [has] the capacity to feel anything" (pp. 106–7).

Either configuration of the myth can, of course, be handled ironically, undercutting the myth itself as hopelessly flawed, which some playwrights indeed hold. Others, however, propose that history itself has erected a barrier between the present and the dream, that in the movement from the agrarian frontier and garden to the industrialized urban centers too much has transpired to regain the vision. As was true for Gatsby, what is sought for is already receding, temporally in the past and geographically farther away.

Although William Saroyan refused the prize, disclaiming any sympathy with patronage for the arts, *The Time of Your Life*, one of the more original American plays and one of several notable barroom dramas in American theatre, was named winner of the drama Pulitzer for 1940. In the tradition of the Whitmanesque celebration of democracy and equality, it proclaims American self-reliance and extolls the work ethic: "You can't enjoy life unless you work."[5] But if *Life* finally asserts a transcendental optimism, it does so mainly by the force and coloration of Saroyan's personality that can snatch the material from darkness and despair. An impressionistic mood-piece owing its loose structure to the influence of vaudeville, its almost childlike—some mistakenly claim naive—outlook makes it the most assertively positive of all the Pulitzer plays treating the

American Dream; appearing as it did between the great Depression and America's entry into a new world war, it does not, however, neglect the presence of evil.

Joe, the resident "philosopher" at Nick's waterfront saloon in San Francisco, possesses a sense of the innately wonderful in people (something that Emily in *Our Town* cannot achieve until she dies). Nick, too, shares this conviction and exhibits the corresponding instincts, being moved to tears by beautiful music though he does not know why. Joe feels guilt for some unspecified past transgression evidently connected with how he attained his money, always tainted anyway since it is gotten at the expense of the have-nots; the judgment that Saroyan places on money, as inherently suspect and only existing through oppression, casts a Marxist tinge over his work: "Money is the guiltiest thing in the world. It stinks" (p. 35). The saloon, in fact, serves as a refuge for the downtrodden and abused, though the outside world cannot be kept from invading the barroom. The fact that violence and force are essential for preserving civilization reveals that something is seriously amiss in the universe outside this microworld.

Joe watches over the others who enter his world: over Tom, if not an innocent still a kind of holy fool, and over Kitty, the whore with a heart of gold. In Kitty, Joe discovers beauty where none should exist, just as each of the other characters has the spark of something salvific or redemptive: Dudley is set afire by love for a woman, Harry possesses a sort of defensive black humor, Wesley can dance, Willie is vitalized by the challenge of the electric games. From them, Joe learns "how full of goodness life is" (p. 34). Kitty's childhood "dream of grace," of a "home," of being an actress and someday marrying a doctor makes her special and helps her retain her innocence. Joe supports her in her illusory belief that she was a burlesque queen and not a hooker, a belief that Blick, the man in black, tries to undermine. Blick—clearly analogous to Hitler—is the force of disharmony, of chaos and old night who enters Nick's place. Joe, who ordinarily spends his life waiting while he sends Tom on numerous errands, willingly, however, takes up a gun against Blick, although it falls to Kit Carson, an old teller-of-tall-tales dressed in white, to kill Blick in a shootout. Which, if any, of Kit's tales before this event are true remains unclear; yet there is no doubt that the one about killing Blick is, and this gives a retrospective validity to the others. Saroyan thus emphasizes the continuing value of the mythicizing imagination, especially in a skeptical age that thinks it can survive without myth, by reinterpreting the myth of the past to energize the present. Joe tells Kit that "living is an art" and that "it takes a lot of rehearsing" before it is perfected and made right, which definitely applies to Joe who only gradually "get[s] to be himself" (p. 26).

The other passwords of Joe's philosophy are the need for a sense of self-worth—which he supports in Tom and Kitty who eventually marry—and the need to live "a civilized life," which "means a life that cannot hurt any other life" (p. 17). The facts of life itself test his philosophy; as Dudley's girlfriend, Emily, asks, how can one love knowing that death is "*our end?*" Or as the Arab who acts as a choral figure says, warning of absurdity and meaninglessness that lie just around the corner both metaphysically and politically, there is "no foundation. All the way down the line" (p. 20). To act or to not act may be just the same in the end. Yet in the face of these truths, mankind must go on in hope, as exemplified by Willie, the last pioneer against the new frontier of mechanization, of technocracy, who finally defeats the machine, American flags popping up to announce his victory. From an allegorical point of view, the power of darkness and despair will always remain present as a challenge. Saroyan, therefore, presents his play to the audience as a reminder of the old inspiring faith, a gift equivalent to the music box carousel Kitty receives. Indeed, the entire play could be performed on a merry-go-round, which would convey much of its special charm. Seen in that light, Saroyan's play as toy would symbolize the almost biblical childlike innocence that must be sustained if the dream is to remain operative.

To move from *Time of Your Life* to *How to Succeed in Business Without Really Trying,* the 1962 award winner over both Williams's *Night of the Iguana* and Paddy Cheyevsky's *Gideon,* is to turn from the sentimental to the satiric. With music and lyrics by Frank Loesser and libretto by Abe Burrows, Jack Weinstock, and Willie Gilbert, *How to Succeed* is a brisk, brash farce that contributes nothing new to the musical as a form; it is, in fact, a throwback to the slick, character-as-caricature musicals of the 1920s and early 1930s like *Of Thee I Sing.* In his review of this "non-romantic musical," Henry Hewes judges it "a belated but merry funeral service for Horatio Alger"[6]—a tenable viewpoint, surely, but perhaps far from the minds of the audiences who kept it running for over 1,400 performances. If the Horatio Alger figure, the simultaneously beguiling and roguish J. Pierpont Finch, is, on the one hand, reduced to absurdity, on the other he demonstrates that it still remains possible to take on the system and beat it, thus making it likely he will be applauded for his vices—particularly in an age when most individuals are fighting for upward mobility. In his rise to the top, guided by voice-over passages from Shepherd Mead's book subtitled *The Dastard's Guide to Fame and Fortune,* Finch makes the expense-account audience an accomplice in his game of one-upmanship as he rapidly climbs the ladder from window washer to mailroom clerk to head of personnel to director of advertising to chairman of the board of the Worldwide Wicket Company. A likeable office Machiavel, for whom the end justifies the means, he capitalizes on the stupidities of others in a cutthroat climb to the top. Although the cronyism and buddy system receive satirical send-ups along the way, Finch ultimately does arrive at the pinnacle, reassuring for an audience content to have the specific "evils" of Madison Avenue undercut while still seeing preserved intact the abstract possibility of achieving fame and fortune. For the authors *not* to have it both ways would be to court audience dissatisfaction and rejection.

The love interest essential to a musical is provided by Rosemary, a woman militant feminists would love to hate. She delights in the role of wife, and marrying Finch means that the other secretaries can live vicariously a Cinderella-like existence. The romantic imagination of these girls, who "want to see his highness / Married to your lowness," is brilliantly satirized in their song "Cinderella Darling": "You're a real, live fairy tale; / A symbol divine. . . . / Of glorified unemployment."[7] Miss Hedy LaRue, the dumb but buxom blond secretary and mistress to the company president, provides the indispensable complication of a romantic triangle. Finch uses her in his media blitz to appeal to the sex and greed of the TV-obsessed audience. The predictable fiasco is set straight by a pure coincidence when the aged Mr. Womper, who discovers he is a fellow-alumnus of Finch from Old Ivy, takes Hedy for himself and hands the running of the company over to Finch. The secret of Finch's success is a heady egotism, coyly dramatized in a love song to himself, "I Believe in You." Sung to his image—the only self he any longer knows—in an imaginary executive washroom mirror that allows him to face the audience and thus include them in his tongue-in-cheek accolade, it is an exaggerated paean to American individualism and self-reliance. Because the audience need to see the self-indulgent expression on Finch's face as he sings, having him look into the auditorium solves a practical dramatic problem; on a deeper level, he sees himself in the audience, and they in turn recognize in him a reflection of themselves. Anyone infected by the American Dream possesses at least a bit of the J. Pierpont Finches of this world. Yet *How to Succeed,* while entertaining, makes no attempt to alter an audience's preconceived attitudes, which the remaining five works about the American Dream to varying degrees do.

Willy Loman and his son Biff in *Death of a Salesman* might be said to embody, respectively, the two versions of the American myth: the one for whom the dream is irretrievably lost; the other for whom paradise exists to be regained. Arthur Miller's 1950 Pulitzer Prize drama might, in fact, be seen as a play about America, about the gradual deterioration of the dream into nightmare. Willy's ancestors represent and recreate within themselves different stages in the country's history: Willy's father as the last of the pioneers, a hardy, self-reliant carver and peddler of flutes who made his way west across the continent; his brother, Ben, as a self-made capitalist and living proof of the rags-to-riches romance who went to Africa and discovered diamond mines. By the time, though, that Willy, as a salesman who lived through the Depression and World War II, tries to make the dream of Benjamin Franklin, Ralph Waldo Emerson, and Horatio Alger operative, it has been reduced and even become debased.[8]

Even though Miller gives his protagonist the surname "Lowman" ("low" or common man), Willy refuses to think of himself, or allow others to consider him, as "little." The dream of being Number One propels him, and the tenacity with which he pursues the dream in itself makes him nonordinary. Like all salesmen, Willy must sell himself, so his self-image depends more than usually is the case on support from the outside. When others begin to doubt that self, so too does Willy, which is the point he has reached as the play opens. To dramatize this mental disorientation and spiritual dislocation, Miller adopts a somewhat expressionistic form, in which memories of the past and the reality of the present weave in and out, through free association, to reveal the guilt-ridden, accusatory, ruminative process of Willy's mind. The play's structure is not a sequence of flashbacks, Miller insists, but instead a "mobile concurring of past and present."[9] Rather than through exposition, the past becomes tangibly present for Willy and the audience in something akin to acted-out soliloquies. So *Salesman* is a subjective drama, analogous to a first person limited point of view in fiction. Yet the dramatic form itself precludes the solipsistic effect often felt in the first person narrative: seeing events acted out on the stage surrounds them with an aura of objectivity, making them seem not as subjective and allowing the audience to gain sufficient moral perspective on the character.

If his heroes were isolates, Willy is a family man through-and-through. His sons are very much a part of his dream; he has done everything for them, not only to live again through them, but also to earn their love through the granting of material things. He wants them to like him (his motto is "Be well liked and you will never want"[10]), but he confuses being liked with being loved. He does not realize that sometimes one must be not liked and criticized in order to be loved, because a totally uncritical love can be destructive rather than creative. Although the insistence of his wife, Linda, that "attention must be paid" (p. 443) to Willy who is a human being and so cannot be thrown out "like an old dog" commands assent, her unquestioning and unswerving support for him in his dream/delusion throughout their marriage has, in effect, exacerbated his problems.

Miller might well have named his work *Fathers and Sons,* for numerous such relationships are embedded in its texture: not just Willy with each of his boys or Willy with his father; but Ben, Howard, and Charley as surrogate fathers to Willy; and Bill and even Bernard, though he is the same age, as substitute fathers for Biff. Willy feels temporary about himself partly because of the lack of any close relationship with his own father, and he himself fails as father to his sons. He continually instills in them the wrong values, condoning their using any means, including cheating and petty thievery, to get ahead. Generally in American drama, the failure of the American Dream links up closely with the failure of fathers to instill the proper values, including a respect for the affective side of human nature which is often considered unmasculine and so sacrificed to aggression and greed. Willy's boys fail him as well, literally deserting him in the restaurant scene, but more deeply by other acts of rejection. Son Happy, a womanizer, is unhappy despite his material success; liked less by Willy, he is yet more like Willy and his Uncle Ben, retaining to the very end the conviction, ill-founded, that he can be Number One.

Biff, whose story Miller develops so fully that he becomes a dual protagonist, has been spiting his father for years, blaming Willy's failure for his own. When he walked in on his father and another woman in a Boston hotel room, Biff discovered what every son discovers of every father: he fails to live up to the ideal of virtue the child expects. But Miller asks, as he does in the earlier *All My Sons*, what right a son has to bring a father to judgment and if, in doing so, he does not himself incur some guilt. Before the incident in the hotel, Biff was the Adonis-like high school football hero, whose trophy still gleams in the house; afterwards, his idol tarnished, he gave up and became a drifter, never making it in the real world as neighbor Charley's son Bernard does. Equally destructive can be unreal expectations by the parents. Biff finally desires not success in any material terms, as Willy would have it, but to be out-of-doors, away from the city, to work the earth with his hands; he possesses a kind of Thoreauvian nostalgia for the garden, not understanding (as Nick Carraway does) that the garden has receded behind him. He does, nevertheless, achieve self-knowledge, recognizing that he has tried to be what he really has no desire to be and finally telling Willy that they are a "dime a dozen" and should "take that phony dream...and burn it" (p. 470). Willy, too, longs to retain some vestige of the garden within the urban setting, pathetically planting a few carrot seeds in the moonlight in a yard almost totally encroached upon by towering apartments. At times, accompanied by flute music, a scrim of golden-green leaves covers the set, yet this simply supports the sense that the dream of the garden is an illusory patina over the urban economic jungle.

Willy chose, against these stirrings of his inner nature, the pull of material success, which reveals a moral littleness in him. Partly he is the victim of a society infested by the success syndrome, but mostly he is the victim of himself and his choices; he reaches no epiphany and is still as devoid of self-knowledge at his suicide as he was all along, thinking that Biff will love him for the insurance money—which Miller connects linguistically with Ben's diamonds that the audience knows do not shine. The father dies so that the son might live, but the sacrifice is partially blighted. Willy dreamed of a funeral like Dave Singleman's, not understanding that Singleman, as his name indicates, was the exception to the rule, the extraordinary one. At Willy's funeral in the play's "Requiem," only a few gather to hear the choral comments by the other characters that readjust the work's focus from Biff's rebirth back to Willy's death. If society is to blame, then Willy can only be pitied. Yet if that is the case, then Miller has provided an indictment of the perversion of those ideals that America has for so long pursued, which makes *Death of a Salesman* a drama as much about the decline of the American Dream as about the demise of Willy Loman. The works that follow in its path might be seen as variations on Miller's *Dies Irae* for the American Dream.

Frank Shelton suggests that "the agrarian dream, based on concepts other than material success, had a force and a possibility for Biff lost to the Americans of *That Championship Season*,"[11] Jason Miller's 1973 award-winning drama. In this structurally old-fashioned play, touted as "essentially a workingman's play...a 'popular' work...for the people of America,"[12] four members of a championship high school basketball team from twenty years ago gather at their Coach's home, as they do every year, to celebrate the final game by replaying it in memory—with the trophy as chalice and grail—and to draw up the plans for their current contest, the reelection of a mayor who once had his "freakish-looking" mongoloid child placed in an institution to safeguard his own public image. The team forms a microcosm of middle-class America; of Polish, Irish, and Italian extraction, they trade ethnic jokes and slurs, à la Archie Bunker, and yet they put on a united front against Jews, Communists, and blacks. The mayor, George, in campaign rhetoric redolent of the Nixon/Agnew years, promises "four more years of serenity and progress" (p. 49). Phil, carrying on with George's wife, will contribute to the campaign if he can keep open the strip mines he leases from the city, while James hopes to receive George's endorsement as school superintendent.

The Coach, symbolically being eaten away by cancer, inhabits the past, as if time stopped on the day the championship was won. Attempting to reinvigorate his peculiar, exclusivist brand of the American dream, he chooses for heroes a motley mix: John Kennedy, Joseph McCarthy, Father Coughlin and, though unnamed, Vince Lombardi. A combination prophet and patriarch, the Coach is a surrogate father-figure/priest-confessor to his perpetually adolescent boys who also live in the past, fixated on a win that was a fraud and a sham, accomplished when the fifth team member, Martin—absent from the reunion—broke the ribs of the black center on the opposing team. Martin's absence symbolizes the moral vacuum in America, the loss of values corroding the national fiber. The alcoholic Tom feebly attempts to fill in for that absent conscience. Paradoxically, sobriety means deception and lies, while alcoholism permits insight and truth. Like the clear-sighted Claire in Albee's *Delicate Balance*, Tom stands on the sidelines (when he is not drunkenly falling down the stairs), acting as a moral referee trying to goad these men into an admission of the corruption beneath the veneer. That Tom comes closest to being the ethical norm in the play further underlines the moral vacuity of America.

Violence never hovers far away in this macho domain punctuated with locker-room lingo, and the playwright intimates that the aggression inherent in competitive sports relates to the other acts of violence that pervade the country. Sports no longer provide the only or even the most important way these men channel their aggressions, for in their estimation everything assumes the aura of a game: politics is a game—"just another way of makin' money" (p. 46); war is a game, and they think that any way it is played is fair, so long as their side comes up the winner. This world built on the male myths of power and dominance allows little, if any, room for the tenderer emotions of love and compassion. In fact, the world of the play is a world without women—and the women mentioned are not women who really have the capacity to love. In this masculine wilderness, the affective side of human nature ordinarily associated with feminine sensitivity is almost entirely missing, creating an unbalanced and faltering familial and social structure.

Almost a generation earlier, Arthur Miller portrayed the American success syndrome—the need to amass money as proof of character, to be well-liked at the expense of moral virtue, to prove love for family by bestowing on them material goods—as misdirected and ultimately self-defeating. In his plays, however, the sons bring the father to task if they find him not living up to an ideal of conduct. In *That Championship Season*, the surrogate sons for the most part refrain from judging the substitute father for his moral failure, either because they cannot recognize it or because they know that their own failure is equally as great. Jason Miller, though, implicitly does pass a judgment upon these men; the play, as John Simon remarks, "tells grass-roots America that it stinks."[13] Yet the audience's attitude might be just as schizoid as that fostered by *How to Succeed*; it appears likely that a certain segment of the audience might, at the end, be caught up in the communal spirit of win-at-any-cost and rally round the Coach and team. Though the dramatist intends to undercut the myth—or at least the perversions and excesses to which it is frequently subjected—he might, for at least some in the audience, unwittingly reinforce it. The myth of champions, even of tarnished ones, still exerts a powerful hold on the national consciousness. Still another part of the audience, those who share the playwright's basic assumptions, can leave the play reassured that their worst fears about the decline of America are true, feeling vindicated and morally superior to the characters. Such moral chauvinism serves, however, only as a sentimental salve.

David Mamet's *Glengarry Glen Ross,* the drama winner for 1984, presents, like *That Championship Season* of a decade earlier, a world of prejudiced, mean-spirited, what's-in-it-for-me men, a world utterly lacking in feminine sensibility. Unique among the Pulitzer plays since it opened originally in London, followed by a run at Chicago's Goodman Theatre before reaching New York, Mamet's work would automatically have elicited comparisons with Arthur Miller's award-winning drama of thirty-five years before even if a much-heralded revival of *Death of a Salesman* had not been running simultaneously on Broadway. Mamet's Loman-like peddler of property is Shelley "the Machine" Levene, now a down-on-his-luck, almost-out real estate salesman begging his office manager for the "leads" that will give him an opportunity to be back "on the boards." Levene finds himself caught in a catch-22 dilemma: in a business where the bottom line is "Always be closing," he can only make a sale if he is given good prospects; but he will only get those leads if he first finalizes some deals. Preaching the old-fashioned wisdom that "a man's his job,"[14] Levene attributes his former success to skill rather than luck. Believing in oneself furnishes the key, and making a sale requires missionary zeal to convert clients into buying what they do not really want. So desperate has Levene's situation now become that he not only offers Williamson, the office manager, a bribe for each name plus a percentage of his commission, but also allows Moss, another salesman, to implicate him in a plan to break into the office and steal the list of prime prospects. When Levene is found out, he tries without success to buy off Williamson for an even higher price. Williamson knows, however, that no matter how good Levene's leads, he no longer has what it takes; Levene's near-religious exhilaration over believing he has reclaimed his spot on the boards evaporates when Williamson reveals that the buyers' checks always bounce, that they just enjoy talking with salesmen.

If Levene offers an insight into what selling once was but can never again be, Moss, who considers himself as little better than a hustler for the pimps who own the business, underscores just how demeaning the salesman's job has become in today's cutthroat wasteland. The only avenue left to regaining his selfhood and escaping the enslavement that the salesmen themselves help perpetuate resides in striking back by hurting the company owners, Murray and Mitch, who, significantly, remain faceless and unseen. When Moss first attempts unsuccessfully to convince Aranow—who, like Levene, is also unable to close—to become his accomplice in robbing the office, his pitch sounds like that of a salesman pressuring a client; and if Aranow had agreed, he would have been bilked out of his fair share just like many clients at the hands of sleazy salesmen are.

A salesman who does succeed in closing—and winning a Cadillac—is Richard Roma, though his victory, too, is short-lived. If Levene's credo of salesmanship, no matter how zealously applied, has been made obsolescent by the changing times, Roma's creed is a purely rationalistic and self-serving one; salesmen, like others, must be as the times are, greedy and vulgar and petty, doing whatever is necessary for their own security. Denying the existence of any absolute morality in favor of a relativistic ethic of the jungle, Roma sets up his private situational morality as the only code, "do[ing] those things which seem correct to [him] *today*" (p. 49). Emotional bonds between people exist to be broken; pragmatic bonds for using and abusing another to the best advantage wait to be forged. When Williamson, however, jinxes Roma's big sale so that the client will have it nullified, Roma excoriates him for being a company man, and a peculiar and paradoxical camaraderie grows up amongst these men ordinarily at each other's jugular. In this world which is "not a world of men" but an adventureless "world of clockwatchers, bureaucrats, and officeholders," salesmen "are the members of a dying breed" and "have to stick together" (p. 105). They have acquired on the streets an ability to think on their feet, a skill Williamson can never learn because, as Levene asserts in a speech that ironically incriminates himself, you can only "know the shot" by living. These salesmen are actors who, Iago-like, exploit their gifts and take great delight in their performance, no matter how nasty the tactics; greed has not had such a thoroughly good time trying to make a killing on the American stage since Hellman's *Little Foxes*. Yet the torrent of words reveals the shallowness and powerlessness of these salesmen; their scatological language—which some reviewers hailed as a poetry of profanity—is finally as limited as they are.[15]

As an outsider, Williamson can have no notion of the bond these men form with one another. A salesman "can't exist alone," but must go all out "with" and "for" the "partner [who] depends on [him]" (p. 98)—because it is "us" against "them," the salesmen against the managers, the little men against the entrepreneurs. But Roma denies this bond with his fellow salesmen almost as quickly as he espouses it. Before he knows that Levene has become a thief, he marvels at his gifted way with phony words and promises to take the older man on as his partner—by which he means that he will take half of Levene's leads along with all of his own. So in *Glengarry Glen Ross* (named for the tracts of Florida real estate of dubious worth that these salesmen foist upon naively unsuspecting customers), the society that victimizes is composed of individuals who victimize. The play intentionally cuts two ways: the audience feel the same contempt for the managers that these salesmen do; yet by linking themselves with the salesmen as victims out for redress at any price, they become the objects of Mamet's indictment. Mamet's work is finally, however, a slight drama, remarkable more for its extreme realism, for the almost cinematic conciseness and swiftness of its first act—three scenes in a Chinese restaurant (though its second act is considerably more conventional)—and for its pervasive odor of despair than for any startling new insight.

Whereas *Glengarry Glen Ross* seems clearly a post-Watergate play (complete with a break-in for a list of names), the unspoken national nightmare behind Sam Shepard's *Buried Child* is undoubtedly the Vietnam War, which continues to haunt America's conscience. In his 1979 prize-winning tale of a midwestern family living on a dark, rain-sodden, and, until now, barren earth, Shepard pursues the age-old notion of the sins of the fathers being visited upon the children, of the seeds of corruption planted in the past coming to fruition in the present. Shepard displays a peculiar power in his highly symbolic family-problem plays such as this and the earlier *Curse of the Starving Class* of allegorizing the American experience, of deflating the myth of America as the new Eden and showing the new American Adam as the perpetrator of a new Fall from grace. The one outsider who visits the farm that Dodge and his descendants inhabit clings to a mental image that it will resemble a Norman Rockwell cover, something out of "Father Knows Best" or "Ozzie and Harriet" transported from the Pacific coast to the heartland. Shelly, that outsider, holds out the only possibility for new blood mixing with old to somehow redeem the fetid atmosphere, but it is finally a futile hope since her boyfriend, Vince, the youngest male, is cut from the same cloth as his father and grandfather, as the visual rituals of the play make clear.

Except for the lengthy interspersed poetic monologues that have become something of Shepard's trademark, *Buried Child* uses the Ibsenite ploy of a secret only gradually revealed to the audience as its dominant structuring device. Dodge, the decrepit patriarch, sits virtually immobilized before the TV set during the entire course of the play; debilitated by smoking and drink, he feels "invisible, displaced." While his harridan of a wife, Halie, is off running around with the effete local minister, Father Dewis, their sons parade through the house: Tilden, once an all-American fullback, now mentally imbalanced; Bradley, a partial amputee whose wooden leg becomes a darkly comic weapon. The family talk also of the dead Ansel, a high school basketball hero who died in the war, not on the battlefield but in a motel room, and whose memory Halie intends to commemorate through "a big, tall statue with a basketball in one hand and a rifle in the other."[16] As Dodge remarks, there is no necessary connection between "people propagating and lov[ing] their offspring" (p. 46), and surely no love is lost between this father and his sons. It is, in fact, the lack of love to which Shepard, like Jason Miller, largely attributes the decline of the family and, by extension, the gradual diminishment of America; as Mel Gussow aptly comments, *Buried Child* is "a wake for the American dream."[17] Halie, blind in other ways, is clearsighted enough—if somewhat hypocritical—to smell "the stench of sin in this house" (p. 50), to see that sports and war, the arenas in which men traditionally prove themselves, are hollow. The men, rather than heroic, are now vicious and savage, consumed by drugs and sex. She asks pointedly, "What's happened to the men?" (p. 58)—and Vince, the youngest generation on stage, will clearly not regenerate things. The motif that sounds throughout the drama is a plaintive "Where have all the fathers gone?" During the play, several ritual burials of the father occur: Tilden enters with corn from the garden, husks it, and covers Dodge with the shucks; later, Dodge is covered with Shelly's rabbit fur coat, with a blanket, and with a rose from the hand of Halie. Bradley comes in and, in the dark of night, stealthily shears off his father's hair, signifying a removal of potency.

The corn and later carrots that Tilden brings in have mysteriously sprung up in profusion out of the mud behind the house, where no crops have been planted for decades. But this profusion of vegetation must be seen as ironic; it has literally been fertilized by the corpse of a baby resulting from an incestuous relationship between Tilden and Halie, killed and buried out back by Dodge to protect the family's reputation. Bradley's comment that a veritable "paradise" has grown up outside the house calls attention to this as a fallen paradise, a wasteland never to be reclaimed. That the past cannot be buried forever is symbolized when the crazed Tilden carries in the mud-covered skeleton at play's end. Vince, the only possibility for the future, lies down at the conclusion, taking exactly the same posture as the recumbent Dodge; he sees himself as the inheritor of the house and embraces the connection with his father and grandfather. Halie speaks to him as if he were Dodge, using exactly the same words she addressed to the now-dead father at the beginning of Shepard's foray into the American Gothic, which initially holds a kind of grotesque fascination but whose action becomes frenetic near the end.[18]

Surprisingly for a musical, America's longest-running Broadway one expresses a vision, in the tradition of *Death of a Salesman* and its followers, more dark than light. Conceived by Michael Bennett, with lyrics by Edward Kleban, music by Marvin Hamlisch, and book by James Kirkwood and Nicolas Dante, *A Chorus Line*, awarded the drama prize for 1975, pictures the surrender of America's absolute faith in the myth of success. In a theatre/audition hall, seventeen gypsies vie for the eight available places in the chorus of a Broadway-bound musical. The nature of a chorus demands that there be no dancing "to a different drummer" or marching to variant tunes for those finally chosen; they must blend together into a whole by moving in synchronization. Virtually every song reiterates this necessity of molding oneself into a socially and professionally acceptable person by masking individual idiosyncracies and covering over one's psychic needs in the name of art—of conforming, in short, to expectations imposed from without.

Locating the action on a stage without scenery contributes to the illusion of an unplanned, improvised audition. But the premise of the entire proceedings—namely, that the director (heard mostly in a disembodied voice from the back of the theatre) would put this potential chorus line on the couch, as if he were a psychologist or priest-confessor—seems extremely artificial, even stilted at times. Worse still, many of the confessions border on banality: the girl whose mother uses her as a substitute to achieve what she was not able to in her youth; the girl born to save her parents' marriage; the self-denigrating homosexual who learns to accept himself and whose father finally calls him "my son" only after seeing him in drag. The photographs from their résumés that all of the dancers hold up in front of their faces bring surface up against substance, since the résumé is for each of them "a picture of a person I don't know."[19] Like Willy Loman, the dancers must sell themselves if they are to succeed. But if an actor/dancer ordinarily adopts the mask of a character while onstage, here the dancers remove the masks that everyone (the audience included) wears to face the world. Once unmasked, the dancers' overriding and universal desire to "find a place to fit in" becomes clear. For example, one not exceptionally attractive female discovered that "different is nice, but it sure wasn't pretty," another rejected method acting because "she couldn't do what everyone else could," and still another resorted to silicone treatments and plastic surgery to make her body fit the standard measurements for a job. Everyman and Everywoman will likely find elements of himself or herself somewhere up on the microcosmic stage, or at the very least empathize with this enforced conformity. This central motif of the sameness that the egalitarian ideal has come to entail reaches its apex in the conflict between Cassie, who in the past was a lead dancer, and Zach, the director who was her lover. Zach argues her inability to return to the line: "You don't fit in. You don't dance like anybody else—you don't know how." Cassie counters that she need not "prove anything anymore," does not wish to excel, and can be special *within* the chorus line, thus commiserating with those who no longer put stock in the dream, those for whom the passing of time involves not only physical loss but diminishing goals. What Cassie is willing to settle for is what the audience must settle for as well.

In the old-fashioned production number that serves as the show's breathtaking finale, all of the dancers, dressed in identical silver lamé top hat and tails, join in a precision dance in perfect unison; with no one out of step, they resemble a well-oiled machine doing a show-stopping routine. The number they dance to, entitled simply "One," accepts the dark underside of America's egalitarian ideal: there can be only "one singular sensation, and you can forget the rest." Those in the chorus line, and most in the audience, are among all the rest, limited to being "second best." The audience thus see images of themselves up on the stage, recognizing that their belief in unlimited opportunity and the possibility for success is illusory, that most are *not*—indeed cannot be—the singular "one." And the mirrors that serve as a backdrop for the finale reinforce this realization, forcing upon the audience the self-reflexivity peculiar to Modernist art. Not only do the mirrors give the illusion of added size and dimension to this production number, but those in the audience see themselves as a mass of people reflected in the same image that catches the anonymity of the members of the line. While the music makes this a celebratory occasion, a more somber mood resonates in the realization that, for most people, ever being special is just a mirage. Confronting the self in a mirror in this metatheatrical musical destroys distance and turns the green world of the theatre—the world of illusion—gray or even black. Individual fame is elusive: the collectivity of common people form only the background of the dance and not the center of it. The glamour and glitter and glory of this dance are finally themselves an illusion, since this production number is merely being rehearsed to serve as the climactic showstopper spotlighting the star of an escapist musical comedy of the kind American audiences have always loved the best. So *Chorus Line* ends on a note of tension between the thrill of art and the terror of anonymity.

Miller's *Death of a Salesman* stands at the center of these plays about the American Dream, since it contains within itself a dual perspective on the myth of the American Adam. One of its protagonists, Biff, seems to believe that the dream can be recaptured; the older, Willy, knows that it is too late for himself but hangs on to the delusion of possibility for his son. Miller himself appears, nevertheless, to favor the opposite stance that the dream is irretrievably lost, as do several of the other dramatists whose works are treated here. Most of these plays, in fact, provoke a dual response in their audiences, intimating that their cherished belief in the opportunity for success is illusory, destroyed by the very same system founded to guarantee it; at the same time, they generate sympathy for those characters who still try to actualize the dream in their own lives. This ambiguity makes these dramas, as a group, among the densest of all the Pulitzer winners.

Atypically, *The Time of Your Life* does, indeed, propose that the dream is still alive and operative, but because the play is an allegorical fable with a heavy aura of fantasy, it today seems pervaded by sentimental, wishful thinking. Admittedly, *How to Succeed in Business* makes believe that everyone can climb the ladder of success unimpeded and arrive at the top, yet the authors handle their hero ironically, with tongue-in-cheek, and he sees himself that way as well. Furthermore, rising involves dishonesty, or at least taking advantage of others; any means of getting to the top is fair. *That Championship Season, Buried Child,* and *Glengarry Glen Ross* all argue even more emphatically than *Salesman* that the dream has died—if it ever lived—not only perverted but irreparably debased; the little private immoralities of their characters reflect a larger social and national corruption. Finally, *Chorus Line* questions whether in a democratic, not to say egalitarian, society the kind of success that accrues to being number one preached by the prophets of the American Dream is not, in fact, inimical. The garden that is America, these playwrights emphasize, is not pristine, but a home for fallen humankind. The myth was never anything more than a myth, unrealizable from the very beginning because it failed to adapt itself to human nature. If the myth might once have been potentially creative, it has long since become destructive and had best be laid to rest. As Biff urges Willy, "Take that phony dream and burn it" (p. 470).

Although Arthur Miller employs the stage in an antirealistic, and even at times expressionistic, way in order to dramatize the inner life of Willy Loman and his mental disintegration which blurs the distinction between then and now, dream and reality, *Death of a Salesman* is not nonrealistic in the strict sense of acknowledging the presence of an audience—at least not until possibly the "Requiem" which forms the coda to the drama and which is played on the forestage or apron. By potentially implicating the audience as mourners at Willy's grave, the "Requiem" not only lays to rest the man, but also the myth by which he (and the audience) live: everyone, just as Willy does, must dream ("It comes with the territory" [p. 472]), but the dream is almost certain to be denied by history or circumstances. In the other "salesman" play, *Glengarry Glen Ross,* Mamet, while clearly intending that his real estate men be seen as actors who role-play, deceive, and otherwise employ a bag of verbal trickery to effect their sales, does not directly cause his audience to think of themselves as an audience in the way that both *How to Succeed* and *Chorus Line* do through their use of onstage mirrors. When Finch gazes admiringly at himself in the mirror that has no glass (which means that he looks straight out into the auditorium), the audience look approvingly back at him through the other side of the glassless mirror, seeing him as a reflection of themselves—and his faith in the unlimited possibility of rising to the top as their faith. In *Chorus Line,* the mirrors on the stage that reflect (and simultaneously multiply) the line of dancers also send back to the audience an image of themselves: just as the dancers in the chorus submerge their individual freedom and identities to move in perfect unison—so that each is all and all is each—the rows of viewers are, during their time in the theatre, as in life, an anonymous mass, any distinctiveness blurred. The audience, by virtue of their reflection in the mirror, become analogous to the dancers, all toeing the line under the control of an unseen force, none standing apart from the others as the "one."

The Varieties of Religious Experience

Despite several factors—strict separation between church and state and the absence of a national religion, the lack of any solid tradition of religious drama, the inheritance of the Puritan suspicion of things theatrical, the small number of influential Art Theatre movements, the emphasis on the commercial aspects of production—the modern American professional theatre can still boast of a strong and vibrant group of what might broadly be called religious dramas. In "Patterns of Belief in Contemporary Drama," George Kernodle proposes a method of categorization for these plays, "distinguish[ing] three main approaches to religious drama in this age. The first way is to dramatize biblical events in the idiom and psychology of the present day. ...The second approach seeks an exaltation in method, as well as subject" by "fus[ing] modern poetry and modern stage techniques with the method of the miracle plays. ...The third method is to dramatize a contemporary religious problem."[1] Although among the Pulitzer plays representatives of the first and last of these approaches—for example, Marc Connelly's *The Green Pastures* and Albee's *A Delicate Balance*—come readily to mind, it remains more difficult to find a clear-cut example of the second, if only because saints' plays per se have never been abundant in America (where the "saints" tend more often than not to be political figures such as Lincoln). Yet the particular direction of American religious drama as evident in the Pulitzer plays can perhaps best be appreciated not by employing Kernodle's approach that divides plays according to type, but by charting the central motifs and issues that pervade these works: first, the tension between the God of the Old Testament and the New and the notion of an evolving deity; second, the contention between predestination and free will; third, the problem of reconciling the existence of suffering and evil with the concept of a loving God; and fourth, the perplexing question of how, indeed whether, man can know the Unknowable and the related issue of whether man receives revealed truth through institutionalized religion or personal inspiration.

Although Kernodle's capsule judgment of Marc Connelly's *The Green Pastures* as "the masterpiece of [the first] method . . . considered by many the finest play of the twentieth century,"[2] by now surely has been proven excessive, Connelly's 1930 drama does furnish a convenient beginning for considering the notion of a developing godhead. Although Connelly, by basing his work on Roark Bradford's *Ol' Man Adam an' His Children*, was, strictly speaking, ineligible for the Pulitzer which was to go only to an "original" stage work, he does significantly alter Bradford's perspective to mark it as his own. Indeed, changes from Bradford's 1928 book, subtitled *Being the Tales They Tell About the Time When the Lord Walked the Earth Like a Natural Man*, are legion. Connelly is more selective of events from the Old Testament, omitting, for instance, any dramatization of Abel's murder, the Ten Commandments, and the parting of the Red Sea. He deals with the New Testament not at all, except through the Negro spirituals that charmingly, if anachronistically, proclaim that the day of salvation has already dawned and through the narrator's vision of the crucifixion with which *Pastures* closes. Furthermore, his comedy is less broad than Bradford's—the girl Cain marries is not a gorilla in a tree, and Noah's problems with drink and a nagging wife in Connelly's less matriarchal and sexually open society are not so pronounced. Connelly's dramatic version adds a haphazardly used frame with Mr. Deshee, the preacher, conducting Sunday school classes, so that the acted-out Bible stories become a type of dream vision for the audience who see, as it were, with the eyes of children. Finally, Connelly removes almost entirely the separatist aspect of Bradford's work, which ends by asserting the chosen status of the black people; Bradford's Lord tells "Nigger Deemus," who denigrates himself and believes that blacks should be denied the right of discipleship: "'Dat's de very rock I been huntin' for all dis time. Nigger Deemus, set dat rock down right yar and now and build me a church on yit.'"[3]

Structurally, *Pastures* is a mini-mystery cycle (thus harkening back to the origins of English-language drama), although Connelly, limiting his scope essentially to the Old Testament, takes as his hero not Christ but rather Yahweh, anthropomorphised into a folksy southern black patriarch. Moreover, Connelly's God, instead of possessing an essence fixed from all eternity and simply doing things to his creatures, actually learns from man. The more God is humanized in this fashion, the easier it becomes for man to see himself as godlike and be assured of his own dignity—particularly appealing to audiences during the Depression when everyone seemed the slave of the economic system. In the traditional medieval mystery cycle, as in the Bible, the New Testament God of Mercy is already implicit in the Old Testament God of Wrath, since in Genesis God promises to send a redeemer; humankind, as a result, lives in expectation and later fulfillment of that assurance. In *Pastures*, however, there exists no such promise before the exile from the Garden, which increases the play's tension since Yahweh must somehow resolve the conflict within himself over how to respond to his recalcitrant creatures.

In this scheme, a fallible God reacts with anger and despair to his mistakes and those of his creatures and depends upon an evolving mankind to point the way towards perfectability, as Shaw's Life Force does in *Back to Methuselah*. Man's success in meeting the challenge towards betterment depends, however, not on the growth of mind and will, as in Shaw, but on some very American values of hard work and self-reliance in the face of the temptation to simply enjoy life. Adam is a fieldhand, a type of black Everyman, but his descendants, the Cains of this world, give themselves over to the pursuit of pleasure; studs, dandies, and city-slickers, they carouse and gamble and drink and fornicate and kill, culminating in the combined Babylon and Sodom and Gomorrah of the nightclub scene. Looking down on mankind, "De Lawd" becomes so distraught over their sinfulness that he wishes to cast them aside and start over. But Hezdrel, an apocryphal character of Connelly's creation and a second Adam—whose consciousness has actually evolved to a higher level than God's—instructs God about the nature of forgiveness and the creative value of suffering rather than the destructive use of force. At the end, God experiences a sudden intuition that "even God must suffer"[4] and so consents to send his Son to die for mankind, "terrible burden" though it is. For God willingly to suffer in this way consoles man in his own trials, making him less alone. As Dietrich Bonhoeffer writes, "Only a suffering God can help." Not only does Connelly envision a dynamic God who unifies his play in a way that none of the medieval cycles really coheres, but he also helps revitalize the biblical myth for an age of unbelief and for a down-to-earth people. In doing this, however, he unintentionally resorts to racial stereotyping (blacks are a rowdy, womanizing lot who conceive of the afterlife as a celestial fishfry) that renders the work virtually unplayable today.

Given the staunch Calvinistic bias of the nation's theological heritage, the polarity apparent in *Pastures* between the God of Retributive Justice and the God of Love recurs frequently in American drama. It adumbrates what is arguably the weakest play ever to win a Pulitzer, Hatcher Hughes's *Hell-Bent fer Heaven*. This 1924 folk melodrama stresses how the evangelical spirit—essentially populist and anti-intellectual in its impetus since it gives witness to the egalitarian principle that anyone may undergo conversion—can, like any good, be perverted by an excess of zeal. The hypocritical Rufe, "hell-bent fer [sic] heaven... sence he got that camp-meetin' brand o' religion,"[5] embraces totally the doctrine of predestination, in both the spiritual and the material realm, which means that the just and righteous God whose "instrument" he claims to be can be made the scapegoat for the many ugly and un-Christian methods Rufe employs to win Jude Lowry away from Sid Hunt. In Rufe, Hughes welds together several readily identifiable character types: he is partly the deprived orphan taking vengeance on everyone around him for the love denied him as a child; partly the Vice figure, glorying in the confusions he can cause; partly the Archfiend or Tempter provoking Sid and Jude's brother Andy to turn against and kill one another; partly even the disguised Antichrist, whose justification is that "I've been about my Master's business!" (p. 264). Set against Rufe and his deterministic theology are both Sid, whose "God helps those who help themselves" ethic implies the need for human initiative, and Andy, who denies that God plays any part in human actions—he will take full responsibility and go to hell by his own free choice. Poised against what he considers the perverted theologies of the others is David, Sid's grandfather, who rejects Rufe's religion as "a stench in the nostrils o' God" (p. 242) while he professes the efficacy of an old-fashioned, muscular Christianity.

Yet Hughes places an onerous burden on any audience if he expects they will sympathize with David in his insistence that no one release Rufe from the cellar where he will surely drown, since that would interfere with God's "chance" to inflict punishment. Apparently, David sees no moral inconsistency in claiming that God's providential pattern is at work in the encroaching floodwaters and at the same time considering himself the instrument of the Lord's will by turning his back on Rufe—thus rendering his notion of Christianity hardly more humane than the sinner's. Hughes intends that the close of his play function on a mythic as well as a literal level, with the Deluge come again. Here, however, the Remnant who are saved seem hardly better than the evil one washed off the face of the earth by the wrathful God who speaks (as he stereotypically does in many plays) through thunder and lightning, darkness and wind, leaving the audience with no very consoling image of the deity. Earlier, Sid's mother, the normally pacifistic and pietistic Meg, even raised the unsettling possibility that if God demands vengeance then there might not be a God at all; significantly, the sentiments of this usually "religious" woman are echoed by Rufe himself, who finally dies in a paroxysm of alternately damning God for letting the wicked prosper and of denying God's existence for not saving him from the flood. If taken seriously, much of *Hell-Bent fer Heaven* becomes patently ridiculous; only if played in a broadly comic vein could it feasibly succeed in not alienating its audience. Yet the text of this unpleasant play provides no clue that would justify a satiric reading of the deranged Rufe or suggest he be seen as a figure of comic derision rather than religious psychosis.

Some playwrights question whether a God less harsh and more loving than Hughes's might not exist. As W. David Sievers remarks, "if there is one persistent theme in O'Neill it is the search for godhead—male or female"[6]—male or female gods in Eugene O'Neill being associated with the vengeful versus the compassionate. The notion of a "female" Godhead operates in O'Neill since, to the residue of Puritan thought in his dramas, O'Neill adds the remnants of a conservative Irish Catholicism, characterized by an ardent devotion to Mary—almost a Mariolatry—reflected in a preponderance of female archetypes, Jungian anima figures, and Earth Mothers. In its outlines, the plot of *"Anna Christie,"* awarded the 1921 prize, owes a debt to nineteenth-century melodrama: a prostitute with a heart of gold returns home to her father, who forbids her to marry the sailor she comes to love. But the triangular conflict between Anna, her father, Chris Christopherson, and Matt Burke could also be regarded as a conflict between the Father and the archetypal Mother/Sea for control of the child, especially because of the close association between Matt and the sea that brings him to Anna after his boat capsizes in a squall. The father, captain of a barge, has—like Maurya in John Millington Synge's *Riders to the Sea* (a work to which the early O'Neill seems indebted)—fared badly at the hands of what he calls "dat ole davil [sic] sea,"[7] which has claimed his father, brothers, and two sons as its victims. To protect Anna from the sea's influence and break the hold it apparently possesses over his family, Chris sent her to live on a farm, which only resulted in her loss of innocence. Chris regards the sea as a villain, blaming it for all the evil in the world; it is a malevolent force which, he feels, has nothing to do with God, but is connected instead to some inscrutable fate or chance. Chris thinks he has adequately accounted for all of experience in terms of a simple division between black and white, but believing in such a Manichean duality leaves no room for any mystery or ambivalence in the universe.

The religion of Matt Burke, the blustering, highly romantic Irish sailor, comes across as every bit as reductive, though it has more to do with traditional Catholicism, to which a dose of predestinarianism has been added; according to his unexamined faith, he will suffer damnation just for loving a Lutheran. Unlike Chris, Matt accepts the possibility that the sea can be a positive force; to die in it will give him (in another echo of Synge) a "good end...quick and clane [sic]" (p. 168). His belief in Providence is, nevertheless, a purely mechanical one—God's will is what brought him through the fog to Anna—and he reduces the crucifix to an object of superstition. But mostly Matt regards the sea as a place of freedom from constraint and materialism.

Because of her past experiences, Anna hates all men, giving the play a Strindbergian complexion. Claiming that nobody owns her, she insists on belonging only to herself. She, too, searches for freedom from the things that have caged her in—the house in the country, the jail—and like Matt discovers that freedom in the sea. Disagreeing with Chris that the sea is totally malevolent and that the fog is its worst trick, Anna actively seeks out the sea as a source of wonder and mystery where she can find union with something outside of herself and belong to a force that she can immerse and even annihilate herself in. The sea, like love, cleanses her from guilt. Anna, therefore, does not consider the sea as simply either good or bad; even the fog potentially can bring transcendence and reconciliation. Nor does she subscribe to the fatalism of Chris or pay to free will the lip service that Matt does. Instead, she develops a metaphysic which posits that fate is character and character is fate. While it may be true that "things happen" to her (such as Anna's helplessness against corruption on the farm), it remains equally true that she is capable of choice up to a point—yet that precise point has been decided by earlier existential choices that shaped her character. Humankind, therefore, lives both free *and* determined. When Chris and Matt go off to sea together at the end, Anna accepts her fate as the woman who waits and most likely mourns; she is free to be alone (not the same thing as being lonesome) and to suffer. She submits herself to the sea come what may. But in so doing, she finally belongs totally to herself, breaking out of apparent meaninglessness to achieve a near Sisyphean acceptance.

The implied criticism of the doctrine of predestination in *Hell-Bent fer Heaven* and *"Anna Christie"* continues in the most impressive drama on a specifically religious subject so far produced by an American and the one that has generated debate even among theologians: Archibald MacLeish's 1957 award winner, *J. B.* As Connelly does, MacLeish returns to medieval drama for the form of his framed play. A retelling of the Book of Job in modern dress, this poetic drama is technically a mystery play; yet it is just as indebted, if not more so, to the morality tradition with its contest between God and Satan over the soul of Everyman, in this instance a successful businessman first seen celebrating with his family that American feast which expresses most forcibly the connection between spiritual election and material prosperity—Thanksgiving Day. The stage set establishes the link with medieval drama: inside a microcosmic "circus tent" stands a "sideshow stage" or "platform" called "Heaven," with a "table" nearby named "Earth."[8] This is not, as in medieval times, an age of faith, but the postbomb nuclear age of anxiety; inside the tent are castoff vestments like the accoutrements of wornout religions, and in the last lines, J. B.'s wife, Sarah, muses about the church candles and the stars that have been extinguished in this God-is-dead, indifferent universe. (In *The Flowering Peach*—to which the drama jury voted a Pulitzer in 1955 only to have the advisory board, wisely in this case, reverse its decision and award the prize to *Cat on a Hot Tin Roof*—Odets also alludes to the atomic age, with the Flood serving as an allegory of nuclear destruction in a modern mystery play that converts the Noah story into Jewish family drama.) J. B.'s recurrent imagery of dungheaps and cesspools decidedly pictures a modern wasteland; moreover, one of the characters echoes the metaphysical *angst* of the Absurdists: "We never asked him to be born . . . / We never chose the lives we die of. . . / They beat our rumps to make us breathe" (p. 144).

J. B. plays itself out concurrently on several levels. The first of four conflicts involves an acting contest between two old and out-of-work performers: the balloon-seller, Mr. Zuss, who believes that God's ways, though inscrutable, are still providential, and the disillusioned cynic, Mr. Nickles, who holds that consciousness of one's suffering, while it validates one's humanity, simultaneously denies any possibility of happiness. But once Nickles dons the Satan mask and Zuss the mask of God for the play-within-the-play, the masks assume a power of their own, raising the conflict to a battle between supernatural forces for J. B.'s allegiance. That an unseen "Distant Voice" controls both these masks indicates that Nickles and Zuss live in the grip of some power larger than themselves, that their roles have been thrust upon them. But for the actor playing the role of J. B., the role and the reality have been identical from the start: to be human is to be Job, for to be is to suffer. There have been and always will be Jobs.

The third conflict occurs between a capricious God, who indiscriminately visits suffering upon the good as well as the bad, and J. B., the modern Everyman, who dares demand logic and meaning as opposed to whim and irrationality. Insofar as this conflict pits God against Job, it adds nothing to the biblical myth, in fact lopping off a great deal by, in Samuel Terrien's formulation, "deliberately ignor[ing] or distorting the figure of the 'impious' Job which is the focus of the ancient Hebrew (3:1–42:6)," so that ultimately "the repentance of J. B. loses its *raison d'être* since it does not follow a display of Promethean arrogance."[9] Because the modern J. B. and God, unlike their biblical counterparts, never speak together, that tension must be concretized through the fourth—and apparently central—conflict between J. B. and Sarah, whose notions of religious belief radically differ. J. B., although not a born-again Christian, is a staunch Calvinist, certain that, though he did nothing to deserve election, he is predestined for salvation. In return, J. B. thanks his Creator by joyfully immersing himself with a childlike curiosity and exuberance in the simple things of life, worshipping God through his creation. Yet Mr.

Zuss probes to the heart of J. B.'s beliefs: "A poor man's piety is hope of having / a rich man *has* his—and he's grateful" (p. 46).

As opposed to J. B., his wife, Sarah, argues for a moral system based on willingly returning something to God. But as loss after horrendous loss befalls them—the death of a son in war, the loss of another son and daughter in an automobile crash, the assault and murder of still another daughter, the death of their youngest child, an explosion that reduces J. B.'s business empire to rubble—she moves closer and closer to despair, finally admonishing her husband to "curse God and die." For commonsense says that if God is responsible for the good, then he is equally to blame for the evil. Eventually J. B., unconscious of any guilt in his past, can no longer bear the apparent meaninglessness of his suffering. Nor will he be party to the facile rationalizations of the Three Comforters sent by God, rejecting in turn Bildad, the purveyor of historical necessity who argues that guilt is a sociological accident; Eliphaz, the doctor of psychiatry who reduces guilt to a psychophenomenal situation, an illusion; and Zophar, the priest whose doctrine holds that all are born inherently corrupt, but that it is this guilt that somehow raises man above the beasts.

If MacLeish is asking, do any rational grounds for faith exist, the answer would seem to be "no." Man's inability, like that of Shakespeare's Lear, to do anything more than "take upon's the mystery of things / As if we were God's spies" (V, iii, 16–17), does not mean, however, that no supernatural order exists, but only that it is not given to man to understand it. And yet, MacLeish implies that contemporary man yearns for more than that. Sarah, who changes not because things happen to her, discovers the fulfillment of that need by moving from an unquestioning piety through despair to a dynamic new faith in man, a humanism that results from a response to something small in nature not unlike J. B.'s earlier Romantic worship of Nature's God through Nature. Growing in the ashes, she finds a twig from a forsythia tree, a promise that life does spring from death (after the bombing of Hiroshima, certain plants almost miraculously regenerated in profusion). This teaches her not to expect justice, because none exists, providing instead a sudden epiphany into the wonder of man's love for each other: whereas God only exists, man loves, and the latter truth is infinitely more miraculous. The ultimate value becomes then, feelings of the heart, a deification of human affective emotions. If the churches are dark, then "blow on the coal of the heart" (p. 153) and there shall be light. The final image presents a paradise regained, a modern Adam and Eve in a new, humanistic age setting to work, with a renewed faith in the American ideal of self-reliance. Emersonian optimism wins out as the Melvillean emphasis on the presence of darkness fades.

The note of philosophical absurdity sounded as a minor motif in *J. B.* becomes dominant in Edward Albee's metaphysical drawing room comedy, *A Delicate Balance*, the 1967 Pulitzer winner. Not that it is the most nearly Absurd in ideology of all Albee's works, a position *Tiny Alice* of a year earlier holds. In that play, Albee not only attacks head-on the ontological problem of how man comes to know the Unknowable, but also questions whether, in fact, that Unknowable, or only man's idea of it, exists in reality. Focusing on "how much false illusion we need to get through life,"[10] Albee plumbs man's compulsion to concretize the abstract, to personify it through a symbol before he can worship it. Equally it is possible that only the symbol, and not the thing it symbolizes, has any real existence, that, finally, "THERE IS NOTHING THERE."[11] The only reality may be nothing, nonbeing. *A Delicate Balance* treats this problem from a less overtly religious—but no less metaphysical—perspective, through characters who come face-to-face with the Void. The "delicate balance" of the title refers to a condition of stasis and stagnation, a comfortable routine that the late-middle-aged and well-to-do couple Agnes and Tobias cling to and nurture, even though it eventuates in a kind of death-in-life status quo. An appropriate epigraph for this autumnal play of drifting passively through life would be Eliot's "living and partly living."

Albee's external action is simple: into the stately home of Agnes and Tobias and her alcoholic younger sister, Claire, come the oft-married-and-divorced daughter, Julia, and their best friends, Harry and Edna, who arrive one Friday night demanding shelter from the terror. More allegorical personages than fully dimensioned characters, Harry and Edna serve as mirror images of their host and hostess; their "lives are the same."[12] When Agnes and Tobias gaze at them, they see themselves. Harry and Edna suddenly became "FRIGHTENED," and yet "there was nothing," (p. 55)—that is, emptiness, meaninglessness. They arrive bringing the challenge of self-knowledge, which Agnes calls a "plague," for even if she wanted to see herself and how little her life has become, which she does not, it is too late for change, so such knowledge, without any possibility of fruitful action, would be doubly hard to bear.

The terror for Tobias resides in his recognition that if he throws Harry and Edna out, then his entire life—marriage, friendship—has "all been empty," and so in one of Albee's verbal arias he attempts to maintain the illusion of something, of not-nothing, by making them stay. For too long, however, Tobias's life has been one not of grand gestures, but of no gestures at all. His motto, "We do what we can" (p. 19), attests to his refusal to exert himself by going the extra distance required to love instead of just being loved; Claire rationalizes this by saying that, faced with "distasteful alternatives," he makes "the less...ugly choice" (p. 46). Two things aid and abet Tobias in his stasis: his wife, Agnes, and the operation of time upon character and choice. Julia accuses her father of becoming "very nice but ineffectual, [a] gray...non-eminence" (p. 71). The precise moment that occurred can be pinpointed as the death of their son, Teddy, when Tobias relinquished his rightful position as head of the family to Agnes; he explains that it was fear of hurting Agnes again that made him not want another son. Now he claims that Agnes makes all the decisions in the family, though she maintains this is only his illusion, the thing that allows him to not feel guilty for having receded from his position of authority. Agnes, in fact, decries what she sees as an unhealthy imbalance in modern sex roles. The woman, she argues, should not make the decisions, but only hold the reins and steer the route determined by the moral values of the man. Her vocation becomes then, like a fulcrum, to maintain the balance, the evenness in the family, which is only another way of saying that she keeps them from facing the unpleasant truth. Even the haughty grace of Agnes's extremely artificial and studied language reveals the brittle surface shell of their lives.

Like Harry and Edna's visit itself, Agnes's demand that Tobias now decide disturbs him because he does not like being called to task for being neglectful and not returning love. In his desperation to ward off the sense of failure, he begs Harry and Edna to stay, but this is doing too little, too late. His very ability to act has been stultified. As Agnes wisely perceives: "Time happens, I suppose. . . .You know it's going on. . .up on the hill. . .but you wait. . .When you *do* go, sword, shield,. . .finally. . .there's nothing there. . .save rust; bones; and the wind" (p. 169). Life becomes a matter of diminishing possibilities; the road not taken can never be traversed. Every choice one makes limits all of one's future choices, for each time one chooses A over B, one's options at the next moment of choice are automatically halved, as the missed chance can never be recalled. Eventually, with the passage of time, the pattern becomes so firmly fixed that one is locked inside it and it is "too late" to break from it; character is finally determined then as firmly as if it had been fated. This pattern of character as fate and of choices as becoming fewer with the passage of time bespeaks the special formulation that the deterministic philosophy assumes in American drama from O'Neill through Albee to such other recent playwrights as Robert Anderson in *Solitaire/Double Solitaire* and Stephen Sondheim and James Goldman in *Follies*.

Tobias looks at his soul and finds it wanting, and he understands that the nothingness Harry and Edna feared has been inside him, unrecognized all along, and can only be lived with. His tragedy is not that things will never change, but that he now possesses the knowledge that they *can* never change. Agnes blocks out this recognition and reverts to the status quo, reasserting the protective balance in a way that Tobias cannot; she can say, "Come now; we can begin the day" (p. 175), not caring that the night was ironically a time of potential revelation when the ghosts of truth were released, happy only that the terror of the unexpected visit has been put behind. For Tobias, as Claire feared, "THERE IS NOTHING THERE." And he does not even have J. B.'s deified "coal of the heart" to fall back on. Albee uses the religious connotations of the days of the week (Friday evening to Sunday morning) in much the same richly ironic way as Samuel Beckett does in *Waiting for Godot*, which takes place on Saturday, between the despair of (Good) Friday and the hope of (Easter) Sunday. In *A Delicate Balance* not only does no resurrection occur, but none any longer can occur. In this play, it is "too late" even for a secular religion of love to operate and redeem.

If Emerson appears to be the seminal thinker for O'Neill and MacLeish, he fulfills that role even more explicitly for Thornton Wilder, whose *Our Town*, winner of the 1938 prize, is probably the most widely known and revered of all the Pulitzer plays and the one commonly thought to best embody the American spirit. *Our Town* is not, strictly speaking, a morality play—as it loosely has been called—since it features no conflict between opposing forces of light and dark for man's soul. It does, however, present the archetypal journey through life to death of Everyman/Everywoman figures, so the characters tend towards abstraction rather than detailed delineation as individuals, while the action centers on everyday events experienced by all: birth, growing up, marriage, childbearing and rearing, death—all in a mythical and microcosmic town, Grover's Corner, New Hampshire, which seems so real that theatergoers expect to find it on a map. Wilder undercuts the conventions of stage realism, however, to free the theatre from its spatial and temporal limitations by specifying "No curtain" (thus indicating that the action has no beginning and no end but is part of an ongoing continuum) and "No scenery"[13] (thus refusing to localize his events so that they could be occurring in anytown and everytown). Furthermore, he allows only as many props as are necessary for the literal-minded, unimaginative spectators in his audience.

Although the action begins in 1901, *Our Town* is more than an exercise in nostalgic recall of an America now past. Nor is the microcosm of life from the dawn of this century to the outbreak of World War I as inadequate and limited in its awareness of evil and the darker forces of life as some critics would insist, for along with the presence of the town drunk and eventual suicide, Simon Stimson, who is given almost the last—and decidedly downbeat—words in the play, there are gossip and backbiting, partial lack of communication among family members, death in childbirth and—looking forward since the action per se ends in 1913—war. Quite clearly, Wilder presents life "after the Fall."

Basically, *Our Town* is not as simplistic a play as it has sometimes seemed, but rather a philosophical examination of time and the proper way of seeing experience, expounding the necessity for escaping from the narrow, myopic view of existence and embracing, with the poet's help, a God's-eye perception of human history. Wilder concretizes his attitude towards time as a continuum through the way he conveys events that occurred prior to or will happen after the twelve-year scope of the action. Not only does Professor Willard give a lengthy report about the geological formation of the earth and the anthropological data of the area ("some of the oldest land in the World" inhabited as far back as "the tenth century" [p. 157]), but the linguistic nuances of the Stage Manager's choice of verb tenses in the opening frame point to a perspective both inside secular time and outside of time, transcending it; he reports: "First automobile's going to come along in about five years—belonged to Banker Cartwright"; or "There's Doc Gibbs comin' down Main Street now. . . . Doc Gibbs died in 1930"; or talking about Joe Crowell, "Goin' to be a great engineer, Joe was. But the war broke out and he died in France" (pp. 6–8).

Wilder's Stage Manager, with his understated, homespun New England manner, performs several functions: narrator, bridging shifts in time and place, setting the scene for the audience; actor of minor roles—drugstore owner, preacher at the wedding of Emily Webb and George Gibbs; chorus, philosophizing for the audience. Distanced from the action filtered through his eyes, the audience begin to see with his perspective. He possesses a godlike omniscience, overseeing the progression of history as God would. The theatergoers, too, Wilder intimates, must develop this kind of sight, which is the same type of vision that the audiences at medieval mystery cycles experienced when they saw the whole scope of sacred history. In a seemingly inconsequential exchange in the play, Wilder verbalizes the idea on which his entire drama pivots. George Gibb's younger sister, Rebecca, tells him about a letter sent by a minister to a friend of hers when she was sick: "on the envelope, the address was like this: It said: Jane Crofut; The Crofut Farm; Grover's Corner; Sutton County; New Hampshire; United States of America;. . .Continent of North America; Western Hemisphere; the Earth; the Solar System; the Universe; the Mind of God" (p. 28). Wilder, who himself played the part of the Stage Manager for a while in the Broadway production, tells his audience that if they could only penetrate the understanding of God where everything—from least to most, from smallest to largest, past, present, and to come—exists simultaneously in a purposive, providential order, then they would live life wholly, and even be able to cope with death.

The play's tension arises because, paradoxically, this vision necessary for living can only be attained after death. That is man's tragedy. Emily dies giving birth, at once an image of mutability but also of the way in which life coming out of death is a part of the natural cycle. Only after she dies—when "something way down deep that's eternal about every human being" can "come out clear" and "get weaned away from the earth" and be reunited with something larger—does Emily, granted the opportunity to relive "an unimportant day" in her life, see that that day is "important enough" (p. 58), that "earth" is "too wonderful for anybody to realize" (p. 62)—except maybe "the saints and poets." Death has lost its "sting" for her; the individual spirit can be reunited with the World Spirit, with the evolving Life Force that is the "real hero" of the play. Wilder's religion is basically pantheistic, a kind of vague Emersonian Transcendentalism; the ideal is union with the "mind of God," which only death—or the mystical vision of the poet—can effectuate.

A number of critics have pointed recently to something that has been suspected now for a long while: the really distinctive hallmark of drama on this side of the Atlantic is its emotional power; substantial intellectual inquiry, except in the rare philosophic work such as O'Neill's *The Iceman Cometh* or MacLeish's *J. B.*, has never been of paramount importance in much of American theatre—though the Pulitzer plays do have a better record on this count than might first have been expected. As Ned Rorem states the situation: "American theatre has little to do with mature philosophic analysis and much to do with the pure energy one finds in animals and children. [Our dramatists] never spark the theological fireworks of a Mauriac, a Montherlant, a Cocteau, a Claudel, even a Sartre."[14] Yet, if there exists any group of Pulitzer dramas that shows American playwrights flexing their intellectual muscles, it is the religious dramas that—in pursuing answers to some of man's most perplexing epistemological and theological questions—reveal a speculative thrust courageous for the commercial American theatre, while reflecting the pluralism (evangelicalism and Calvinism, mysticism and Transcendentalism, humanism and atheism, agnosticism and Absurdism) that has always characterized the nation's beliefs.

The image of the deity that emerges from these plays is of a much humanized Godhead, himself undergoing a progressive growth and evolution (*Our Town*), perhaps even in response to the example set by mankind (*Green Pastures*). If *Hell-Bent fer Heaven* closes as it opens with a harsh God, vengeful and capricious, *"Anna Christie"* and *J. B.*, positing Nature as revelatory of God and communion with nature as a means of reaching union with the divine, both elevate human love, the heart's affection, as modern man's primary deity. Man's love not only copies but even substitutes for God's. If some of the characters in *"Anna Christie"* do not completely escape a belittling belief in predestination, Anna herself moves beyond this by understanding that to accept one's fate is to affect one's fate and thus secure freedom and dignity. Since *A Delicate Balance* proposes that with the passage of time man's opportunity for free choice grows progressively less, finally ceasing to be effective in altering character, it is the darkest of these dramas. The love that could have saved in the absence of God was withdrawn long ago, leaving an emotional and spiritual void—what *J. B.* would have ended with were it not for the redemptive power of human caring.

J. B. and *Green Pastures*, the two works from this group that employ framing devices to remind their audiences that they are in a theatre watching a play, offer diametrically opposite types of "faith": the former, an anxious, skeptical stance appropriate to a nuclear-age *theatrum mundi;* the latter, a simple, unquestioning belief such as would be conveyed in a bible school class. *Green Pastures* and *Our Town*, the most popular of these works with audiences at the time of their initial productions, are the brightest, both offering a hopeful glimpse of an afterlife in union with either an anthropomorphized God or a generalized World Spirit, each benign in his own way. Audiences in a skeptical contemporary age, however, may well find the darker works like *J. B.* and *Delicate Balance* more convincing precisely because they *do* rest upon unfathomable mystery rather than enforce any easy closure. Although *J. B.* does confirm that human love can, to borrow Octavio Paz's phrase, "re-sacrilize society," it neither denies the fact of suffering nor offers any rational explanation as to its "why," while *Delicate Balance*, where love has failed, offers no exit from its self-imposed hell except entrance into an equally bleak unknown. Even the apparently light *Our Town* closes with a subtle intimation of darkness. Although no curtain rises to signal the play's beginning, one does materialize at the end: "The Stage Manager appears at the right, one hand on a dark curtain which he slowly draws across the scene" (p. 64). By masking that part of the stage where what only "the saints and poets" can ordinarily see has just been played out, Wilder stresses that humankind's normal condition is to live with blinders over its eyes, keeping veiled what only art in this life and a mystical oneness in the next can reveal.

9

The Idea of Progress

The notion of progress that has intrigued and motivated humankind throughout history might be seen as a secularized version of the search for the Kingdom of God—secularized because the promised end is utopian and this-worldly rather than otherworldly, remaining in the finite sphere. And yet, since progress is thought of in terms not only of social but of intellectual and moral advance as well, requiring the ascendancy of reason over passion and of altruism over egoism, a link exists between confidence in progress as an end and a recognition of some providential design. Whereas J. M. Bury in his *Idea of Progress: An Inquiry into Its Origins and Growth* expresses doubt that classical and medieval civilizations even thought of progress in human terms, more recently Robert Nisbet in the *History of the Idea of Progress* hypothesizes that an "abandonment of faith in the idea of progress"[1] characterizes contemporary society. Arguing that modern man has jettisoned valuing the past; has deserted reason, knowledge, and the ideal of community for the irrational, the hedonistic, and the egocentric; and has come to think of Western civilization as a corrupting influence on the rest of the world—and that all of these tendencies find reflection in a debilitating lack of religious conviction in the sacred and the mythological—Nisbet believes that "disbelief, doubt, disillusionment, and despair have taken over—or so it would seem from our literature, art, philosophy, theology, even our scholarship and science" (p. 318). Although much recent Continental and even British drama bears out Nisbet's assertion, the plays in this chapter generally belie that assumption, but perhaps only through a willful myopia or desperate act of courage on the part of their authors.

Thornton Wilder won his third Pulitzer (his second for drama) in 1942 for *The Skin of Our Teeth*, a truly original American play and one that the author claims "held all the implications that were real to me: man's spiral progress and his progression through trial and error."[2] Like Shaw's *Back to Methuselah*, with which it shares structural, philosophical, and tonal affinities, *Skin* displays the influence of the medieval mystery cycles, recounting human history in capsule form—here in a style akin to the comic strip—from the beginning of time to the present and on into the future. But as a mystery cycle it has been largely secularized, dealing with the Ice Age, the Deluge, and the War, any war, as natural and social history, though it does speak to the twentieth century's need for reinvigorating myth by drawing on the Garden and Noah episodes of Genesis, with the characters existing between paradise lost and paradise regained. *Skin* is cyclic and comedic in its overall structure, ending in guarded optimism; and each act, like three variations on a theme, recapitulates the movement of the whole: Wilder's family of man, the Antrobuses, begin each act on the upswing, reach a low point through either a natural disaster and/or human culpability, and then end having narrowly muddled through by "the skin of their teeth"; in each instance, the temptation is overcome, sinful action somehow compensated for.

In its techniques, *Skin* reflects the influence of Surrealist art, previews the multimedia theatrical effects of the 1960s and 1970s, and even hints at some Absurdist drama in the vein of Ionesco. The scenery with its angles askew, the lantern slides projected onto the set, the talking dinosaur and mammoth who share the Antrobus house, the cardboard cutouts, and the lights and noises all help contribute a carnival atmosphere while establishing the aura of a dream that happens without conscious control. Furthermore, the impression Wilder creates of watching an impromptu presentation reflects Pirandello's influence. Mr. Fitzpatrick, Wilder's director/stage manager, not only stops the play so that he can rehearse volunteers taking over the roles of sick actors but, like the manager in *Six Characters in Search of an Author* and Hinkfuss in *Tonight We Improvise*, is satirized for his prosaicism; even the costumer, Ivy, understands the play and the dramatist's erudite allusions better than he does. Lily Sabina Fairweather, temptress, mistress, camp follower, and maid, steps out of character and, as the actress Miss Somerset addresses the audience, telling them not to trouble themselves over the meaning of this play she hates. She requests that they "pass up [their] chairs" for firewood to "save the human race"[3] and at the end sends them out of the theatre to complete the action: "We have to go on for ages and ages yet. You go home. The end of this play isn't written yet" (p. 137).

Within the framework of his comic allegory of humankind's journey, Wilder's characters assume an archetypal dimension; each member of the Antrobus family represents an aspect of the individual man's or woman's personality. Mr. Antrobus, former gardener (Adam), self-made man, inventor of the wheel, the lever, gunpowder, the singing telegram, the brewing of beer, and grass soup, is the power of intellect, a force for either creation or destruction. Appreciating the wisdom of the past, he will not tolerate the burning of Shakespeare's works even to provide warmth during the Ice Age, for without books "it isn't worthwhile starting over again"(p. 125). Mrs. Antrobus, inventor of the apron, the hem, the gore and the gusset, and of frying in oil, is humankind's affective side; her watchword is the "family" and the "promise" of love between husband and wife that helps them endure suffering. As one who insists that women must be themselves and not the subservient objects the media extoll, she emphasizes woman's role as transmitter of the Life Force, "why the whole universe was set in motion" (p. 114). Lily Sabina (Lilith), with her philosophy of "just enjoy your ice cream while it's on your plate" (p. 72), embodies the hedonistic pleasure principle, although she has become cynical about the "dog-eat-dog" world. The Antrobuses' daughter, Gladys, conveys hope for the future, symbolically appearing with a baby after the war. Their own son, Henry (Cain) represents the strong, unreconciled evil always present in the world, the anarchic principle that misuses freedom while refusing to accept responsibility. Although he kills his brother and the boy next door (earning the mark of "C" on his forehead), hits the Negro with his slingshot, and becomes the enemy in the war, he is taken along on the Ark, as is Sabina, in act 2.

In act 3, the actors playing Henry and Antrobus break out of their stereotypes and become dimensioned characters in order to reveal the root of the tension between them: something in the attitude of the actor playing Antrobus reminds the actor playing Henry of "being hated and blocked at every turn" (p. 132) by authority figures, and so they clash. Through this, the person playing Antrobus comes to a recognition of his own "emptiness" because he has "ceased to *live*." At play's end, Antrobus knows that he will eventually endure and prevail, "that every good and excellent thing in the world stands moment by moment on the razor-edge of danger and must be fought for. . . . All I ask is the chance to build new worlds and God has always given us that" (pp. 135-36). Mrs. Antrobus echoes Shaw when she insists, "this world has a work to do and the will to do it" (p. 129). Yet Wilder, like Shaw, has often been criticized for an optimism that seems out of keeping with the facts—*Skin* opened only a year after Pearl Harbor, but was more popular in Germany right after World War II than in America during the War—though he does not allow a belief in scientific and intellectual progress to deflect him from admitting and examining the existence of evil. Whether or not one accepts Wilder's optimistic philosophy of spiral progression or not, *Skin* remains a richly imaginative play, the seminal text of self-consciousness in the American theatre.

For critics to call *The Effects of Gamma Rays on Man-in-the-Moon Marigolds,* Paul Zindel's Off-Broadway work and the 1971 prize winner, "honest" or "engaging" creates the impression that here is a work which pretends to be nothing other than what it is: a stark if overly familiar family-problem play about life's ability to sustain itself against great odds—doing for a particular family something of what Wilder does for the universal family of man in *Skin*. Zindel, though, appears to have pretensions to something more, attempting to impart additional weight to his basically simple characterization and content through overblown stage trickery. Originally produced at Houston's Alley Theatre, *Effects* too obviously recalls Williams's *Glass Menagerie* in its character configurations and stylistic techniques: both concern a mother, who lives mostly on dreams, and two children, one healthy, the other not; both households lack a father, through either death or desertion; in both, a gentleman from the outside world helps, or thinks he helps, one of the children. The stylistic similarities are even more pronounced: in both, the stage setting, while essentially realistic—an apartment in St. Louis, a vegetable store in New York—is used in a nonillusionistic fashion, particularly as regards lighting and music. In *Menagerie,* the nonrealistic elements, including the images and legends flashed on a screen, are integral to the play as "memory" occurring in Tom's mind. In *Marigolds,* however, such devices as recorded voice-overs (sometimes used pretentiously as when a character's voice reverberates electronically) and blackouts and spotlighting of characters (equivalent to cinematic fade-outs and close-ups) seem superimposed upon a fragile content that cannot support them, as if the form could supply a weightiness the content does not itself merit. Zindel seems interested in the techniques in and for themselves, simply as a means of avoiding straight realism.

Furthermore, perhaps because Zindel usually writes novels for adolescents, the abundant symbolism in *Marigolds* frequently lacks subtlety. The mother, Beatrice, for example, to assuage her guilt over having sent her own father off to a sanatorium, cares for the senile Nanny who, with her "smile from a soul half-departed" and her "shuffling motion that reminds one of a ticking clock,"[4] serves as a walking personification of death and of how affluent Americans (her daughter is "Miss Career Woman") mistreat their aged parents. More compellingly, the once orderly vegetable store now symbolically reflects the clutter and refuse of Beatrice's psychic and emotional life. With her motto "just yesterday," Beatrice lives on reminiscences of things *past*—a word prominently displayed on a placard at the high school science exhibit—on would-have-beens and should-have-beens. All her life she has romantically dreamed and schemed, yet she has seldom carried through on her plans, some of them, like turning the run-down store into a neighborhood tea shop, slightly outrageous. Like Willy Loman, Beatrice tends to blame something outside herself for her failure, though she accurately assesses the way that a competitive, success-oriented society attempts to force everyone into a predetermined mold, decrying the lack of tolerance and the levelling down to sameness and mediocrity that, paradoxically, is a part of the American system: "If you're just a little bit different in this world, they try to kill you off" (p. 84). Difference may threaten the status quo and not be easily handled or accommodated, yet Zindel argues not only that some differences are beneficial but that variation rather than sameness is essential for there to be progress.

Although Zindel's exposition leaves some past events annoyingly obscure, it seems to have been criticism by the father she idolized that began Beatrice's descent into a present condition she characterizes as "half-life" and "zero." One day she hitched up the horses and rode through the streets selling fruit, to be met by her father's stern rebuke; ever since, she has dreamed of riding a shiny wagon pulled by white horses, only to see the forbidding figure of her father look on disapprovingly. She married badly, merely to please her father, but then no man could live up to her dream. After she took her father off to the hospital, she had the horses "taken care of"—a cycle of failure, guilt, and still more failure.

The cycle of parent destroying child continues in Beatrice's erratic relationship with her daughters, shifting suddenly between compassion and bitterness—in much the way that the pet rabbit is alternately loved and then hurt. Beatrice's older daughter, the mentally disturbed Ruth who was traumatized by contact with death and violence, tells tales, craves the attention of men by flaunting her sexuality, and appears just as destructive and vindictive as her mother; when she cannot have what she desires, she ruins it for everyone else. The younger Tillie, in her awkwardness and unprettiness and firm grasp on reality, stands as Ruth's opposite and a living denial that one need be determined by heredity and environment. Tillie discovers a much-needed father figure in her high school teacher (unfortunately named Mr. Goodman), who introduces her to the word *atom*, which she comes to love. The notion that everything in the universe, herself included, is somehow connected with every other thing from the moment of creation enthralls her; it provides a fixed point of reference and a feeling of importance. For her science project, she exposes marigold seeds to radiation, which need not produce sterility and may even yield a positive effect: while those that receive little radiation are normal and those exposed to excessive radiation (like Beatrice and Ruth) are killed or dwarfed, those subject to only moderate radiation produce mutations, some of which (like Tillie, who has experienced very detrimental influences but has emerged relatively unscathed) are good and wonderful things. Against all odds, Tillie not only survives but actually thrives.

Finally, though, Zindel's optimism does not grow organically from the play. Some might argue that Tillie's (and the playwright's) optimism, because it is won with so much difficulty and is so at variance with the adverse and negative atmosphere from which she arises, is therefore all the more impressive and no more facile or unwarranted than Wilder's. The widely divergent perspectives of the two writers, however, militate against this: where Wilder discerns a pattern of ultimate success after repeated failures over the entire sweep of human history, Zindel ties his faith and hope to a specific—and atypical rather than representative—household that he then proposes as symbolic and universally applicable. Though Zindel seems to find little difficulty in asserting this optimism, an audience might have a considerably harder time assenting to it.

Produced by Eva Le Gallienne's Civic Repertory Theatre, Susan Glaspell's *Alison's House* took the 1931 honor over more highly regarded works such as Maxwell Anderson's *Elizabeth the Queen* and Lillian Riggs's *Green Grow the Lilacs*. Glaspell loosely bases her drama about the relationship between the writer and society and the means by which the poet can transcend time and attain immortality on the life of Emily Dickinson. Alison's poetry becomes for Glaspell what classical literature is for Wilder and what Tillie's imaginative interpretation of experiential data is for Zindel—a bright spot in, even proof of, humankind's progress. Set on December 31, 1899, the turn of the century that will see the Victorian age give way to the Modern, the play focuses on the Stanhope family's decision to sell the ancestral home where Alison, dead for eighteen years, lived and wrote. Glaspell strikes a Chekhovian note at the beginning of act 2 with the arrival of the Hodgeses, who have purchased the house as a summer resort and their announcement that they will chop down the trees (à la *The Cherry Orchard*); the play stands then, like the Russian master's, as a swan song for a way of life being replaced by more commercial enterprises, though Glaspell's attitude, like Chekhov's, is ambiguous: both the old and new ways have their good and bad sides.

Glaspell builds her well-made play, like those of Ibsen's middle period, on a long-hidden secret: the truth about Alison's love for a married man. The central conflict resides in a dispute among the family, some of them excessively circumscribed by a repressive concern—even obsession—with social propriety, over whether a cache of autobiographical poems through which Alison sublimated that love should ever be published. In short, does Alison (and, by extension, any writer for whom the autobiographical impulse is central) belong to the family or to the world? The playwright's *raisonneur,* the outsider and journalist/poet, Richard Knowles, provides the answer—"to the world"—at the outset, so even though the exact content of the poems remains hidden, the dramatist's stance is immediately clear, diluting audience interest. Furthermore, there exists within the Stanhopes a too-neat melodramatic division between the good (who share Knowles's viewpoint and happen all to be of the younger generation) and the others with narrow, self-serving concerns.

The patriarch, Mr. Stanhope, argues that Alison correctly chose duty and Puritan respectability over happiness (what Ibsen calls "the joy of life") by denying her love and abiding by the social code. Stanhope's daughter, Elsa, in a play so overly dependent on parallel plots and foil characters as to be contrived, did what Alison would not; true to her inner feelings, she "betrayed" the family by running off with a married man. Her libertinism particularly galls Stanhope, since he stayed with his wife even though he, too, loved someone else. Alison's spinster sister, Agatha, who devotes her life to insulating the dead poetess's memory from the world, effects the strong curtains of acts 1 and 2. In the first instance, she attempts to set fire to the house; in the second, she does a courageous about-face and, evidently recognizing Elsa's kinship with her dead aunt, gives her the leather portfolio containing the poems of loneliness and love. Elsa senses Alison's living presence in the poems and finds reading them a mystical experience, attesting to the way that a frustrated love—"death for Alison"—can be transformed into art—"life eternal." The family's secretary, Ann Leslie, most persuasively challenges Stanhope's demand that the poems be burned (incredibly, he even threatens to kill his son, Eben, over this). By falling in love with Knowles, who also was almost engaged to someone else, Ann repeats the pattern of Elsa and Alison, but in a manner that allows the play to end happily without violating conventional tastes and mores. The three women are kindred spirits, and the two younger ones make visible a central figure who never appears through even so much as a portrait on the stage. Moreover, Ann becomes like a surrogate daughter to Stanhope, since it was, incredibly, her mother he once loved, thus permitting the play to conclude on a note of reconciliation between "father" and "daughter," old age and youth, as the old century makes way for the new. The bells at the final curtain may signal the passing of a century, but Alison's life will not pass away, for, as a suddenly magnanimous Stanhope says, taking the errant daughter Elsa in his arms, "If she [Alison] can make one more [gift] from her century to yours, then she isn't gone. Anything else is—too lonely."[5]

Compressed into a one-act play, a form that Glaspell excels at in *Suppressed Desires* and *Trifles, Alison's House* would be immeasurably improved. What continues to be most noteworthy about it is the way that so many of the subjects pursued in the Pulitzer plays over the decades here converge: the new woman whose values are a beacon for the future; the artist as quasi-mystical singer for society; and the tempering of harsh paternalism through compassion, often learned from the child. From this point of view and in its tameness and capitulation to commercialism and conventionality, it stands as unexceptional Pulitzer material.

Tad Mosel's *All the Way Home* continues the turn from progress in global terms to progress in particular instances apparent in Zindel's and Glaspell's works, focusing on how the presence in memory of a now-dead family member invigorates and inspires those who come after. Mosel adapted his 1961 play from James Agee's 1956 novel, *A Death in the Family,* making it the second time that a stage version of a previous winner of the fiction Pulitzer carried off the drama award (*South Pacific* was the first). As is true with several of the prize plays of the 1960s and 1970s, the scope of Mosel's dramatization seems geared more to television than to stage, but it faced virtually no competition. Arriving on Broadway at the start of a decade of racial unrest and political upheaval, a work set in the South (Knoxville, 1915) might be expected to exhibit a more sustained social conscience than the mild reflection of antiblack prejudice as a gang of white boys taunt Rufus for having a "nigger name"—but that constitutes Mosel's only bow to contemporaneity.

In adapting Agee's novel, Mosel made three substantive changes. First, instead of beginning his play with the automobile accident in which Jay Follett dies, he tells the events chronologically, which helps ensure rising tension and suspense. Second, he shrewdly makes no attempt to include, through a narrator or some other device, Agee's interpolated poetic passages. Finally, and most important given the new thematic emphasis on the cyclic nature of life and regeneration, he has Jay die while his wife is still pregnant, whereas in the book, Jay leaves both Rufus and a baby daughter; as two of the characters remark, "people go on dyin'" and "being born."[6] If Mary's pregnancy emphasizes the "being born," several things other than Jay's fate express the "dyin'": the Negro spirituals and folk songs that Jay and Mary sing to Rufus; the profession of Jay's brother, Ralph, an undertaker, though so uncomfortable with death that he compensates through drink and flashy cars; and the advanced age (103) of Great-Great Granmaw. Senile and unaware of her older descendants, she responds immediately to the presence of her great-great grandson, Rufus; when he was born, she wrote a postcard to Jay and Mary saying that she had been "borned again," thus underlining Mosel's motif of children as a means of conquering time and gaining immortality. Her grandson (Rufus's grandfather) predicts after their visit that the hand of death is approaching the family; ironically, the relatively young Jay dies returning from a visit to his sick father.

Mosel underscores the fact that Jay's death has an enriching and liberating impact on Mary by her echoing a line of his that encapsulates the play's central perception. Early on, Jay remarks philosophically about the processive nature of life: "We come from people, Mary, and in time they fall away from us. . . . We give birth to others, and in time they *grow* away from us" (p. 67). Near the end, Mary, having learned the lesson well, says virtually the same thing: "People fall away from us, and in time, others grow away from us. That is simply what living is, isn't it?" (p. 165). Mosel symbolizes this intuition through both an inanimate and an animate object: the sound of the train that frames the play at beginning and end embodies continuous movement in a cyclical fashion; and the butterfly that settles on Jay's coffin and then flies "straight up into the sky" (p. 164) holds a multiplicity of meanings. When told about it by his Uncle Andrew, Rufus associates the butterfly's delicacy and dependency with the baby to be born; to most, it might signify Jay's soul or spirit flying free. The skeptical Andrew, whose distaste for orthodox religion is only exacerbated when Father Jackson refuses to officiate at the unbaptized Jay's funeral, sees the episode with the butterfly as a miracle revealing Nature's God. Mosel confirms the persistence of Jay's life and system of values after death through other less tangible means than Rufus and the unborn child. Mary and her devout Aunt Hannah, for instance, suddenly experience an intimation of immortality, becoming sharply aware of the dead Jay's presence in the house and inviting that presence to return and be there often.

Mary's religious beliefs mature through the testing of her faith that Jay's death unleashes. Whereas the guiding principle from her Catholic upbringing was always the necessity to grow away from oneself to God, the more humanistically oriented Jay looked with sadness on the way most people move away from their essential selves with the passage of time and the accommodations and compromises living requires. More staid and introverted than the sensual, pleasure-loving Jay, Mary recalls while awaiting confirmation of his death all his inclinations she tried to curb; she now rejoices in his love of life, hoping that "he looked death itself in the face. In his strength" (p. 161). While Mary never sheds her belief in an other-worldly supernatural, she does, by the play's end, discern the religious dimension within the this-worldly order that Jay and Andrew see all along. An additional visual symbol concretizes Mary's insight. When she hears that Jay is dead, she takes Andrew's portrait of him and stores it away, finding in it nothing of the man he was and refusing in her anguish to have God in place of a flesh and blood husband. But later, certain that Jay's presence will indeed return, Mary places the painting on display, indicating not only her acceptance of his death but her understanding as well of the premise on which the artist depends: that the tangible, physical artifact can somehow convey the inner spiritual reality. In a gentle coda, all the members of the five generations of the Folletts and Lynches, those alive and those dead and those yet to be born, come on stage as Mary tells Rufus about the love that will be the beginning of his own family and a continuation of the lives of his parents, and also his link with the entire human family. If Mosel's play sometimes veers towards sentimentality, it is more often distinguished by the honest sentiment of the ending and frequently touching.

If Wilder, Zindel, Glaspell, and Mosel all look to future progress in various guises, Michael Cristofer sees the source of progress in the fulfillment of one's highest potential in the here-and-now with no assurance of anything to come. One of the characters in his 1977 Pulitzer play, *The Shadow Box*, remarks without the least trace of irony about the "huge market for dying people right now. My agent assured me."[7] Elizabeth Kübler-Ross's influential contribution to the literature of thanatology, *On Death and Dying*, appears to have strongly influenced Cristofer's drama in subject and structure. Seemingly the playwright sets out to accomplish in the dramatic mode what Kübler-Ross does in her clinical report that delineates the five stages in the process of dying: first, denial that this is happening; second, anger and rage at life being cut off, coupled with envy and resentment of those who will live on; third, bargaining for more time; fourth, depression, or the preparatory grief resulting from the final separation from everyone and everything that must be left behind; and, finally, acceptance or detachment—the readiness for death. Much of Kübler-Ross's volume consists of transcribed interviews between doctors, chaplains, and dying patients, and Cristofer employs a similar interview format as his chief structural component, creating a variation on the rotating point of view. During the play (though less frequently in act 2), each of the three patients and one of the five family members/survivors in turn repair to a downstage "interview area" to face questioning either by an unseen miked voice emanating from the rear of the auditorium or by an onstage interviewer, thus bringing the audience up onto the stage as if they were that interviewer. Yet the technique of the Interviewer, along with shifting the audience's attention among the three locations where the action occurs simultaneously, at the same time distances—as a Brechtian device would—by interposing a wall between the audience and the characters, preventing excessive sentimentality. Since the Interviewer is evidently a doctor or a psychiatric counselor, the device creates the impression for the audience of seeing these lives with something approaching scientific objectivity. This generates tension between empathy and detachment, similar to that experienced by those whose vocation demands that they deal with dying, which has been called the "last taboo" in America.

The characters and their lives are not, however, as compelling as the form, having more than a little of the stereotype about them: a disillusioned middle-aged father of a guitar-strumming teenage boy; a crochety old woman given to crude language and tyrannizing over her long-suffering spinster daughter; a homosexual writer formerly married to a boozy and sexually athletic woman. The first of these, Joe, with his house hemmed in by other structures, his unfulfilled dream of escaping the city for a farm in the country, and, most of all, his sense of how little his life adds up to, follows the pattern of Willy Loman too closely. Though "scared" and angry at the prospect of death, he has attained an intellectual understanding of it as part of a universal cyclic pattern, though he has not yet arrived at the point of acceptance, for he cannot tell his son, Steve. Nor can his wife, Midge, accept the approaching end, refusing to enter the cottage where death dwells, since once she is denied her familiar role of wife she fears that nothing will remain to define her existence. Yet both change; he will tell his son, and she will not make Joe die "alone."

If Joe has moved beyond denial, Felicity, for whom senility means a blurring of past and present, is at the bargaining stage; she will not die until her long absent and favorite daughter, Claire, whom she exiled for running off with a boy, returns to be forgiven. But Claire has long been dead, the letters from her actually written by Agnes. In her devotion to a mother she no longer loves, Agnes sacrifices her own life; the emptiness that waits for her is effectively suggested by her singing "Holy God, we praise thy name," in counterpoint with Felicity's risque ditty, "Roll me over in the clover." Although Agnes claims she does not want the process of dying to go on, she continues to give Felicity hope since her only role is that of martyr. Ironically, the letters she regularly composes reveal her own emotional starvation: "When I look out the window, nothing is there. . . . I think it's because I miss you because it hurts not being close to you" (p. 81).

Even in the potentially explosive portions of the play focusing on the male lover, the ex-wife, and the writer, Brian, through whom Cristofer conveys his central idea, the emphasis remains on situation rather than depth of characterization. Mark jealously hangs on to Brian, blaming him for dying and thus denying him the chance to pay back all that he "owe[s] him." Like the survivors in *All Over,* Albee's tauter and less sentimental drama about dying (and death-in-life), most of Cristofer's survivors selfishly think first only of themselves. Brian, aware of death as life's only certainty and knowing "most of us spend our entire lives trying to *forget* that we're going to die" (p. 14), is still terribly afraid of that last fraction of a second: "You're absolutely alone facing an absolute unknown and there is absolutely nothing you can do about it. . .except give in" (p. 38). His response, rather than a *contemptus mundi,* is to write with a prodigious energy and otherwise gluttonously experience everything lest he die having missed something. Whereas once he only intellectualized life, recently he has come to feel it and live it with a childlike—though not childish—and Wilderian sense of wonder: "The universe isn't a syllogism, it's a miracle" (p. 15). The unasked question is whether that revelation will not make it even more difficult to let go.

The play concludes with a lyrical, antiphonal coda in which all of the characters chant their "yes" to life, echoing isolated lines of dialogue from earlier in the play—a shift towards stylization that Cristofer hints at near the end of act 1 when conversations from all three groups of characters interweave. Brian's voice dominates at the end: "But if I *am* dying...I must still be alive," and so he will savor "this moment" (p. 85). If this were Cristofer's only insight, the resolution would be affirmative but the revelation meager—hardly more than what Wilder arrived at thirty years earlier in *Our Town*—and the play would better deserve some critics' accusations of glibness and triteness. Yet, on a deeper level, Cristofer underlines a disturbing paradox about the human condition that involves the limitations of art and the nature of language. As a writer, Brian has a "faith" in words; even though "they don't add up as neatly as they used to," still "eventually they have to mean *some*thing" (p. 14). Language, generally thought of as one of man's most important distinguishing characteristics, fails, however, in the face of something as human as death. So Cristofer, wedding form to meaning, must break free of a realistic use of language in the play's coda and enter the realm of the poetic. What he sees is the awful discrepancy between the revelation and the limited means at man's disposal for conveying it—a chasm that only a supreme work of art can bridge. *The Shadow Box*, whose title indicates both "delineat[ing] a tiny scene and throw[ing] light on it so you can see it more clearly" and also "'shadowboxing'—fighting an unseen enemy,"[8] falls short of that. It might have been more commanding were it less saccharine and better shaped, if the bits and pieces of these people's lives reverberated more consistently off one another and if there had been more instances when the verbal images and icons interfaced poetically as they do in the luminous conclusion.

Whereas *All the Way Home* and *The Shadow Box* reach towards poetry in their codas, Edward Albee's *Seascape*, winner of the 1975 Pulitzer for drama, seems, as Brendan Gill writes, like "some superb long poem" throughout.[9] Almost the entire first act, concerned (as *Delicate Balance* is, too) with the effects of time on human choice and the possibility for change, is a "two-character play," taken up with middle-aged Nancy's and Charlie's diametrically opposed viewpoints on where they go from here. As Charlie languishes on the seashore, he revels in the prospect of painlessly easing out of the picture by withdrawing from all purposive activity. Feeling existential man's *angst*, terrified by "deep space? Mortality?

Nancy... not... being with [him]," and the possibility that even life itself might be just "an illusion," he yearns for "death [as a] release" since he has "lived all right."[10] Given Charlie's desire to spend his waning years wasting away, Nancy chides him, "all *you* want to do is become a vegetable. ...a lump" (p. 42). Lying just beyond the sand dunes in the stage set is the sea, archetype at one and the same time of both life and death; once symbolic of Charlie's life-wish, it now encapsulates his willed movement towards inertia and death. It is a place as well where one can, Charlie thinks, retreat into a premoral condition, free from the terror that is an inescapable part of life which Albee concretizes through a recurrent sound effect: four times "a jet plane is heard from stage right to stage left—growing, becoming deafeningly loud, diminishing" (pp. 3, 14, 53, 130).

Nancy insists that they not spend what time they have left in a retreat from life, embracing an inactivity that would be tantamount to condemning themselves to a "purgatory *before* purgatory," demanding instead, "we will do something" (pp. 10–11). She believes that man must create his own happiness by making a Kierkegaardian leap of faith and finding some positive value. Whereas Charlie, afraid of change, desires stasis, Nancy accepts flux as the necessary precondition for growth and progress. She has barely completed her admonition that they act when the opportunity to respond to "something new" startlingly presents itself with the appearance of "two great green lizards" (p. 120), which confirms the distinctive parable-like tone of the play. Leslie and Sarah "Lizard" exist at some prehuman stage on the evolutionary ladder. Instead of functioning as mirror images of what Charlie and Nancy now are, they serve as reminders of the older couple's origin for, as Charlie remarks, "there was a time when we *all* were down there" (p. 138). If life in the sea is unterrifying because a known quantity, it is also restrictive; as Sarah points out, they outgrew it and "didn't feel [they] *belonged* there any more" (p. 136). They experienced, as Nancy would put it, the dissatisfaction that can be redirected in either a positive or negative way but which is essential for there to be progress. Leslie and Sarah's predicament—attracted by the temptation of passively settling in and thus settling for less than a full life—parallels Charlie's.

Significantly, Charlie, himself afraid, convinces Leslie and Sarah to remain up on earth rather than return to their familiar habitat. In the moment of convincing them, he experiences a regenerative epiphany, moving from his customary stance of "put off" and "make do" to beginning again. Recognizing that what separates man from lower forms of existence is his "aware[ness that he is] *alive,* [and] that [he is] going to die" (p. 149), Charlie realizes that in order to help Leslie and Sarah complete their physical and psychological transformation, he must make them experience truly human emotions. Playing on Sarah's fear that Leslie will leave her and not return, he deliberately makes Sarah cry which, in turn, causes Leslie to become so defensive and angry that he hits Charlie and chokes him. Having tasted these dark human emotions of sorrow and wrath, Sarah and Leslie want more than ever to go back to the prehuman security of the sea. What quenches their fear is Nancy's and Charlie's pleading with them not to retreat and extending their hands in a human gesture of compassion and communion—clearly a visual echo of the dramatic gesture that concludes *Who's Afraid of Virginia Woolf?*, voted the 1963 drama Pulitzer by the jury but denied it by the advisory board. In helping Leslie and Sarah take the mythic journey from the womb into the world that, however traumatic, must at some time be taken, Charlie simultaneously leaves behind his earlier attempts to escape from life and asserts once again his will to act. Since Albee presents Charlie not only as an individual but also as a representative, middle-aged Everyman fallen prey to ennui and despair, Leslie's "Begin" on which the curtain falls signifies an act of faith and hope uttered for himself and Sarah and Charlie and Nancy, as well as for all humankind who, with the passage of time, must be periodically rescued from the temptation of being "half in love with easeful death" and inspired to re-embark on its arduous journey despite the inherent dangers.

The two parable-like plays that frame this chapter, Wilder's *Skin of Our Teeth* and Albee's *Seascape*, approach progress from a global or universal perspective. Reportedly, it was Wilder who first suggested that Albee take up playwriting, and *Seascape*, Albee's most optimistic drama so far, might be seen as homage to Wilder, since it contains verbal, tonal, and philosophical echoes of the older dramatist's works. Nancy's words about being given the time to "try something new" could be considered Albee's confirmation of the belief in progress through trial and error that Wilder espouses through the Antrobus family, as well as Albee's challenge to mankind to change and expand if they are to advance. Zindel's *Effects of Gamma Rays on Man-in-the-Moon Marigolds*, Glaspell's *Alison's House*, Mosel's *All the Way Home*, and Cristofer's *Shadow Box* all narrow their perspective to focus on the individual's experience as a link with the progress of the human community. It is perhaps not surprising that three of these plays (those by Cristofer, Mosel, and Glaspell) focus on death and dying, which would seem to call into question and even threaten modern man's hope for physical and spiritual progress. In his treatise *Eternal Life? Life After Death as a Medical, Philosophical, and Theological Problem*, the German theologian Hans Küng draws a connection between man's declining faith in "the god Progress"—his "belief in a continually better life with the aid of science and technology"—and the search by the young to discover "the missing sense of life" and among the old "to come to terms with the meaning of death."[11] Whereas the adolescent Tillie in

Marigolds achieves a feeling, however slight, of some form of godlike immortality through her link with matter which, once created, can never be destroyed, the dying characters in *Shadow Box* ask what, beyond acceptance of their condition, can be affirmed, answering simply living fully and living well. In *Alison's House*, the positive value in the face of death comes through art (poetry) and in *All the Way Home* through offspring—both ways of attaining immortality. All these works inquire into what basis exists for affirmation, what possibilities for human achievement and perfectibility remain in the face of nihilism and the very human fact of man's finitude.

The most substantial challenge these playwrights face comes in trying to effect some reconciliation between death and the ideal of progress, especially this-worldly progress. If *Man-in-the-Moon Marigolds,* with its focus on progress, and *Shadow Box,* with its focus on death, each brings its audience up onto the stage so to speak (the first as spectators at the high school science fair; the second as the interviewers), *Skin of Our Teeth* takes the play, instead, out into the audience, both literally by extending the action to planted actors and props in the auditorium and metaphorically by encouraging the theatergoers to help write "the end[ing] of this play" (p. 137) through the way they live. The abrupt, almost cinematic "blackout and silence" that precedes the starting again of this play that "must go on for ages and ages yet"—and that is analogous to the Stage Manager's drawing the black curtain across the acting space at the end of *Our Town*—reiterates that mankind's movement forward (and upward) is only wrenchingly achieved. Rather than processive from birth through life to death, as it is for the individual, progress for man as social being and historical force is cyclical, a matter of uncertain starts, continual misfires, and constant beginnings over again with each circle of the spiral coiled tightly next to the one just below it. In the face of such evidence, collective mankind must see beyond the constant tension between hope and despair as it moves forward towards some promised end, just as individual man must see through—and perhaps beyond—death by wholeheartedly embracing his life and his art.

From Modernism to Metatheatre— Art and Artists in Modern American Drama

From the earliest Pulitzer dramas to the most recent, a repeated motif in these works—whether primarily about women or romantic delusions or the ethic of happiness, about war or politics, about the American Dream or religion or the idea of progress— is a concern with the nature of art and the role of the artist. Surprisingly, this holds true even about several plays that succeed mainly as popular entertainment, such as *Harvey* or *The Teahouse of the August Moon*. It is not simply that many of these works employ a nonrealistic form or use illusion-destroying devices to remind the audience of being in a theatre watching a play as, for example, *Our Town* or *Talley's Folly* do. Beyond this, they make the theatre itself or the act of going to the theatre part of their subject and demand that the audience consciously think of themselves *as* an audience, thereby establishing a link between these works for the stage and other forms of Modernist art. This ultimately pushes the theatre into the realm of metatheatre, with metatheatrical elements evident where one would hardly expect to encounter them, in such otherwise realistic, even naturalistic, plays as *The Subject Was Roses*.

In his lectures on *"Modernism" in Modern Drama*, Krutch examines Modernism almost exclusively from an ideological point of view, applying the tag to those works from Ibsen on in which he discerns an awareness of the "irrational element" that reflects the disorder of a mechanical, "meaningless universe where all is relative"[1]—a perspective that sees Modernism feeding eventually into Absurdism; among the Pulitzer dramas,

The Shrike with its world as asylum and *J. B.* with its postapocalyptic universe, on that basis would be, for example, Modernist in their sensibilities. Pirandello, the high-priest of Modernism in drama (as are James Joyce in fiction, Ezra Pound in poetry, Pablo Picasso in painting, Igor Stravinsky in music, and Albert Einstein in science) uses his plays to explore the relativity of truth, the falseness of reality and the "realness" of illusion, the mutability and becomingness of existence, and the fragmentation of man and the "dissolution of the ego." Yet Pirandello's seminal contribution to dramatic Modernism was not only epistemological but, more importantly, technical and stylistic as well. As Maurice Beebe indicates, the movement evidences a "pre-occupation with form: in its studied self-consciousness and reflexivism, it displays a concern with its own creation and composition."[2] Malcolm Bradbury and James McFarlane hypothesize that this obsession with "the problem in the making of structures" can be traced, at least in part, to the writers' awareness of "the irrationality of a mechanistic universe." In an effort, then, "to redeem...the formless universe of contingency,"[3] the playwright, in McFarlane and John Fletcher's words, makes "the world within the theatre walls...the only genuine world."[4] Because of this emphasis on form, on the medium of expression, Modernist drama is, of its very nature, metatheatrical as it was for Pirandello, whose most influential works become aesthetic inquiries into the nature of the theatre. It is this aspect of Modernism that Krutch's definition does not adequately encompass.

In *J. B.*, for instance, not only do the moral "lights" in the world seem to have gone out in a postbomb era, but that world is a theatre and that theatre is the world (a *theatrum mundi*); in short, "the stage [is] a world in itself" (p. 511). And in *The Shrike*, while the world seems overrun by a Kafkaesque insanity, the asylum is also a theatre in which the inmates are watched just as the audience watch the characters—and as the audience themselves as actor/characters in the larger world outside the theatre's walls can be sure that they, too, are being watched. What distinguishes most of these American dramas reflecting the Modernist impulse from other expressions of Modernism in fiction, poetry, and the other visual arts, however, is that even though the playwrights' handling of form often "elevates aesthetics to a primary position," their philosophic stance tends to remain traditional and teleological, and thus comforting and reassuring to the audience. What they present on the stage continues to be an imitation (*mimesis*) of reality, of a "sense-accessible world" ordered so that "time [is] linear, space fixed, cause/effect operable."[5]

Of the fifty-seven plays that have won the Pulitzer Prize for drama in the almost seventy-year history of the award, no fewer than two dozen address in dramatic terms what might broadly be called aesthetic issues: the nature of the theatrical experience, the relationship between the play-within-the-play and the audience's perception of itself as audience, the nature and function(s) of art, the vocation and role of the artist. A few of these works, such as *Men in White* with its operating room/theatre and *'night, Mother* with its bedroom/inner stage, make audiences conscious of stage space. Several others comment implicitly on the theatrical experience as illusory, creating in the process an awareness either of the separation between the theatre and the world or of the way in which the theatre is the world or vice versa. *South Pacific, Teahouse of the August Moon,* and *Talley's Folly* all establish locations that function as onstage stages, "green worlds" (Bali Hai, the teahouse, Uncle Everett's boathouse) where characters can escape from the deficiencies of the real world, whether racial prejudice or excessively materialistic goals, just as an audience can seek temporary forgetfulness within the walls of a theatre. Yet in none of these three is the audience permitted to forget for long that a world exists outside and that they must resume their place in it once the theatrical diversion ends. In *Harvey,* the "green world" is unexpectedly the sanatorium where—in a commonplace in drama—man's foolishness proves wise and man's illusions are nurtured as a lifesaving grace, thus making it analogous to the healing aspect of the theatre. The sanatorium in *The Shrike,* though also presented as a theatre where the patients role-play for the benefit of the psychiatrists, is hardly a "green world" of pleasant escapism; instead, it possesses a nightmarish, almost surrealistic quality that, rather than contrast with, actually replicates and exaggerates the dark, alien world outside the theatre where people prey on one another and assume a myriad of at times contradictory roles. Role-playing itself becomes thematic in two Pulitzer plays; in *Idiot's Delight,* the ability to shift easily in and out of a mask comprises a method of survival in a hostile world, while in *J. B.* to be human means to be permanently cast in the role of sufferer from which there is no release.

In a number of works that observe the conventions of stage realism as well as in a larger group that violate them, the Pulitzer dramatists cast their audiences in the role of audience. This involves more than simply recognizing the presence of an audience, as happens in *The Skin of Our Teeth, The Great White Hope, No Place to Be Somebody,* and *A Soldier's Play* when the viewers become the object of Brechtian distanciation and/or preachment, though it may at times mean little more than breaking the convention of the fourth wall by playing directly to the audience, as John and Timmy do during their vaudeville routine in *Subject Was Roses.* In five of the prize-winning works, however, a visible or implied onstage audience expands to include, by implication, the theatergoers in the auditorium: in *Green Pastures,* they become part of the Sunday school class gathered at Mr. Deshee's feet; in *Idiot's Delight,* they form part of the cabaret audience for Harry Van and his bevy of chorus girls; in *South Pacific,* they become one with the American troops watching the musicale;

in *The Effect of Gamma Rays on Man-in-the-Moon Marigolds,* they are among those present at the high school science competition; and in *The Shadow Box,* they become associated with the unseen Interviewer probing the feelings of the dying patients. Two plays go a step farther than this: in *How to Succeed in Business Without Really Trying,* the audience see in Ponty's expression as he gazes out through the frame of a mirror that holds no glass a reflection of themselves, still pursuing the widespread 'dream of success—that will finally receive a death-dealing blow in *A Chorus Line* a decade and a half later. For in that metatheatrical musical, not only do the audience associate themselves with the director who literally joins them out in the orchestra for much of the show, but they actually see themselves as watchers in the onstage mirrors, so that their own lack of specialness as anonymous rows of common people becomes visible at the very same instant that they recognize just how far removed each of the dancers in the line onstage is from being that "one, singular sensation."

It is, of course, natural for writers to ponder their role as artists and to question the function of art, both in the abstract and vis-à-vis their audiences, and in this the authors of the Pulitzer plays are no different. Surprisingly little consideration, however, is devoted to the specifically social uses of art in these dramas, although *No Place to Be Somebody* does hint at writing as sublimation for revolutionary violence. What theorizing does arise through the characters tends to be more philosophical. Three of the works propose art as a means of transcendence: in *Alison's House,* poetry, while serving as a sublimation for repressed sexual passion, provides a means of escaping time and achieving immortality; in *The Diary of Anne Frank,* writing functions not just as a way of leaving something permanent behind after death but, more importantly, as a means of understanding suffering and coping with the dark impulses in man's nature; in *Our Town,* the poet's vision becomes, like the saint's, a perspective freed from the narrow confines of secular time, able to see the sacred in the profane, the smallest aspect of everyday life as charged with wonder. Both *Look Homeward, Angel* and *All the Way Home,* though admitting the difficulty of reaching a transcendent vision in art, at least allow for that possibility: the stone angel in the first is more than just a shadow of the ideal form, while the portrait in the second becomes an outward sign of an inner spiritual presence. Only *Shadow Box* seems to capitulate to the improbability of ever making the word become flesh, at the same time that it proposes a desperate volubility as the only—albeit ultimately futile— defense against mortality; Brian tries to make up in words for what he is losing in time.

Among the Pulitzer dramas are a number of portraits of the artist, including the Stage Manager in *Our Town,* who conveys an image of the artist as godlike in his omniscient and benign detachment; the poetess in *Alison's House*, who becomes a sacred singer for mankind; the young artist-of-fact in *Anne Frank;* and the incipient writers in *Picnic, Angel,* and *Subject Was Roses,* who all need to break free from their families to enter fully upon their vocation; Robert in *Beyond the Horizon,* for whom art is a source of mystic communion with nature; and Blanche in *Streetcar Named Desire,* whose "magic" protests against succumbing to a demeaning vision of mankind, just as Harry Van's "artistry" in *Idiot's Delight* serves as a jeremiad to a civilization on the brink of catastrophe. But the fullest of these portraits of the artist are to be found in O'Neill's *Strange Interlude* and, especially, his *Long Day's Journey Into Night,* as well as in Sondheim and James Lapine's *Sunday in the Park with George.* When Charlie Marsden in *Interlude* turns to "the book of us" as the source for the story he will write (indeed, the entire play might be seen as that book, in much the same way that *Remembrance of Things Past* is itself the novel that Marcel is ready to begin writing at the end of Proust's work), he does what O'Neill himself will do in writing his autobiographical *Journey.* Just as Charlie, by telling the story, finally realizes his full potential as an artist and thereby enables Nina Leeds to bring her life to completion and rest in peace, O'Neill, by dramatizing the story of "all the four haunted Tyrones,"[6] can at last exonerate himself and reach a measure of reconciliation with his dead, who always inspired his work.

Clurman writes that *Long Day's Journey Into Night,* which posthumously won Eugene O'Neill his fourth Pulitzer in 1957, examines "loss of faith"[7]—in religion, in family, in art. This loss arises essentially from a failure to be true to, or to doubt, one's calling or vocation. To the degree that the cliché "living is an art" conveys any truth, then all the Tyrones (like all humankind) are artists shaping a life, creating an essence that is an artifact in the theatre of the world. In a more specialized sense, however, at least three of *Journey's* four main characters are, or were, artists or potential artists; the fourth (Jamie) lacks—and this causes the peculiar malaise and vindictiveness of his life—any positive calling or vocation at all. Yet, although *Journey* concerns itself very centrally with the nature of art, with the creative act, and with the role of the artist—and affords, together with *Sunday in the Park,* the most mature reflection on all these motifs in American drama—it can only be considered Modernist in philosophy if Krutch's terms are applied very loosely to this play of loss and waste and regret. And it is not at all metatheatrical in its techniques: the audience do not think of themselves as an audience even when, at the end of act 2, Mary soliloquizes for their benefit; nor do they think of themselves as absolving priests or therapists, even admitting that the pattern of the play, particularly of act 4, is a series of confessions that are virtual monologues—a structural device Jamie calls attention to when he claims to have "gone to confession" to Edmund. *Journey* remains quintessentially a realistic, albeit symbolically realistic, drama (when critics refer to it as the "best play" of the American theatre, they frequently add the proviso "in the realistic tradition"); and O'Neill's embracing of the techniques of realism, after long years of experimentation with such modes as expressionism, masked drama, and interior monologues, reflects his ideological and aesthetic posture: there exists an experiential reality outside of the self that can be grasped, that can be known, that must be lived in. The reality, nevertheless, is not all: there exists a suprareality that can be momentarily plumbed and revealed by the visionary artist who is granted the power to see—the highest calling.

The cynical nonartist, Jamie, a hack actor haunting Broadway backstages, living in the shadow of his illustrious matinee-idol father, is, like all the members of this "haunted" family, filled with resentments: against his father for his miserliness and for forcing him into a profession he did not choose and in which he is not equipped to succeed; against his mother for her drug addiction and her favoritism towards her younger son; against Edmund for being the favored and, on top of that, for precipitating the mother's dependency on morphine through his birth. In Jamie's relationship with Edmund, the complex pattern of love/hate feelings that simultaneously binds this family together yet tears them asunder best reveals itself; these people use each other as scapegoats, blaming one another rather than taking responsibility for their actions. Jamie admits, finally, to having deliberately attempted to ruin Edmund's life out of spite by creating a monster in his own flawed image: "I'll do my damnedest to make you fail. Can't help it. I hate myself. Got to take revenge" (p. 166). Yet he "run[s] the risk" of rejection by confessing the truth to Edmund as a proof that he loves his brother more than he hates him. Jamie at least lives without illusions, accurately assessing himself. If their incessant recitations of apt lines from Shakespeare and the pre-Raphaelites and Aesthetes frequently reveal the men in this acting family as poseurs, there is nothing phony—however maudlin—in Jamie's rendition of Dante Gabriel Rossetti's "'Look in my face. My name is Might-Have-Been; / I am also called No More, Too Late, Farewell'" (p. 168).

"Too late" becomes, in fact, a *leitmotif* in *Journey*, especially as regards the parents, and it helps define the tragedy of waste and regret that seems endemic to modern American drama. Life becomes a matter of arrivals at self-knowledge that are doubly painful because they are achieved only after any chance that they could be acted upon in a beneficial manner is long past. In a pattern that Albee echoes in *Who's Afraid of Virginia Woolf?* and *Delicate Balance* and that goes back in O'Neill as far as *"Anna Christie,"* choices made long ago combine with the passage of time to limit man's present options; as Mary Tyrone regrets: "None of us can help the things that life has done to us. They're done before you realize it, and once they're done they make you do other things until at last everything comes between you and what you'd like to be, and you've lost your true self forever" (p. 61). James understands too late not simply his stinginess in material things with those he loves, or even the source in his own youth for his excessive penuriousness and fear of the poorhouse now, but that he sold out as an artist for the promise of money; he might have become an actor of the magnitude of Edwin Booth, yet he settled instead for being a matinee-idol in melodrama: "What the hell was it I wanted to buy," he muses, "that was worth—Well, no matter. It's a late day for regrets" (p. 150).

Mary, too, was untrue to her vocation, allowing what O'Neill in *Strange Interlude* terms the "curse of the romantic imagination'—in this case, marriage to a dashing actor—to deflect her from her dual vocation as pianist and nun. As a visual symbol of the way past choices influence present realities and of the fact that "the past is the present. . . . It's the future, too" (p. 87), in the play's ineffably sad closing scene, Mary enters, drugged and trailing behind her her wedding dress (analogous to the laudatory notice predicting a brilliant career as a classical actor that James has kept all these years) to recall that she "fell in love with James Tyrone and was so happy for a time" (p. 176). The split between innocent convent girl of the past—who would have worn a wedding dress as the bride of Christ had she taken her vows—and edgy drug addict of the present appears constantly in her face; she can only recapture the composure of the past through drugs that blot out the present, but to do that results in a loss of faith in self. In her self-recognition, which occurs earlier than that of the men, Mary admits to being a "lying dope fiend," totally dependent upon the Blessed Virgin as the only hope for reclaiming faith in herself and gaining back her soul. Like the encroaching fog, drugs blot out the reality, but not totally, for the foghorn, which Mary hates, is always there to beckon her back.

Significantly, Mary keeps referring to her lost glasses; she cannot see under the influence of drugs, or, happily, only sees what she wants to. She welcomes the ever-increasing fog that blinds. But just as self-knowledge comes to the three men in the darkest night, so, too, O'Neill suggests that in life—itself normally like a foggy night—the artist can discern the light. Edmund, experiencing a lack of confidence in himself as an artist and a death wish only vaguely suggested by his consumption, yearns to be lost in the fog and the sea, the mother of all: "As if I was a ghost belonging to the fog, and the fog was the ghost of the sea. It felt damned peaceful to be nothing more than a ghost within a ghost" (p. 131). If the sea, however, archetypally is death, it is also life, and even more than that, the source of the mystic vision. In a passage of reverie, Edmund tells James about being on board a ship and reaching a sense of union with the cosmos: "I belonged. . .within something greater than my own life, or the life of Man, to Life itself! To God, if you want to put it that way" (p. 153). At other moments when he was near the sea, the veil would suddenly lift, and he would see, in the words of Saint Paul, face to face instead of through a glass darkly: "Like a saint's vision of beatitude. Like the veil of things as they seem drawn back by an unseen hand. . . . For a second, there is meaning! Then the hand lets the veil fall and you are alone, lost in the fog again" (p. 153). Life without art is, then, like a fog in which man perceives only the surface rather than the essence beneath. With art, and through the artist, truth can be illuminated; the suprareality under the surface appearance can be clarified and grasped. Edmund doubts his ability to do more than "stammer" out a "faithful realism" as one of God's fog-bound creatures; the artist's material, because visionary, is intractable. For the artist the problem remains always how to make the word flesh. In a formulation reminiscent of O'Neill's, William Carlos Williams speaks about the difficulty of achieving the poetic, which he calls the only "fit medium": "In our family we stammer unless, / half mad, / we come to speech at last."[8] In O'Neill's dark-night-of-the-soul play, although three souls without the poet's visionary gift are found sadly wanting, "all four haunted Tyrones" still manage "to come to speech at last."

In their 1985 prize-winning musical, *Sunday in the Park with George*, lyricist/composer Stephen Sondheim and librettist/director James Lapine also express the notion of the artist as seer, though even more obviously than *Journey* theirs is a work about the nature of the creative process itself. And as Frank Rich, calling Sondheim "as adventurous and as accomplished an author, playwrights included, as Broadway has produced over the last two decades," rightly claims, "'Sunday' is itself a modernist creation, perhaps the first truly modernist work of musical theater that Broadway has produced."[9] Sondheim and Lapine turn to an imaginative recreation of the creative processes of a real artist, George Seurat, painting his masterwork, *A Sunday Afternoon on the Island of La Grande Jatte*, as the basis for their reflection upon how personal and aesthetic problems merge for the creative genius. The image of what Peter Brook calls "the empty space" is an extremely potent one in the modern theatre; it is the stage space that must be peopled through the artist's imaginative faculty as he or she makes what wells up from his or her mind and heart visible to an audience. *Sunday in the Park* begins—and ends too—with "a white stage," here the painter's "blank page or canvas" waiting to be filled. "The challenge," says George, is to "bring order to the whole / Through design / Composition / Tension / Balance / Light / And harmony."[10] In the brilliant *coup de théâtre* that concludes act 1, the audience literally see, through a magical combination of real characters and painted cutouts, Seurat's most famous painting created and frozen on the canvas that is the stage. But if art is permanent, it is not life, which is never so ordered, composed, and harmonious. The characters in the painting understand that the gain in conquering time involves a diminishment in lived life—that to remain forever "frozen" is the price they pay for their apotheosis in art. Even Dot, George's mistress and the mother of his child he will not even glance at, so absorbed is he in his work, feels used by the artist who is "so cold," "so controlled," sufficient unto himself, and so she moves on to someone else. Her very name, of course, indicates that she will be "studied," objectified and distilled into the dots of "color and light" that Seurat put on his canvases—so that the viewers' eyes would fuse and harmonize them—in a technique that came to be known as Pointillism; similarly, the musical notes and lyrics, often of one syllable, are the "dots" through which Sondheim composes *Sunday:* "blue / Purple yellow red water"; "green / Orange violet mass / Of the grass." Just as the museumgoers find Seurat and his paintings without "passion" and conclude that he lacks "life in his art" or even "in his life," critics of the American musical theatre oftentimes judge Sondheim as too emotionally detached, as a songwriter who, like the Seurat he creates, is "all mind / No heart," so his and Lapine's fictionalized artist may be partly self-portrait and self-explanation. Paradoxically, then, one of Sondheim's most deliberate and reserved scores might also be one of his most personal, an analogue for the way that the artist sometimes must bring his feelings under strict control so that others might feel.

Understanding character, like understanding painting (or any work of art) is all a matter of the perspective from which one looks. When Dot accuses George of "hid[ing] behind painting because [he] care[s] about nothing," he responds, "I am not hiding behind my canvas—I am living in it"—apparently finding it necessary to deny himself a full emotional life outside of it. Seurat, and by implication any artist, must simultaneously be both connected and detached; there must always be a part of him standing aside and looking, for his "mission [is] to see"—and to see well always to some degree requires treating objects as people and people as objects, animating the first and de-animating the second. *Seeing* forms the necessary prelude to creation, to making, if not from nothing as the archetypal creator/artist did, then from "flecks of light": "Look I made a hat / Where there never was a hat," Seurat sings with wonder and fulfillment.

The second (and less innovative) act of *Sunday* jumps forward a century, from 1884 to 1984, when another young artist named George— presumably the great-grandson of Seurat and Dot—demonstrates his Chromolume, a huge domed machine from which emanates a spectacular sound and laser-light display (Seurat himself always preferred to be called a chromo-luminarist). Here the chic world of art and high culture is deservedly satirized. The artist is now lionized and fawned over, himself turned into an object who is as much on exhibition as are his creations; it is a world of celebrities and promoters and hype, and to sell himself, to survive, the artist must often compromise his integrity. Feeling that his gift has faded, George returns to Paris, where high-rise buildings obscure the park of his ancestor. In his artistic dark-night-of-the-soul, he feels "alone," "afraid," "adrift," "aground," doubting whether he will leave behind any work of value since he has stopped "stretching his vision in every direction." He reads "Lesson #8" of Dot's grammar book, left him by his grandmother Marie, where he finds still visible on the endpapers the loving notes Dot wrote about Seurat. Because Seurat once taught Dot how to concentrate on reality and "see," she will now, in turn, act as George's muse. All that is necessary is that he, as artist, keep seeing so that he can help others to see. She encourages him, "Stop worrying where you're going— / Move on. / If you can know where you're going, / You've gone. / Just keep moving on." Even if the choice of what to create next proves wrong, the act of choosing is itself a good, for life itself means moving on, and so the artist as seer must "look forever." The newness of what he has to say is neither important nor unimportant; the obsession with newness as an end-in-itself in art is, indeed, just a fad. All that matters is that he create "harmony" out of chaos, that he impose a meaning upon existence by taking the infinite number of "possibilities," the dots, and arranging them in an ordered pattern of "color and light" on the once "blank white canvas"—just as Sondheim and Lapine create a play text by composing dots of sound and sense to fill the empty space of the stage; just as the audience existentially write the text of their own lives by choosing and moving on.

Although both *Long Day's Journey Into Night* and *Sunday in the Park* define the artist's vocation in terms of "seeing," Sondheim and Lapine's vision of the artist is, finally, very different. O'Neill's artist figure penetrates through the surface to reveal the reality, or better, suprareality, already there beneath it and to help the audience share in the illumination by seeing it, too. Sondheim and Lapine's artist figure, on the other hand, uses experiences impressionistically received in order to construct a new reality not there before; in this way, he is much more actively the creator, guiding the audience to perceive phenomena from a new angle of vision, but one which potentially changes with each viewer. It is the difference, in short, between the Romantic conception of art and the Modernist.

O'Neill's Romantic image of the poet's vision as parting the veil of fog to reveal what lies beneath—analogous to the Biblical concept of seeing things face to face rather than as reflections in a mirror—has several antecedents in traditional Western thought, among them the writings of Plato, Friedrich Nietzsche, Emerson, and Percy Bysshe Shelley. In his "Defense of Poetry," for example, Shelley speaks of the poet as one who "participates in the eternal, the infinite, and the one" and of poetry as "something divine" that "strips the veil of familiarity from the world and lays bare the naked and sleeping beauty which is the spirit of its forms."[11]

Sondheim encapsulates his image of the artist in the first act song, "Beautiful," sung by Seurat and his mother. His mother seems bewildered by change, by time passing, and by "towers" (specifically, the Eiffel Tower) "Where there were trees." Whereas she can discover beauty only in the natural, Seurat can see it in the manmade as well: "What the eye arranges / Is what is beautiful." The artist not only "holds the mirror up to nature" by reproducing reality, but "revise[s] the world," constructing a new reality of his own. Along with stopping time by bringing permanence where once there was change, the Modernist artist, rather than just shadow forth preexisting forms, revealing their beauty, actually devises new forms that are beautiful in themselves. The Modernist artist, as maker of a new reality that did not exist before, sees that it is good, precisely because, though it harmonizes, it refuses to deny "tension" and remains open-ended: "White. A blank page or canvas. . . . So many possibilities."

Along with the influence of the philosophers and poets, the Pulitzer plays, as has been hinted, oftentimes reflect the stamp of the masters of modern drama in their techniques and concerns, of Ibsen and August Strindberg, of Chekhov and Shaw, of Bertolt Brecht and Pirandello. Nor are many of these works, despite the tendency of critics to consider American drama an ugly stepchild rather than a legitimate heir, divorced from the wider tradition in American literature; there is much, for instance, of Nathaniel Hawthorne and even some of Herman Melville and Edgar Allen Poe and William Faulkner in Tennessee Williams, much that mirrors Emerson in O'Neill, Wilder, and Albee, and more than a little of Walt Whitman in Saroyan and Miller. But that would be another and larger story. What the story told here demonstrates is the rather unexpected emphasis, even in plays of a mainly popular appeal, on aesthetic issues, dramatized through a variety of self-conscious and self-reflexive means.

Recently, J. L. Styan issued a challenge for developing a practical theory that would undertake the "especially difficult. . .task" of "demonstrat[ing] how metadrama works in practice."[12] If the two dozen Pulitzer dramas that focus, in passing or in full, on art and the artist might constitute the raw data for such a theory, they also reveal an American drama that, because conscious of its form, is perhaps much more akin to experimental fiction than has previously been admitted. What is more, because their forms are less closed, these plays require an audience to collaborate actively in the creating of their fictions. The spectators complete, if they do not construct, these fictions, and in that—rather than in in complexity of ideas or systems of thought—resides what has always made American theatre engaging and exciting.

Writing about Tennessee Williams's *Out Cry*, one of the most obviously and obsessively metatheatrical of recent American dramas, C. W. E. Bigsby delineates an aesthetic of the viewer applicable to many of the

Pulitzer plays: "The audience is... invited to collaborate in the process of invention, and therefore, of course, to theatricalize itself. ...The curtain, the interface of fiction and reality, becomes itself a fiction. The two worlds can no longer be kept apart."[13] When, in addition, the audience is made aware of themselves as observers, then the theatrical space extends beyond the stage and across the footlights, so that the auditorium itself is transformed into a stage, with the theatergoers becoming the locus for a new action. In *Notes and Counter Notes,* Ionesco proposes that "to renew one's idiom or one's language is to renew one's conception or one's vision of the world. ...Any new artistic expression enriches us by answering some spiritual need and broadens the frontiers of known reality."[14] The nonverbal idioms of many of the Pulitzer dramas—the language of mirroring props and the language of the stage space—encourage the audience to reflect upon themselves as an audience. To confront the self within the theatre from this new perspective is to engage, after the entertainment ends, in an epistemological inquiry about the fragmentation into surface and reality, about the dissociation between observer and observed, and about the aesthetic experience as a potential means of coming to know and define (and possibly even re-create) the self.

Appendix

A CHRONOLOGICAL LIST OF THE PULITZER PLAYS

1917	No prize
1918	*Why Marry?* by Jesse Lynch Williams
1919	No prize
1920	*Beyond the Horizon* by Eugene O'Neill
1921	*Miss Lulu Bett* by Zona Gale
1922	*"Anna Christie"* by Eugene O'Neill
1923	*Icebound* by Owen Davis
1924	*Hell-Bent fer Heaven* by Hatcher Hughes
1925	*They Knew What They Wanted* by Sidney Howard
1926	*Craig's Wife* by George Kelly
1927	*In Abraham's Bosom* by Paul Green
1928	*Strange Interlude* by Eugene O'Neill
1929	*Street Scene* by Elmer Rice
1930	*The Green Pastures* by Marc Connelly
1931	*Alison's House* by Susan Glaspell
1932	*Of Thee I Sing* by George S. Kaufman, Morrie Ryskind, and Ira Gershwin
1933	*Both Your Houses* by Maxwell Anderson
1934	*Men in White* by Sidney Kingsley
1935	*The Old Maid* by Zöe Akins
1936	*Idiot's Delight* by Robert E. Sherwood
1937	*You Can't Take It With You* by Moss Hart and George S. Kaufman
1938	*Our Town* by Thornton Wilder
1939	*Abe Lincoln in Illinois* by Robert E. Sherwood
1940	*The Time of Your Life* by William Saroyan
1941	*There Shall Be No Night* by Robert E. Sherwood
1942	No prize
1943	*The Skin of Our Teeth* by Thornton Wilder
1944	No prize
1945	*Harvey* by Mary Chase
1946	*State of the Union* by Howard Lindsay and Russel Crouse
1947	No prize

Appendix

1948	*A Streetcar Named Desire* by Tennessee Williams
1949	*Death of a Salesman* by Arthur Miller
1950	*South Pacific* by Richard Rodgers, Oscar Hammerstein II, and Joshua Logan
1951	No prize
1952	*The Shrike* by Joseph Kramm
1953	*Picnic* by William Inge
1954	*The Teahouse of the August Moon* by John Patrick
1955	*Cat on a Hot Tin Roof* by Tennessee Williams
1956	*The Diary of Anne Frank* by Frances Goodrich and Albert Hackett
1957	*Long Day's Journey Into Night* by Eugene O'Neill
1958	*Look Homeward, Angel* by Kitti Frings
1959	*J. B.* by Archibald MacLeish
1960	*Fiorello!* by Jerome Weidman, George Abbott, and Sheldon Harnick
1961	*All the Way Home* by Tad Mosel
1962	*How to Succeed in Business Without Really Trying* by Abe Burrows, Jack Weinstock, Willie Gilbert, and Frank Loesser
1963	No prize
1964	No prize
1965	*The Subject Was Roses* by Frank Gilroy
1966	No prize
1967	*A Delicate Balance* by Edward Albee
1968	No prize
1969	*The Great White Hope* by Howard Sackler
1970	*No Place to Be Somebody* by Charles Gordone
1971	*The Effect of Gamma Rays on Man-in-the-Moon Marigolds* by Paul Zindel
1972	No prize
1973	*That Championship Season* by Jason Miller
1974	No prize
1975	*Seascape* by Edward Albee
1976	*A Chorus Line* by Michael Bennett, James Kirkwood, Nicholas Dante, and Edward Kleban
1977	*The Shadow Box* by Michael Cristofer
1978	*The Gin Game* by D. L. Coburn
1979	*Buried Child* by Sam Shepard
1980	*Talley's Folly* by Lanford Wilson
1981	*Crimes of the Heart* by Beth Henley
1982	*A Soldier's Play* by Charles Fuller
1983	*'night, Mother* by Marsha Norman
1984	*Glengarry Glen Ross* by David Mamet
1985	*Sunday in the Park with George* by Stephen Sondheim and James Lapine
1986	No prize

Endnotes

Chapter 1

1. Henrik Ibsen, *A Doll's House*, in *The Complete Major Prose Plays*, ed. Rolf Fjelde (New York: New American Library, 1978), p. 193.
2. Janet Brown, *Feminist Drama: Definition and Critical Analysis* (Metuchen, N. J.: Scarecrow Press, 1979), pp. 1, 2, 15–16.
3. Virginia Woolf, "Professions for Women," in *The Death of the Moth and Other Essays* (New York: Harcourt Brace Jovanovich, 1970), pp. 237–38.
4. Virginia Woolf, *A Room of One's Own* (Harcourt Brace Jovanovich, 1929), p. 115. Further references appear in the text.
5. Jesse Lynch Williams, *Why Marry?*, in *The Pulitzer Prize Plays 1918–1934*, eds. Kathryn Coe and William H. Cordell (New York: Random House, 1935), p. 8. Further references appear in the text.
6. Zona Gale, *Miss Lulu Bett: An American Comedy of Manners* (New York: D. Appleton, 1921), p. 7. Further references appear in the text.
7. Quoted in August Derleth, *Still Small Voice: The Biography of Zona Gale* (New York: D. Appleton-Century, 1940), p. 146.
8. Marsha Norman, *'night, Mother* (New York: Hill and Wang, 1983), p. 3. Further references appear in the text.
9. Robert Lowell, "For the Union Dead," in *For the Union Dead* (New York: Farrar, Straus & Giroux, 1964), p. 71.
10. Dylan Thomas, "Do Not Go Gentle Into That Good Night," in *The Poems of Dylan Thomas*, ed. Daniel Jones (New York: New Directions, 1971), p. 207.
11. George Kelly, *Craig's Wife*, in *Pulitzer Plays*, p. 343. Further references appear in the text.
12. Brown, p. 12.
13. Mary McCarthy, *Theatre Chronicles: 1937–1962* (New York: Farrar, Straus, 1963), p. 101.
14. Winifred Dusenbury, *The Theme of Loneliness in Modern American Drama* (Gainesville: University of Florida Press, 1960), p. 170.
15. Joseph Kramm, *The Shrike* (New York: Random House, 1952), pp. 81, 87. Further references appear in the text.
16. Kitti Frings, *Look Homeward, Angel*, in *50 Best Plays of the American Theatre*, Vol. III (New York: Crown, 1969), p. 276. Further references appear in the text.

17. D. L. Coburn, *The Gin Game* (New York: Drama Book Specialists, 1978), pp. 42, 45. Further references appear in the text.
18. Owen Davis, *Icebound,* in *Pulitzer Plays,* p. 214. Further references appear in the text.
19. Tennessee Williams, *Cat on a Hot Tin Roof* (New York: Signet, 1955), p. 85. Further references appear in the text.
20. See, for example, Foster Hirsch, *A Portrait of the Artist: The Plays of Tennessee Williams* (Port Washington, N. Y.: Kennikat, 1979), pp. 48, 52.
21. Arthur Miller, "Why Write for Theater? A Roundtable Report," *The New York Times,* 9 February 1986, 2, 30.

Chapter 2

1. Quoted in C. W. E. Bigsby, *A Critical Introduction to Twentieth-Century American Drama,* Vol. 2, *Tennessee Williams/Arthur Miller/Edward Albee* (Cambridge: Cambridge University Press, 1984), p. 304.
2. Eugene O'Neill, *The Iceman Cometh* (New York: Vintage, 1957), p. 258.
3. McCarthy, *Chronicles,* (see chap. 1, n. 13), p. 78.
4. Mary Chase, *Harvey,* in *50 Best Plays,* Vol. II, p. 122. Further references appear in the text
5. Lillian Herlands Hornstein, "'Though This be Madness': Insanity in the Theater," *College English,* 7, 1 (October 1945), 10.
6. Quoted in John L. Toohey, *A History of the Pulitzer Prize Plays* (New York: Citadel, 1957), p. 200.
7. Eugene O'Neill, *Beyond the Horizon,* in *Pulitzer Plays,* p. 72. Further references appear in the text.
8. Jane Bonin, *Major Themes in Prize-Winning American Drama* (Metuchen, N. J.: Scarecrow Press, 1975), p. 22.
9. Toohey, p. 128.
10. Zöe Akins, *The Old Maid* (New York: Samuel French, 1951), p. 40. Further references appear in the text.
11. Quoted in W. David Sievers, *Freud on Broadway: A History of Psychoanalysis and the American Drama* (New York: Hermitage House, 1955), p. 354.
12. William Inge, *Picnic* (New York: Dramatists Play Service, 1955), p. 12. Further references appear in the text.
13. Dissatisfied with the "fortuitous ending" of *Picnic* written under the pressure of upcoming rehearsals, Inge "rework[ed]" the play into *Summer Brave,* which he thought a "more humorously true" version that "fulfill[ed his] original intentions" (New York: Random House, 1962, p. ix). In it, Madge, instead of going off with Hal, stays to work in the five-and-dime, ogled and pursued by the boys.
14. Tennessee Williams, *A Streetcar Named Desire,* in *50 Best Plays,* Vol. III, p. 375. Further references appear in the text.
15. Harold Clurman, *The Divine Pastime: Theatre Essays* (New York: MacMillan, 1974), p. 12.
16. Tennessee Williams, *The Night of the Iguana* (New York: Signet, 1961), p. 117.

17. James G. Watson, "The Theater in *The Iceman Cometh:* Some Modernist Implications," *Arizona Quarterly,* 34, 3 (Autumn 1978), 233.
18. Foster Hirsch, *Who's Afraid of Edward Albee?* (Berkeley: Creative Arts Book Company, 1978), pp. 24, 26.
19. Edward Albee, *Who's Afraid of Virginia Woolf?* (New York: Atheneum, 1962), p. 3.

Chapter 3

1. Joseph Wood Krutch, *The Modern Temper* (New York: Harcourt Brace Jovanovich, 1957), p. xi.
2. Walter Meserve, "An American Drama 1920–1941," in *The Revels History of Drama in English: American Drama,* Vol. VIII, ed. T. W. Craik (London: Methuen, 1977), p. 235.
3. George S. Kaufman and Moss Hart, *You Can't Take It With You,* in *50 Best Plays,* Vol. I, p. 136. Further references appear in the text.
4. Reported in John Hohenberg, *The Pulitzer Prizes: A History of the Awards in Books, Drama, Music, and Journalism Based on the Private Files over Six Decades* (New York: Columbia University Press, 1974), p. 99.
5. Sidney Howard, *They Knew What They Wanted,* in *Pulitzer Plays,* p. 308. Further references appear in the text.
6. Elmer Rice, *Minority Report: An Autobiography* (New York: Simon and Schuster, 1963), p. 237.
7. Elmer Rice, *Street Scene,* in *Pulitzer Plays,* p. 557. Further references appear in the text.
8. Dusenbury, *Loneliness,* (see chap. 1, n. 14), p. 114.
9. Beth Henley, *Crimes of the Heart* (New York: Viking Press, 1982), p. 23. Further references appear in the text.
10. Harold Clurman, *The Fervent Years: The Story of the Group Theater and the Thirties* (New York: Hill and Wang, 1957), p. 120.
11. Sidney Kingsley, *Men in White,* in *Pulitzer Plays,* p. 633. Further references appear in the text.
12. Eugene O'Neill, "Memoranda on Masks," in *American Playwrights on Drama,* ed. Horst Frenz (New York: Hill and Wang, 1965), p. 10.
13. Eugene O'Neill, *Strange Interlude,* in *Pulitzer Plays,* p. 538. Further references appear in the text.

Chapter 4

1. Bernard F. Dick, *The Star-Spangled Screen: The American World War II Film* (Lexington: University of Kentucky Press, 1984), pp. 146, 255.
2. John Patrick, *The Teahouse of the August Moon,* in *50 Best Plays,* Vol. III, p. 195. Further references appear in the text.
3. Quoted in Walter J. Meserve, *Robert E. Sherwood: Reluctant Moralist* (New York: Pegasus, 1970), p. 116.

4. Robert E. Sherwood, "Preface" to *There Shall Be No Night*, in John Mason Brown, *The Ordeal of a Playwright: Robert E. Sherwood and the Challenge of War* (New York: Harper and Row, 1970), pp. 138–39. Further references appear in the text.

5. Robert W. Sherwood, *Idiot's Delight*, in *Three Dramas of American Realism*, ed. Joseph Mersand (New York: Washington Square Press, 1961), p. 40. Further references appear in the text. (*Dance a Little Closer*, an Alan Jay Lerner and Charles Strouse musical updating *Idiot's Delight* to an age threatened by nuclear destruction, managed only a brief run on Broadway in the spring of 1983.)

6. Lowell, *Union*, (see chap. 1, n. 9), p. 70.

7. Frances Goodrich and Albert Hackett, *The Diary of Anne Frank*, in *50 Best Plays*, Vol. III, p. 225. Further references appear in the text.

8. Bruno Bettelheim, "Business as Usual," in *Rhetorical Considerations*, ed. Harry Brent and William Lutz (Cambridge: Winthrop, 1980), p. 384.

9. Arthur Miller, *After the Fall* (New York: Bantam, 1967), p. 30.

10. Lillian Hellman, *Watch on the Rhine*, in *Six Plays* (New York: Modern Library, 1960), p. 296.

11. Frank Gilroy, *The Subject Was Roses* (New York: Random House, 1965), p. 142. Further references appear in the text.

Chapter 5

1. Doris E. Abramson, *Negro Playwrights in the American Theatre 1925–1969* (New York: Columbia University Press, 1969), p. 8.

2. Richard Rodgers, *Musical Stages: An Autobiography* (New York: Random House, 1975), p. 222. In his autobiography, *Josh: My Up and Down, In and Out Life*, the musical's director, Joshua Logan, lays claim to having supplied much of the libretto: "After three fourths of the first act, I realized Oscar was throwing me lines for Emile Debecque, Bloody Mary, and sometimes for Captain Brackett, and I was doing all the rest" (New York: Delacourte Press, 1976, p. 222). Although he feared "'no one will ever know I wrote a word of it,'" at Rodgers and Hammerstein's own insistence, his name was added to the award citation (Hohenberg, *Prizes*, [see chap. 3, n. 4], p. 201).

3. Richard Rodgers and Oscar Hammerstein II, *South Pacific*, in *Six Plays* (New York: Modern Library, 1959), p. 294. Further references appear in the text.

4. Lanford Wilson, *Talley's Folly* (New York: Hill and Wang, 1979), p. 35. Further references appear in the text.

5. Quoted in Abramson, p. 276.

6. Clinton F. Oliver, "The Negro and the American Theater," intro. to *Contemporary Black Drama from "A Raisin in the Sun" to "No Place To Be Somebody"*, eds. Clinton F. Oliver and Stephanie Sills (New York: Charles Scribner's Sons, 1971), p. 24.

7. Paul Green, *In Abraham's Bosom*, in *Pulitzer Plays*, p. 396. Further references appear in the text.

8. Gerald Weales, *The Jumping-Off Place: American Drama in the 1960s* (New York: Macmillan, 1969), p. 292.

9. Howard Sackler, *The Great White Hope* (New York: Dial Press, 1968), p. 186. Further references appear in the text.

10. Quoted in Oliver, p. 19.
11. Quoted in Oliver, p. 20.
12. Larry Neal, "The Black Arts Movement," *The Drama Review*, 12, 4 (Summer 1968), 33.
13. Charles Gordone, *No Place to Be Somebody* (Indianapolis: Bobbs-Merrill, 1969), p. 39. Further references appear in the text.
14. Walter Kerr, "Not Since Edward Albee...," *The New York Times*, 18 May 1969, D22.
15. Charles Fuller, *A Soldier's Play* (Garden City: Nelson Doubleday, 1982), p. 3. Further references appear in the text.
16. August Wilson, *Ma Rainey's Black Bottom* (New York: New American Library, 1985), p. 25.

Chapter 6

1. Alexis de Tocqueville, *Democracy in America*, trans. George Lawrence (New York: Harper & Row, 1966), p. 231.
2. John Stuart Mill, *On Liberty*, ed. David Spitz (New York: W. W. Norton, 1975), pp. 62–63.
3. George S. Kaufman, Morrie Ryskind, and Ira Gershwin, *Of Thee I Sing*, in *Pulitzer Plays*, p. 729. Further references appear in the text.
4. Quoted in Toohey, *History*, (see chap. 2, n. 6), p. 109.
5. Maxwell Anderson, *Both Your Houses*, in *Pulitzer Plays*, p. 773.
6. Quoted in Cornelia Otis Skinner, *Life with Lindsay and Crouse* (Boston: Houghton Mifflin, 1976), p. 200.
7. Howard Lindsay and Russel Crouse, *State of the Union*, in *50 Best Plays*, Vol. III, pp. 185, 200. Further references appear in the text.
8. Jerome Weidman, George Abbott, and Sheldon Harnick, *Fiorello!* (New York: Random House, 1960), p. 9. Further references appear in the text.
9. Hohenberg, *Pulitzer*, (see chap. 3, n. 4), p. 48.
10. Robert E. Sherwood, *Abe Lincoln in Illinois*, in *50 Best Plays*, Vol. II, p. 309. Further references appear in the text.
11. Quoted in John Mason Brown, *The Worlds of Robert E. Sherwood: Mirror to His Times 1896–1939* (New York: Harper and Row, 1965), p. 370.

Chapter 7

1. F. Scott Fitzgerald, *The Great Gatsby* (New York: Charles Scribner's Sons, 1925), p. 182. Further references appear in the text.
2. Frederic L. Carpenter, "The American Myth: Paradise (To Be) Regained," *PMLA*, LXXIV, 5 (December 1959), 605–6.
3. George O'Neil, *American Dream* (New York: Samuel French, 1933), p. 17. Further references appear in the text.
4. Edward Albee, "The American Dream," in *The Zoo Story and The American Dream* (New York: Signet, 1963), pp. 106–7.

5. William Saroyan, *The Time of Your Life*, in *50 Best Plays*, Vol. III, p. 35. Further references appear in the text.

6. Henry Hewes, ed., *Best Plays 1961–1962* (New York: Dodd, Mead, 1962), p. 19.

7. Abe Burrows, Jack Weinstock, Willie Gilbert, and Frank Loesser, *How to Succeed in Business Without Really Trying* (London: Frank Music, 1963), p. 87. Further references appear in the text.

8. See Thomas E. Porter, *Myth and Modern American Drama* (Detroit: Wayne State University Press, 1969), Chapter 6—especially pp. 128–31—for a fuller discussion.

9. Arthur Miller, "Introduction to *The Collected Plays*," in *The Theater Essays of Arthur Miller*, ed. Robert E. Martin (New York: Penguin, 1978), p. 133.

10. Arthur Miller, *Death of a Salesman*, in *50 Best Plays*, Vol. III, p. 436. Further references appear in the text.

11. Frank W. Shelton, "Sports and the Competitive Ethic: *Death of a Salesman* and *That Championship Season*," *Ball State University Forum*, 20, ii, 21.

12. Jason Miller, *That Championship Season* (New York: Atheneum, 1972), p. xiii. Further references appear in the text.

13. John Simon, *Uneasy Stages: A Chronicle of the New York Theatre, 1963–1973* (New York: Random House, 1975), p. 464.

14. David Mamet, *Glengarry Glen Ross* (New York: Grove Press, 1983), p. 75. Further references appear in the text.

15. For insightful comments on language in Mamet, see David Denby's "Stranger in a Strange Land: A Moviegoer at the Theater" (*The Atlantic Monthly*, January 1985, pp. 48–49) and Gerald Weales's "American Theater Watch, 1983–1984" (*The Georgia Review*, XXXVIII, 3 [Fall 1984], 594–96).

16. Sam Shepard, *Buried Child* (New York: Urizen, 1980), p. 11. Further references appear in the text.

17. Quoted in Weales, 571.

18. In an article appearing after I wrote these pages, Thomas Nash discusses Shepard's use of myth, although he argues for a symbolic rebirth of a new Corn King (Vince) to replace the old king (Dodge) who dies ("Sam Shepard's *Buried Child*: The Ironic Use of Folklore," *Modern Drama*, XXVI, 4 [December 1983], 486–91).

19. Since no text of *A Chorus Line* has yet been published, the quotations appear as in my viewing notes.

Chapter 8

1. George R. Kernodle, "Patterns of Belief in Contemporary Drama," in *Spiritual Problems in Contemporary Literature*, ed. Stanley Romaine Hopper (New York: Harper and Row, 1957), pp. 203–4.

2. Kernodle, p. 203.

3. Roark Bradford, *'Ol Man Adam an' His Children: Being the Tales They Tell About the Time When the Lord Walked the Earth Like a Natural Man* (New York: Harper and Brothers, 1928), p. 264.
4. Marc Connelly, *The Green Pastures*, in *Pulitzer Plays*, p. 648. Further references appear in the text.
5. Hatcher Hughes, *Hell-Bent fer Heaven*, in *Pulitzer Plays*, p. 237. Further references appear in the text.
6. Sievers, *Freud*, (see chap. 2, n. 11), p. 133.
7. Eugene O'Neill, *"Anna Christie,"* in *Pulitzer Plays*, p. 154. Further references appear in the text.
8. Archibald MacLeish, *J. B.* (Cambridge: Houghton Mifflin, 1958), pp. 2–4. Further references appear in the text.
9. Samuel Terrien, *"J. B. and Job,"* *The Christian Century*, LXXVI, 1 (January 7, 1959), 10.
10. Edward Albee, "Critics are Downgrading Audience's Taste and Have Obfuscated Simple *Tiny Alice,*" *The Dramatist's Guild Quarterly*, II, 1 (Spring 1965), 12.
11. Edward Albee, *Tiny Alice* (New York: Pocket Books, 1966), p. 44.
12. Edward Albee, *A Delicate Balance* (New York: Pocket Books, 1967), p. 171. Further references appear in the text.
13. Thornton Wilder, *Our Town*, in *Three Plays* (New York: Bantam, 1958), p. 15. Further references appear in the text.
14. Ned Rorem, "Tennessee [Williams] Then and Now," *London Magazine*, June/July 1975, 73.

Chapter 9

1. Robert Nisbet, *History of the Idea of Progress* (New York: Basic Books, 1980), p. 318.
2. Quoted in David Haberman, *The Plays of Thornton Wilder: A Critical Study* (Middletown: Wesleyan University Press, 1967), p. 24.
3. Thornton Wilder, *The Skin of Our Teeth*, in *Three Plays* (New York: Bantam, 1958), p. 93. Further references appear in the text.
4. Paul Zindel, *The Effect of Gamma Rays on Man-in-the-Moon Marigolds* (New York: Harper and Row, 1971), pp. 26, 28. Further references appear in the text.
5. Susan Glaspell, *Alison's House*, in *Pulitzer Plays*, p. 691.
6. Tad Mosel, *All the Way Home* (New York: Ivan Obolensky, 1961), p. 32. Further references appear in the text.
7. Michael Cristofer, *The Shadow Box* (New York: Drama Book Specialists, 1977), p. 36. Further references appear in the text.
8. Quoted in Peter James Ventimiglia, "Recent Trends in American Drama: Michael Cristofer, David Mamet, and Albert Innaurato," *Journal of American Culture*, I, 1 (Spring 1978), 198.
9. Brendan Gill, "Among the Dunes," *The New Yorker*, 3 February 1975, 75.

10. Edward Albee, *Seascape* (New York: Atheneum, 1975), pp. 85, 129. Further references appear in the text.

11. Hans Küng, *Eternal Life? Life After Death as a Medical, Philosophical, and Theological Problem* (Garden City: Doubleday, 1984), p. xiv.

Chapter 10

1. Joseph Wood Krutch, *"Modernism" in Modern Drama* (Ithaca: Cornell University Press, 1953), p. 21.

2. Maurice Beebe, "What Modernism Was," *Journal of Modern Literature*, III, 5 (July 1974), 1072–73.

3. Malcolm Bradbury and James McFarlane, eds., "Introduction," *Modernism 1890–1930* (London: Penguin, 1978), pp. 49–50.

4. John Fletcher and James McFarlane, "Modernist Drama: Origins and Patterns," in *Modernism*, p. 510. Further references appear in the text.

5. Chester E. Eisinger, "Another Battle of the Books: American Fiction 1950–1970," *Prospects*, 4 (1978), 268.

6. Eugene O'Neill, *Long Day's Journey Into Night* (New Haven: Yale University Press, 1956), p. 7. Further references appear in the text.

7. Clurman, *Pastimes*, (see chap. 2, n. 15), p. 283.

8. William Carlos Williams, "To Daphne and Virginia," in *Selected Poems* (New York: New Directions, 1968), p. 135.

9. Frank Rich, "A Musical Theater Breakthrough," *The New York Times Magazine*, 21 October 1984, 53.

10. Since a text of *Sunday in the Park With George* was not in print at the time of writing, the quotations appear as in my listening notes.

11. Percy Bysshe Shelley, "A Defense of Poetry," in *English Romantic Poetry and Prose*, ed. Russell Noyes (New York: Oxford University Press, 1956), p. 1101.

12. J. L. Styan, rev. of *Metafictional Characters in Modern Drama, Modern Drama*, 23 (1980), 215.

13. Bigsby, *Introduction*, p. 119.

14. Eugene Ionesco, *Notes and Counter Notes: Writings on the Theatre*, trans. Donald Watson (New York: Grove Press, 1964), p. 102.

Index

Abbott, George, 90
Abe Lincoln in Illinois, 92–94, 95
Abraham Lincoln, 92
Abraham Lincoln: The Prairie Years, 92
Abramson, Doris, 68
Absurdism, 119, 120, 128, 142
Actors Theatre, 44
Adding Machine, The, 16, 42
Advisory Board, xi, 24, 46, 69, 90, 92, 119, 140
After the Fall, 63
Agee, James, 134
Aiken, George, 68
Akins, Zöe, 28–30
Albee, Edward, 12, 14, 57, 79, 97, 104, 113, 120–23, 137, 138–40, 147, 152
Alger, Horatio, 99, 101
Alison's House, 132–34, 140, 141, 145, 146
All God's Chillun Got Wings, 68, 75
All My Sons, 23, 102
All Over, 137
All the Way Home, 4, 134–36, 138, 140, 141, 145
Alley Theatre, 130
American Dream, 96–97
American Dream, The, 12, 14, 97

American Repertory Theatre, 6
Anderson, Garland, 68
Anderson, Maxwell, 29, 40, 53, 57, 87–89, 94, 132
Anderson, Robert, 14, 17, 54, 90, 122
"Anna Christie," 117–18, 125, 147
Appearances, 68
Archetypal imagery, 117, 123, 129, 139, 148
Arena Stage, 76
Art (as theme), xiv, 21, 36, 50, 52, 54, 55, 56, 63, 73, 97, 126, 138, 141, 144, 145–46, 149, 150
Audience (as self-conscious), xiii, 22, 36–37, 66, 83, 84, 110, 111, 125, 136, 142, 143, 144–45, 146, 153
Awake and Sing!, 29, 42

Back to Methuselah, 115, 128
Barry, Philip, 4
Basic Training of Pavlo Hummel, The, 53
Beckett, Samuel, 122
Beebe, Maurice, 143
Behrman, S. N., 4
Belasco, David, 4
Bennett, Michael, 108–10
Best Years of Our Lives, The, 66
Bettelheim, Bruno, 63

Beveridge, Albert J., 92
Beyond the Horizon, 26–28, 30, 35, 36, 37, 92, 146
Bigsby, C. W. E., xiii, 152
Black Arts Movement, 78
Bock, Jerry, 90
Bonhoeffer, Dietrich, 115
Bonin, Jane, xii–xiii, 28
Both Your Houses, 87–89, 94
Boucicault, Dion, 68
Bradbury, Malcolm, 143
Bradford, Roark, 114
Brechtian devices, 4, 22, 54, 56, 66, 76, 77, 81, 83, 136, 144, 152
Brook, Peter, 149
Brown, Janet, 1
Brown, John Mason, xi, 24
Brown, William Wells, 68
Bruckner, D. J. R., ix
Buried Child, 107–8, 111
Burrows, Abe, 99–100
Bury, J. M., 127
Bury the Dead, 53, 57

Cabaret, 58
Caleb, the Degenerate, 68
Campbell, Oscar, x
Capra, Frank, 94
Carpenter, Frederic, 96
Casablanca, 53
Cat on a Hot Tin Roof, 17–20, 21, 22, 34, 41, 119
Chase, Mary, 11, 24–26
Chekhov, Anton, 34, 44, 56, 132, 152
Cherry Orchard, The, 34, 56, 132
Cheyevsky, Paddy, 99
Children's Hour, The, 29
Chorus Line, A, 108–110, 111, 145
Chronicle (history) play, 76, 77, 85, 92, 93
Civic Repertory Theatre, 132
Clurman, Harold, 33, 46, 146
Coburn, D. L., 14–16
Come Marching Home, 90
Communication (as theme), 17, 20, 21
Company, 70

Connection, The, 79
Connelly, Marc, 113, 114–15, 118
Consul, The, 69
Cotter, Joseph H., 68
Craig's Wife, 2, 9–11, 14, 20
Crimes of the Heart, 30, 38, 44–46, 51, 52
Cristofer, Michael, 136–38, 140
Crouse, Russel, 89–90
Crucible, The, 11, 63
Curse of the Starving Class, The, 107

Dance a Little Closer, 160n
Dante, Nicolas, 108–10
Darwin, Charles, 57
Davis, Owen, 16–17, 18
Death in the Family, A, 134
Death of a Salesman, x, 100–03, 105, 108, 110
"Defense of Poetry, A," 151
Delicate Balance, A, 104, 113, 120–23, 125, 126, 138, 147
Democracy in America, 86
Denby, David, 162n
Desire Under the Elms, 18, 40–41
Diary of Anne Frank, The, 4, 61–63, 67, 145, 146
Dick, Bernard F., 53–54, 66
Dickinson, Emily, 132
Doll's House, A, 1
Doonesbury, 94
Drama citation, terms of, xi
Drama Critics Circle, 29, 61
Drinkwater, John, 92
Dublin Trilogy, 42
DuBois, W. E. B., 78
Dusenbury, Winifred, 10, 43
Dutchman, 73, 76, 81

Effects of Gamma Rays on Man-in-the-Moon Marigolds, The, 30, 130–32, 140, 141, 145
Einstein, Albert, 143
Eliot, George, 30
Eliot, T. S., 23, 121
Elizabeth the Queen, 87, 132
Emerson, Ralph Waldo, 101, 120, 123, 125, 152

Emperor Jones, The, 75
Equus, 81
Escape; or a Leap for Freedom, The, 68
Eternal Life?, 140
Evolutionary metaphor, xiii, 35, 50, 57, 60
Expressionistic techniques, 6, 34, 42, 56, 75, 101, 111, 147

Faulkner, William, x, 152
Feminist drama (definition of), 1, 20
Ferber, Edna, 70
Fiddler on the Roof, 90
Fifth of July, The, 72
Fiorello!, 61, 90–92, 94
Fitzgerald, F. Scott, x, 96
Fletcher, John, 143
Flowering Peach, The, 118
Foil characters, 31, 133
Follies, 122
Framed play, 6, 78, 91, 114, 118, 125
Franklin, Benjamin, 101
Freud, Sigmund, 39, 48
Frings, Kitti, 13–14
Fuller, Charles, 80–82, 83
Furth, George, 70

Gale, Zona, 4–6, 8, 17, 18
Game metaphor, xiii, 14, 64, 82, 90, 91, 104
Garland, Hamlin, 16
Gassner, John, xi, 24
Gelber, Jack, 79
Gershwin, George, 69, 86
Gershwin, Ira, 86–87
Ghetto drama, 42
Ghosts, 28
Gideon, 99
Gilbert, Willie, 99–100
Gill, Brendan, xi, 138
Gilroy, Frank, 63–66
Gin Game, The, 9, 14–16, 20, 21
Glaspell, Susan, 26, 132–34, 136, 140
Glass Menagerie, The, x, 14, 25, 31, 65, 130
Glengarry Glen Ross, 105–7, 111
Goldman, James, 122

Goodman Theatre, 105
Goodrich, Frances, 61–63
Gordone, Charles, 78–80, 82, 83
Gorky, Maxim, 42
Grand Illusion, The, 57, 62
Great Gatsby, The, 96
Great White Hope, The, 76–78, 80, 83, 84, 144
Green Grow the Lilacs, 132
Green Pastures, The, 113, 114–15, 125, 126, 144
Green, Paul, 73–75, 77, 78, 83
Griffith, D. W., 16
Group Theatre, the, 46–47
Gussow, Mel, 108

Hackett, Albert, 61–63
Hamlet, 35
Hamlisch, Marvin, 108–10
Hammerstein, Oscar, II, 54, 69–71
Hansberry, Lorraine, 73
Harnick, Sheldon, 90
Hart, Moss, 39–40
Harvey, 11, 24–26, 28, 36, 37, 142, 144
Hassan, Ihab, 44
Hawthorne, Nathaniel, 152
Heartbreak House, 57, 59
Hedda Gabler, 10
Hell-Bent fer Heaven, 115–17, 118, 125
Hellman, Lillian, x, 16, 29, 61, 63, 90, 106
Hemingway, Ernest, x, 30
Henley, Beth, 30, 38, 44–46
Henry V, 53
Herndon, William H., 92
Hewes, Henry, xi, 99
Hirsch, Foster, 18, 36
History of the Idea of Progress, 127
Hohenberg, John, x–xi
Horstein, Lillian, 26
How to Succeed in Business Without Really Trying, 99–100, 104, 111, 145
Howard, Sidney, 40–42, 51
Hughes, Hatcher, 115–17
Hughes, Langston, 68

I Never Sang for My Father, 14
Ibsen, Henrik, 1, 10, 21, 23, 28, 30, 64, 107, 132, 133, 142, 152
Icebound, 16–17, 20, 21
Iceman Cometh, The, x, 23–24, 35, 36, 37, 79, 125
Idea of Progress, 127
Idiot's Delight, 29, 54, 56–59, 60, 66, 67, 144, 146
In Abraham's Bosom, 73–75, 76, 78, 83
Indians, x, 66
Inge, William, 30–33, 158n
Interior monologue, 48, 147
Ionesco, Eugene, 4, 153

J. B., 118–20, 125, 126, 143, 144
Jewett, Sarah Orne, 16
Jones, LeRoi, 73, 76, 81
Joyce, James, 143
Jung, Carl, 39, 117

Kafka, Franz, 11
Kaufman, George S., 39–40, 86–87, 88
Kazin, Elia, 19
Kelly, George, 9–11
Kern, Jerome, 70
Kernodle, George, 113
Kerr, Walter, xi, 80
Kierkegaard, Soren, 139
Kingsley, Sidney, 46–48, 52
Kirkwood, James, 108–10
Kleban, Edward, 108–10
Kopit, Arthur, x, 14, 66
Kramm, Joseph, 11–13
Krutch, Joseph Wood, xi, 38–39, 46, 52, 142, 143, 146
Kübler-Ross, Elizabeth, 136
Küng, Hans, 140

LaGuardia, Fiorello, 85
Lapine, James, 146, 149–52
Le Gallienne, Eva, 132
Lerner, Alan Jay, 160n
Life Force, 115, 125
Lindsay, Howard, 89–90
Little Foxes, The, 16, 106

Little Negro Theatre, 78
Loesser, Frank, 41, 99–100
Logan, Joshua, 160n
Long Day's Journey Into Night, x, 13, 31, 65, 146–49, 151
Look Homeward, Angel, 4, 13–14, 20, 22, 146
Lovely Ladies, Kind Gentlemen, 55
Lowell, Robert, 7, 60
Lower Depths, The, 42

Ma Rainey's Black Bottom, 83
McCarthy, Mary, 10, 25
McCarthyism, 11, 94
McFarlane, James, 143
MacLeish, Archibald, 118–20, 123, 125
Major Barbara, 57
Mamet, David, ix, 105–7, 111
Maugham, W. Somerset, xi
Mead, Shepherd, 99
Melville, Herman, 120
Men in White, 46–48, 51, 52, 144
Menotti, Gian Carlo, 69
Meserve, Walter, 39
Metatheatre, 110, 142–43, 145, 146, 152
Michener, James, 69, 70
Mielziner, Jo, 42
Mill, John Stuart, 85–86, 89, 94, 95
Miller, Arthur, 11, 21, 23, 63, 64, 100–03, 104, 105, 110, 152
Miller, Jason, 103–5, 108
Mirror (as stage prop), xiii, 33, 100, 110, 111–12, 145, 153
Miss Lulu Bett, 2, 4–6, 12, 19, 20, 21, 22
Modernism, 142–43, 146, 149, 151, 152
"Modernism" in Modern Drama, 142
Morality play, 118, 123
Mosel, Tad, 134–36, 140
Most Happy Fella, The, 41
Mourning Becomes Electra, 10, 86
Mr. Smith Goes to Washington, 94
Mulatto, 68
Mystery play, 114–15, 118, 119, 124, 128

Myth, 37, 96, 98, 100, 104, 107, 110, 111, 115, 116, 119, 128, 140

Narrator, 54, 67, 71, 81, 114, 124
Nash, Thomas, 162n
Nathan, George Jean, 26
Native Son, 73
Neal, Larry, 78
Negro Ensemble Company, 83
New Woman, 3, 91, 134
Nietzsche, Friedrich, 151
"Nigger, The," 68
Night and Fog, 63
'night, Mother, 6–8, 11, 15, 20, 21, 22, 30, 144
Night of the Iguana, The, 33, 99
Nisbet, Robert, 127
No Place to Be Somebody, 78–80, 82, 83, 84, 144, 145
Nonrepresentational drama, 51–52, 71, 77, 79, 80, 83, 111, 123, 130, 142
Norman, Marsha, ix, 6–8, 30
Norton, Elliott, xi
Notes and Counter Notes, 153

O'Casey, Sean, 42, 43, 56
Octoroon, The, 68
Odets, Clifford, x, 29, 42, 119
Of Thee I Sing, 69, 86–87, 90, 94, 99
Old Maid, The, 4, 28–30, 35, 36, 37
Ol' Man Adam an' His Children, 114
Oliver, Clinton, 73
On Death and Dying, 136
O'Neil, George, 96–97
O'Neill, Eugene, 10, 18, 23, 24, 25, 26–28, 29, 35, 40–41, 48–51, 52, 57, 68, 75, 79, 86, 92, 117–118, 122, 123, 125, 146–49, 151, 152
Our Town, x, 98, 123–25, 126, 138, 141, 142, 145
Out Cry, 152

Pacific Overtures, 55
Patrick, John, 54
Paz, Octavio, 126
Peterson, Louis, 68

Petrified Forest, The, 29, 57
Phelps, William Lyons, xi
Picasso, Pablo, 143
Picnic, 30–33, 35, 37, 146
Pinter, Harold, 4
Pirandello, Luigi, 23, 128, 143, 152
Plato, 151
Poe, Edgar Allen, 152
Pound, Ezra, 143
Private, 63
Proust, Marcel, 146
Public Theatre, 82

Rabe, David, x, 53, 55, 57, 64, 69
Raisin in the Sun, A, 73
Remembrance of Things Past, 146
Renoir, Jean, 57, 62
Resnais, Alain, 63
Rice, Elmer, 16, 42–44, 51
Rich, Frank, ix, 149
Riders to the Sea, 117
Riggs, Lillian, 132
Rodgers, Richard, 54, 69–71
Room of One's Own, A, 1–2, 4
Rorem, Ned, 125
Ryskind, Morrie, 86–87, 88

Sackler, Howard, 75–78, 80, 83
Sandbox, The, 14
Sandburg, Carl, 92
Saroyan, William, 59, 79, 97–99, 152
Seascape, 138–40
Seward, George, 149
Seyboldt, Mark, 78
Shadow Box, The, 136–38, 140, 141, 145
Shaffer, Peter, 81
Shakespeare, William, ix, 23, 35, 53, 54, 85, 120
Shaw, George Bernard, ix, 2, 58, 59, 115, 128, 129, 152
Shaw, Irwin, 53, 57
Sheldon, Edward, 68
Shelley, Percy Bysshe, 151
Shelton, Frank, 103
Shepard, Sam, ix, 107–8
Sherwood, Robert E., 29, 56–61, 66, 70, 92–94, 95

Show Boat, 70
Shrike, The, 9, 11–13, 14, 20, 21, 22, 25, 143, 144
Sievers, W. David, 117
Silver Tassie, The, 56
Simon, John, x, 18, 104
Six Characters in Search of an Author, 128
Skin of Our Teeth, The, 63, 128–30, 140, 141, 144
Sneider, Vern, 54
Soldier's Play, A, 80–82, 83, 84, 144
Solitaire/Double Solitaire, 122
Sondheim, Stephen, 55, 70, 122, 146, 149–52
Sophocles, ix
South Pacific, xiii, 4, 54, 55, 69–71, 83, 84, 134, 144
Stallings, Laurence, 40, 53, 57
State of the Union, 89–90, 92, 94
Stephenson, Nathaniel Wright, 92
Sticks and Bones, x, 55, 57, 64, 69
Strange Interlude, 49–51, 52, 146, 148
Stravinsky, Igor, 143
Stream-of-consciousness, 49, 52
Street Scene, 42–44, 46, 51, 52
Streetcar Named Desire, A, x, 33–35, 36, 37, 57, 146
Strindbergian battle of sexes, 12, 13, 14, 27, 118, 152
Strouse, Charles, 160n
Stuckey, William J., x
Styan, J. L., 152
Subject Was Roses, The, 63–66, 67, 142, 144, 146
Subplot, 5, 32, 69, 91
Summer Brave, 158n
Sunday in the Park with George, 146, 149–52
Suppressed Desires, 26, 133
Surrealistic techniques, 128, 144
Synge, John Millington, 117

Take a Giant Step, 68
Tales of the South Pacific, 69
Talley's Folly, xiii, 45, 69, 71–73, 83, 84, 142, 144

Tea and Sympathy, 19, 54
Teahouse of the August Moon, The, 54–56, 66, 67, 71, 142, 144
Terrien, Samuel, 119
That Championship Season, 103–5, 111
Theatre metaphor, 5, 11–12, 22, 36, 52, 56, 67, 69, 71, 83–84, 144
There Shall Be No Night, 54, 57, 59–61, 62, 63, 66
They Knew What They Wanted, 40–42, 46, 51, 55
Thomas, Dylan, 8
Thoreau, Henry David, 102
Thurber, James, 9
Time (as theme), xiii, 14, 22, 32, 121–22, 123–24, 125, 132, 134–35, 138, 145, 147
Time of Your Life, The, 79, 97–99, 110–11
Tiny Alice, 120
Tocqueville, Alexis de, 85–86, 89, 94, 95
Tonight We Improvise, 128
Toohey, John, x
Toys in the Attic, 61, 90
Trifles, 26, 133
Trilling, Lionel, 23

Uncle Tom's Cabin, 68

Valency, Maurice, xi
Valley Forge, 29

Waiting for Godot, 122
War movies, 53–54, 66
Watch on the Rhine, 61, 63
Watson, James, 36
Way Down East, 16
Weales, Gerald, 76, 162n
Weidman, Jerome, 90
Weidman, John, 55
Weinstock, Jack, 99–100
Wharton, Edith, 28, 29
What Price Glory?, 40, 53, 57
Whitman, Walt, 97, 152
Who's Afraid of Virginia Woolf?, x, 24, 36, 37, 57, 147

Why Marry?, 2–4, 20, 21, 22
Wild Duck, The, 23
Wilder, Thornton, 63, 71, 123–25, 128–30, 132, 136, 137, 138, 140, 152
Williams, Jesse Lynch, 2–4, 8
Williams, Tennessee, 17–20, 25, 33–35, 57, 99, 130, 152
Williams, William Carlos, 149
Wilson, August, 83
Wilson, Lanford, ix, 71–73
Wings, 14
Winterset, 87
Wolfe, Thomas, 13
Woolf, Virginia, 1, 4, 9, 19, 21
Work ethic, x, 17, 40, 47, 97, 115, 120
Wright, Richard, 73

You Can't Take It With You, 39–40, 51, 52
Young, Stark, xi

Zindel, Paul, 30, 130–32, 134, 136, 140
Zoo Story, The, 79